DATE DUE

Jan 4 5 ‡			
GAYLORD			PRINTED IN U.S.A

Other Books by Arthur H. Lewis

THE AARONSBURG STORY • THE WORLDS OF CHIPPY PATTERSON

ARTHUR H. LEWIS

THE DAY THEY SHOOK
THE PLUM TREE

HARCOURT, BRACE & WORLD, INC., NEW YORK

© 1963 by Arthur H. Lewis

F. 7. 6 3

Library of Congress Catalog Card Number: 63-8101

Printed in the United States of America

For Juliet, Suzy, and Heather with love

The Day They Shook the Plum Tree

A view of the plum tree from a distance

MENTION the names Morgan, Mellon, Vanderbilt, Rockefeller, and Russell Sage to a literate adult and he's likely to think of libraries, art collections, scholarships, medical research, and sociological studies. He may also call to mind a hotel, yacht racing, a late-blooming politician, and—if age and memory serve him well—a lap-climbing midget. It is far less likely that he'll recall a Wall Street emperor, a Pittsburgh monopolist, a hated railroad magnate, a destroyer of small businessmen, and a vulturous usurer.

Time does have its way with us; the founders of these great American fortunes, regardless of how they accumulated their wealth, have finally made a desirable impact on our world through the vast philanthropies conducted in their names and

3

through their wealth. Most descendants of these first-generation pirates have accepted a responsibility to society; these inheritors of vast sums of money bear names that are respected and will be recalled kindly by future generations.

Yet one of the largest of all American fortunes is now almost forgotten less than a dozen years after its distribution. Its major begetter, Hetty Green, surely one of the most bizarre figures of our time, is remembered only by a few. Litigation concerning various aspects of the fortune provided headlines, sometimes of sensational nature, over many years; one action reached the Supreme Court of the United States, involved five states, and established a precedent in law. The many human dramas involved are the stuff of tragedy and of comedy; there is material enough for several novels although, in the guise of fiction, these undisputed facts and real people might prove difficult of belief.

Why, then, should this of all fortunes vanish so swiftly, leaving only barely perceptible traces of its existence? Was it because the last surviving generation knew nothing about money—either how to treat it, earn it, spend it, invest it, or even give it away? Was it because the fortune was built for no other purpose than the blind accumulation of money for its own sake? Vanderbilt wanted railroads and built them; Morgan yearned for power, got it, and used it; Rockefeller gobbled up his lesser competitors, but in so doing developed the oil industry; Mellon advanced the aluminum trust, but he made aluminum almost as popular as steel. Wealth was incidental to their main drives. Only Russell Sage of these five money men shared the obsession of pure dollar greed with Hetty Green. But his heir, his widow, was endowed with vision, wisdom, and will; Hetty Green's heirs were not.

One can approach this strange and true saga in many ways: initially out of curiosity, and a most curious tale it is; as a fragment of Americana, covering, as it does, more than three hundred years in unusual places and often under extraordinary circumstances; and as a human document, for a strikingly broad band of the human spectrum is revealed. Any one of these approaches

4

can be supported by an abundance of fact contained in this record.

Yet one other element forces itself upon the investigator piecing together the story—the question of morality. This is undeniably a cautionary tale; but what is the caution? One response, appropriate to current flip jargon, might be: "What *not* to do with your first one hundred million dollars." More eloquent, and dignified by the trial of centuries, might be Paul's invocation to the convert Timothy: "For the love of money is the root of all evil; which while some coveted after, they have erred from the faith, and pierced themselves through with many sorrows." A historian, a sociologist, and a psychiatrist would each likely enough pry into this area with a different verbal lever to press for particular points of view or, as the case may be, to shun them. This writer, without academic standing in any of those disciplines, prefers to beg the question once he has raised it and to remain, as he intended, merely a reporter. In what complex of human behavior are data ever complete? A reading will confirm that this is clearly a cautionary tale, but the formulation of the caution is left to the reader. It may not prove too easy a task.

In gathering material for this book I have had the help and co-operation of many people. I am particularly indebted to Mary Nims Bolles, Ruth Lawrence Briggs, and Joe Epstein for searching deeply into their memories. To Florence Collis, Renee Marke, and Arthur L. Redstone for their editorial help. To the following distinguished members of the American Bar for helping me to understand the legal technicalities and for making easy my examination of the contents of the court records: Dillon Anderson, John M. Bullard, James A. Dixon, George W. Jaques, Timothy N. Pfeiffer, Ernest Scott, and Harrison Tweed. To Charles J. Lewin, Editor and Manager of the New Bedford *Standard-Times*, and to the following members of the working press: Jack Kofoed of the Miami *Herald*, John McMahon of the Boston *Herald*, and Van G. Sauter and Eugene Galkowski of the New Bedford *Standard-Times*. To Mrs. Muriel G. Thomas, Librarian of the Rockingham

Free Public Library of Bellows Falls, Vermont and to her staff; to Herb Davis and other members of the staff of the Free Library of Philadelphia; to staff members of the New Bedford, Massachusetts, Free Public Library, the Greenwich Public Library, Greenwich, Connecticut, the New York Public Library, the Carnegie Public Library of Fort Worth, Texas, and the Adriance Memorial Library of Poughkeepsie, New York. And to Mr. and Mrs. Herbert Bancroft, Alfred I. Barton, Norris S. Barratt, Preston D. Belknap, Howard A. Chinn, Beeman Fisher, Mary Leslie Fisher, Mr. and Mrs. Bert Hill, Professor Henry G. Houghton, Stephen T. Kelsey, Jr., Dr. and Mrs. Henry S. Pascal, Lino L. Sertel, Mr. and Mrs. B. Karl Sharp, Willard P. Snyder, Mrs. Wynant Vanderpool, F. Lowry Wall, and Miss Blanche Webb.

Reported conversations included herein have been examined, whenever possible, by the actual participants and are as accurate as individual memory and the passage of time allow.

ARTHUR H. LEWIS

Philadelphia, Pennsylvania

Chapter One

At about 5 P.M. on January 31, 1952, William Howell, a messenger boy employed by New York's Chase National Bank, made his accustomed rounds gathering the outgoing mail. Among the thousands of letters he collected were 119 of more than casual interest. They were addressed to a farmer, an engineer, an osteopath, a genealogist, an elderly recluse, New York City's Commissioner of Parks, a gardener, several housewives, universities, old ladies' homes, firemen, and churches, from Bellows Falls, Vermont, to San Francisco, California.

None of the individual addressees and only a few of the institutions were expecting the letters. Certainly young Howell hadn't the slightest inkling that his was almost the final step in the disposition of one of the last, least taxed, and oldest of the great American fortunes, the $100,000,000 Green estate.

7

Begun with "one black cow" bought at Plymouth, Massachusetts, in 1624, the Fortune, then in possession of the prolific and frugal Howland family, grew slowly through the generations. Farming, trading with Indians, slavery, and land sales pushed it to respectable proportions before the French and Indian War was over.

Rum, Russian iron, and the post-Revolutionary merchant marine gave the Fortune added impetus. But it was whaling plus the shrewdness of Black Hawk Robinson that enabled his daughter Hetty, through forgery, perjury, penury, genius, ruthlessness, and physical stamina, to die in 1916 the richest and most detested woman in America and the mother of two children whose lives she had ruined. Since Hetty gave nothing to charity while she lived nobody expected her to give anything to charity when she died. Nobody was disappointed.

Hetty's will put her entire estate into the hands of "Colonel Ned," a six-foot four-inch, three-hundred-pound, wildly eccentric, one-legged son who blithely tossed away $3,000,000 a year on yachts, coins, stamps, diamond-studded chastity belts, female teenage "wards," pornography, orchid culture, and Texas politics, and a frightened, eremitic daughter, Sylvia Wilks who kept a $31,000,-000 cash bank balance that earned no interest. Despite these handicaps the Fortune grew. Protected from within by antenuptial agreements and from without by a brilliant array of legal talent, neither death nor taxes could prevent its expansion until its final dissolution.

So powerful had the Fortune become that even during the death struggle—those months between probation of Sylvia Wilks' will and final distribution of the funds—interest on principal, interest on interest, and interest on interest on interest raised the total by more than $2,500,000.

Who got the fruit the day they shook the plum tree? Millions of dollars went to many who needed it least, parting gestures of a lonely old woman to the few cherished friends she had made in a lifetime. Millions more were bequeathed to distant, unknown, and mostly wealthy relatives who might otherwise have attempted to break the will. Nearly $11,000,000 went to a half-dozen debt-free Episcopal churches whose lists of trustees, vestrymen, and wardens read like a financial *Who's Who* and include Morgans, Vanderbilts, Frelinghuysens, Mellons, and Roosevelts. Almost $8,000,000 was given to four of the most exclusive and best-endowed boys' preparatory schools in the United States. That considerable sums of money went to hospitals, homes for the crippled and infirm, and institutions of higher learning was partially due to the gentle, always indirect persuasion of Sylvia's legal advisers. Those who knew her best said the surest way to get Sylvia to refuse to do something was to urge her to do it.

The reactions of the beneficiaries were not all joyous. Most, of course, were pleased, although Henry Loomis, of Rochester, New York, turned irritably to questioning reporters and piped, "What the hell good is a hundred thousand dollars to a man who'll be eighty-six his next birthday?" And three universities, each promised $30,000,000 in a preceding will, admitted to a certain amount of disappointment when a later and far less generous (to them) testament was found hidden under four cakes of soap in a little-used tin cabinet in Mrs. Wilks' Fifth Avenue apartment.

Blessings, too, were mixed. The New Bedford *Standard-Times* said editorially on May 4, 1953, "The trustees of the Free Public Library are faced with what could accurately be called an embarrassment of riches, a predicament rarely encountered by agencies of City Government." To the trustees' rescue came the thrifty New Bedford city fathers, who found a simple solution to the problem. They lopped off all library funds from the next municipal budget and left that institution considerably worse off than it was before receiving the $1,200,000 bequest.

Some of the lucky ones did not keep their money long. Robert Moses, Commissioner of Parks for the City of New York, merely endorsed his $10,000 check and turned it over to charity the day he received it. Josephine Grinnell Smith, a lovely young New

Yorker in the days of Ward McAllister but an old, near-penniless widow in 1952, was living in one room of her dilapidated mansion in the backwoods of southern New Jersey when her bequest of $100,000 reached her. Mrs. Smith, during a lifetime of gaiety, had gone through two fortunes (Grinnell and Van Rensselaer) and three husbands. She managed to spend her $100,000 in five years and died insolvent in 1957.

Perhaps the most surprised beneficiaries were Sylvia's former employees. One such was Joseph A. Lynagh, who entered the Green service in 1915. He was their bookkeeper, their only one, and worked long hours on a high stool in a dreary, Dickensian office at 111 Broadway where narrow windows looked out over the burial grounds of Trinity Church. His salary, for one who kept track of the flow (there was no ebb) of $100,000,000, was not high. Its peak was reached in 1945, when he was raised to $75 a week. The office atmosphere, Lynagh said, was cold and unfriendly. There was no banter among the four aging employees. Sylvia frowned on camaraderie and frigidly repelled the slightest attempts at intimacy.

Another employee was Dan Chicko, a hard-working Italian laborer at Altacrest, Sylvia's Greenwich estate. His mistress spoke to him twice in his thirty-four years of service. The first time was to tell him he had been docked an hour's pay, forty cents, because he was late for work. The second was to ask him to keep his seven-year-old daughter, Maria, off the premises. "Mrs. Wilks didn't like children," Dan said.

Yet despite her brusque treatment while she lived, Sylvia in death was generous to all who worked for her. Lynagh's bequest was $35,000 and Chicko's $34,000.

Sylvia paid her taxes promptly and honestly, if not without pain, and engaged in comparatively few lawsuits, unlike her embattled mother, for whom litigation and tax dodging occupied many a waking hour. Hetty distributed her boundless hatred fairly evenly between tax collectors and members of the bar, for whom she had a deep abomination. ("Every time a lawyer gets near me I want to throw up.")

Members of the bar returned Hetty's feelings in kind. Frequently a lawyer who had represented Hetty had to hire his own counsel to represent him in order to collect *his* fees. More often than would seem possible a lawyer engaged to defend Hetty in such a suit would wind up in the same awkward position as his erstwhile opponents.

Shortly before the turn of the century the indomitable Mrs. Green was forced to represent herself in a Chicago courtroom. Undismayed, in fact delighted by the prospect of jousting with her enemies personally, Hetty appeared in court dressed in the most ragged garment in her wretched wardrobe. By pleading poverty and persecution she won a verdict from a sympathetic jury, who apparently shared her feelings about lawyers.

Mrs. Green's attitude toward tax collectors was passed on to her son, who traveled hundreds of thousands of miles and spent half a lifetime attempting to confuse revenue agents. That he nearly succeeded is evidenced best by the fact that it took 385 witnesses two years of continuous testimony before a Special Master appointed by the Supreme Court of the United States to determine in which of four competing states the peripatetic Colonel really lived. The final verdict cost one Attorney General the highest office in his state and helped boost another into a Governor's mansion.

However, the Colonel did not inherit his mother's distaste for members of the bar. Some of his best friends were lawyers. As a matter of fact, the Colonel hated almost no one, not even the servants who stole from him, the "wards" who disappointed him, the politicians who defeated him, the merchants who defrauded him, the doctors who failed him, the wife who bored him, and the woman who loved him and abandoned him.

The only apparent exception to the warmth this lonely, troubled, funny, phony Colonel felt for people was his mother. For her, despite vociferous protestations of affection, Colonel (by the grace of a Southern Governor) Edward Howland Robinson Green must have nourished a bitter hatred. Everything he did after she died was a violent protest against this woman whose penury cost him his leg, whose domination cost him his self-respect, and whose money cost him his self-confidence.

How did his sister Sylvia feel about her mother? Only once in a long lifetime did she who shared with her beloved brother Ned the miseries and frustrations of a dreadfully unhappy childhood reveal that she, too, had no love for Mamma. During the famous Green domicile trial Paul A. Dever, Attorney General for the Commonwealth of Massachusetts, asked Mrs. Wilks where her brother had lived at a certain time.

"With my mother," she answered, "if you call that living."

Chapter Two

In a state of dubious preservation, shadowed by Colonel Green's $4,000,000 mansion on Buzzards Bay near Dartmouth, Massachusetts, is an aged wooden farmhouse. The two sharply contrasting houses are in the center of a three-hundred-acre tract known as Round Hills. Until Sylvia donated it to Massachusetts Institute of Technology this land had been in the possession of the Howlands, her maternal ancestors, since the last decade of the seventeenth century. The existing farmhouse was built in 1721, one hundred and one years after the arrival of the first Howland on the *Mayflower* and exactly two hundred years before the Colonel erected his sixty-room stone and marble dwelling.

The mansion is in excellent shape but the farmhouse looks ready to collapse. Hetty, who spent many a childhood summer in

13

it, refused to part with a dime to repair it and the Colonel allotted less than a hundred dollars a year for repairs, which barely kept the roof from leaking.

There are five rooms in the farmhouse including a fair-sized addition built some years after the original structure was completed. For generations, the Howlands were members of the Society of Friends and the new room was added as a meeting place, to accommodate the overflow from nearby Apponagansett, where the mother church stood.

We are indebted to the late William M. Emery, famous New Bedford genealogist (and a $10,000 recipient of Sylvia Wilks' generosity), for a painstaking study of the Howland ancestry. Emery traced the family tree from the birth of Bishop Richard Howland, who was granted a coat of arms by Queen Elizabeth, June 10, 1584, to the death of Sarah C. Howland, October 14, 1918. It may be of interest to those who followed Hetty's career to learn that silver and gold figure prominently in her emblem of heraldry.

John, the *Mayflower* Howland and the first on these shores, was followed in a few years by brothers Henry and Arthur. Henry Howland, Mr. Emery notes, is the one who bought that black cow, and this was the first listed possession of any American Howland.

The Colonel's great-great-grandfather, Isaac Howland, was a well-to-do farmer who had three sons and two daughters. An uncompromising Quaker, he disinherited his youngest son, his namesake, for religious reasons. But by the time old Isaac died, in 1778, young Isaac had far outstripped his father in wealth.

Isaac, the disinherited, went to sea at an early age, became a master mariner and shipowner, engaged in the West Indies trade, and was in at the start of the American whaling industry. He accumulated a considerable amount of money and settled in New Bedford, where he was known as Captain Howland, Sr. He died in 1811 at the age of eighty-five and left a substantial estate to his widow, three sons, and two daughters.

Captain Howland's third child and first son was Isaac, Jr., who

14

was to have the double distinction of founding the great New Bedford whaling firm of Isaac Howland, Jr. & Co., and becoming Hetty's grandfather. Unlike his father, the Captain, a large and powerful man whose commanding presence drew instant respect from his crews and his business associates, Isaac was short and slight. He weighed less than a hundred pounds. But what he lacked in physical structure he more than made up in mental equipment and the quality of endurance.

In its eighty-year history the firm developed the greatest whaling fleet in America. The fame of Howland's ships and the daring crews that manned them spread all over the world. Some thirty-five craft sailed under the company flag. Included in this fleet was the redoubtable *Charles W. Morgan,* last active survivor of the once huge fleet of 426 great whalers that sailed the seven seas and proudly listed their home port as New Bedford.

Venturing forth on voyages lasting from two to four years, the whalers returned to New Bedford laden with sperm oil, whale oil, and whalebone. A successful trip for a bark-rigged whaler, manned by a crew of thirty-five, could mean as much as a $75,000 profit for her owners.

Sometimes, of course, a ship would founder mysteriously in unknown waters and neither vessel nor crew would ever be seen again. But the firm of Isaac Howland, Jr. & Co. suffered remarkably few losses by shipwreck. Competitors considered it lucky. But part of the luck must have been due to Isaac Howland, Jr., himself, who built or bought the sturdiest of vessels, kept every ship of the fleet in the finest condition, and hired the most experienced and bravest of captains and the most trustworthy crews. This policy was carried out long after its founder's death in 1834. Then control passed into the hands of Edward Mott Robinson, a strong, ruthless, domineering, money-loving Philadelphian who increased his normal chances for success in the approved fashion of the times by marrying Isaac's granddaughter.

Abby Howland and Edward Mott Robinson were married December 29, 1833. On January 12, 1834, Isaac died in his New Bedford mansion. His only survivors were his widow, Ruth Butts, whom he had married after the death of his first wife, Abigail Slocum, and two grandchildren, Abby, the bride, and her bed-ridden spinster sister, Sylvia Ann.

Because Isaac had long been aware that Abby was easily influenced and might part with her inheritance by giving something to charity or spending it foolishly in some other unproductive fashion, he kept possession of the actual cash away from her. He put $90,000 of Abby's money in the hands of one partner, Edward Mott Robinson, the bridegroom, whom he disliked but whose business acumen and drive he respected. He put the remainder of Abby's bequest, $40,000, under the trusteeship of a third partner, Thomas Mandell, of New Bedford, who had joined the firm of Isaac Howland, Jr. & Co. in 1819. Isaac had more faith in his other granddaughter, Sylvia Ann, and left her $130,000 legacy outright. Hetty determined to get hold of Aunt Sylvia Ann's cash no matter what the consequences.

During the years Robinson was associated with Isaac Howland, Jr. & Co., the firm prospered enormously. From partners and captains down to the lowliest deck hand, every man in its employ benefited by increasingly successful voyages of the Howland whaling fleet. It was Robinson who bought the *Morgan* for his company after owning a few shares in her himself. Although this ship was by no means the largest to fly the Howland flag, she certainly was one of the most profitable and played a large part in increasing the fortune Sylvia Ann Howland Wilks was to distribute on a January day a hundred years later.

Chapter Three

HETTY was born November 21, 1835. Both her mother and father were devout Quakers. Although most members of the Society of Friends seem to have a strong feeling of responsibility for less fortunate neighbors, social-consciousness is not a requirement for membership. Edward Mott Robinson adhered to the letter of his faith, but his only feeling toward his fellow townsmen was the urge to use them whenever he could to make money for himself, his family, and his firm.

Robinson, nicknamed "Black Hawk" after a wily Indian chief, was hard and cold and had little sympathy for the ailing wife who, having first presented him with a daughter, took to her bed shortly after the death of their infant son. Abby could have no more children and Edward, a tyrant with patriarchal instincts,

17

was a bitterly disappointed man. How many of Abby's ailments were real and how many imagined, perhaps to escape from the domination and scorn of her husband, no one will ever know. The effects upon Hetty would have been the same either way. No softening maternal control was exercised over the child and she grew up as her father wanted her to, absorbing—from the time she could understand at all—his lifelong passion for accumulating money.

Those who had dealings with Hetty Green in later life cannot conceive that she ever had the normal reactions of a child. They picture her as always having been full-grown and ready for battle like the instant warriors who sprang from the dragon's teeth that Cadmus sowed. Yet if we are to believe stories of her early life, objectively written more than fifty years ago, Hetty's responses, at least until she was five years old, apparently were the same as those of other children.

"Much of the early life of Mrs. Hetty Green," said the New Bedford *Times* on July 3, 1916 (the day of Hetty's death), "was spent in her parents' stone mansion at the northwest corner of Pleasant and Campbell Streets, where she and her playmates played with their dolls."

When her mother "didn't feel up to it" and was too busy "doctoring," the little girl was shunted between her grandfather's home, a bright and cheerful house, and her Aunt Sylvia Ann's less pleasant but equally spacious home. Summers were spent at Round Hills.

At the time of Hetty's birth and until the use of petroleum began to close down the whaling industry in the mid-sixties, New Bedford was at its most thriving and exciting best. Its population had grown to 16,000, and while no rival of Boston, sixty miles to the north, it was a far more fascinating community than the state's capital. Basically its people were of early American stock, but the danger and romance of whaling had attracted to New Bedford seamen and adventurers from all over the world, including more than a scattering of Portuguese.

18

Hetty's formal schooling was sketchy, a fact revealed in later life by her impoverished vocabulary and her lack of knowledge of even the fundamentals of grammar and spelling. "Deare Sir," she might scrawl in salutation and conclude a letter with "Youres respectfuly." When she was seven she was sent to a Quaker boarding school operated by Miss Eliza Wing at Sandwich, near New Bedford. She remained there for three years before returning to her father's home. Later, when she was sixteen, she attended a Boston finishing school run for the daughters of wealthy New England aristocrats by the Reverend Charles Russell Lowell and his wife, Anna Cabot Lowell. Hetty stayed here for two years, learning, according to the New Bedford *Standard*, "to dance and to play the piano, two accomplishments that were considered the most genteel for girls of that time."

Hetty's real eduction and the training she was to use in later life came directly from her father. She stayed close at his heels, on school vacations and whenever she had the chance. An accustomed sight to New Bedforders in the forties and early fifties was that of Robinson and his daughter, whose aggressiveness, aptitude for commerce, and obvious desire to emulate her father in every way had stilled forever his wish for a son.

All day long the pair of them—Hetty, tall for her age and leggy, clutching the hand of her six-foot father or trailing behind his hurried steps—went about the town. Their first stop was at the busy offices of Isaác Howland, Jr. & Co., where clerks and bookkeepers sat on high stools keeping records of expenditures and profits. Next they would enter the Howland warehouses, where the overpowering smell of oil was always present. Then on to the huge Howland commissaries, where the tingling scent of spices, gathered from all over the world, blended delightfully with the pungent bouquet of Louisiana perique and Danish cheeses. After this they were on their way to the countinghouses of Pleasant Street, where Black Hawk banked and bought and sold futures. The last stop was at the wharves near Acushnet, where there was always at least one tall ship flying the Howland flag, unloading

19

cargo, or taking on stores. This was Hetty's world and the one she loved best.

In the evenings, when doting mothers read *The Tales of Peter Parley* or Hawthorne's *Wonder-Book for Girls and Boys,* Miss Robinson's fare was of hardier stuff. Almost her first glimpse of the printed word was the financial pages of the New York *Herald,* the New York *World,* and the Boston *Globe.*

"When I was five years old," Hetty once told a reporter, "I used to sit on my father's lap while he read the business news and the stock market reports of the day to me. When I was six I read them myself. And I understood them, too!" This may have been an exaggeration by a couple of years, but you can be sure that when Hetty was an adolescent she wasted no time on *Godey's Lady's Book.*

While the men of New Bedford were amused at the spectacle of the richest girl in town growing up as a hoyden, the aristocratic ladies of that community were shocked by Hetty's dirty, unkempt appearance and her friendship with the social outcasts of the town—"Portagees," dock workers, seamen, and the like. Hetty felt no warm bond of kinship with these lower classes; she simply wanted to learn from them how the Howland wealth was gathered and preserved by its producers and custodians.

Hetty was not unattractive physically. On the contrary, she was beginning to ripen into a tall, full-figured, handsome young woman, with a fine, delicate, peach-colored complexion that she retained even as an old woman. A miniature of Hetty painted when she was about nineteen shows regular features, eyes bright, blue, large, and intelligent, and a bosom full and high.

There was nothing soft and yielding about Hetty, and she grew more and more careless about her personal appearance. Mrs. Robinson, self-effacing and weak, had long since abandoned efforts to cope with her. Attempting to run a household on the strictly limited budget her husband allotted, and sick with real and imagined illnesses, she sought help from her physically weaker but mentally stronger sister, Sylvia Ann. There were times when constantly increasing clashes between strong-willed father and even stronger-willed daughter grew so bitter that Mrs. Robinson would leave home to find a measure of peace in the household of her invalid sister.

Before Hetty was twenty she made two sorties into society, one in Boston and the other in New York. Proper lineage on both sides of her family, coupled with her father's great wealth, made the first possible. The second was achieved through the social prestige of her maternal cousins, the Grinnells, who belonged to the most exclusive set in New York. From Hetty's point of view neither foray was successful and both were a waste of time. She held society in utter contempt and could hardly wait until she returned to the more desirable and familiar surroundings of Isaac Howland, Jr. & Co., and the moneymaking potentials of New Bedford.

Chapter Four

Abby Slocum Howland Robinson died February 21, 1860, at the age of fifty-one without having made a will, an unthinkable condition for any Howland. The $40,000 left to her by her father had tripled under the capable trusteeship of her husband and Thomas Mandell. In addition she had owned nearly $10,000 in real estate. Hetty fully expected to receive the bulk of her mother's fortune. But knowing her father only too well, she realized this could never happen without a bitter struggle and protracted litigation. She was in a real quandary. If she antagonized her father he was quite capable of cutting her off without a cent and thus she could lose nearly fifty times the amount she might gain even if she got all her mother's money.

There was no question in Hetty's mind and also in that of Aunt

Sylvia Ann that Abby's money, "Howland money," should remain in Howland hands. But the odds were too great, and after a vitriolic display of temper Hetty yielded to her father's suggestion that they submit the question of their joint inheritance to a mutually agreed upon lawyer and abide by his decision. Robinson, cognizant of nineteenth-century attitudes toward the paterfamilias, knew beforehand his chances for winning were far better than his daughter's. His gamble paid off and he was awarded all the cash. Hetty received the real estate.

Shortly afterward Robinson sold out his interests in Isaac Howland, Jr. & Co., and left New Bedford for New York. Here he became a partner in the firm of William T. Coleman & Co., shipping merchants "under whose flag," said the New York *Times*, "many a fine clipper put out into the East River for a voyage to foreign shores." Grief over his wife's death was hardly his reason for leaving Massachusetts. Robinson had vision enough to realize that kerosene, rather than whale oil, soon would be lighting the lamps of the world and that the firm which had brought wealth to its owners and fame to New Bedford must soon pass out of existence. With the Civil War driving prices to new highs, Robinson received nearly $5,000,000 for his share. Two years later the firm was liquidated.

Robinson was fifty-nine years old, handsome, virile, and rich. His father had lived to be eighty-five, and his mother, eighty-six. Released from an unsuccessful marriage, with a vision of twenty or more years ahead, there was no reason why he should not begin a new family that might produce a male heir to carry on the Robinson line. Such a thought must have been a living nightmare for Hetty.

Her father's departure for New York left Hetty in the proverbial pickle. Should she follow him to protect her interests by discouraging predatory females who might like to become the bride of this eligible widower? She had seen enough pairs of young New Bedford eyes cast on her father to know that a second marriage was a definite possibility if he were left alone. Or should she stay in New Bedford to make sure that Aunt Sylvia Ann's $2,000,-000 fortune remained in Howland hands (Hetty's) and was not distributed to charity as the invalid had so often threatened it would be?

It is not likely that affection played any part in Hetty's decision to remain, temporarily at least, in New Bedford. She must have concluded that her mother's sister, a bedridden invalid, certainly had a shorter life expectancy than Black Hawk Robinson. Besides, Sylvia Ann was more pliable, or so Hetty thought, and more likely to yield to persuasion than her stubborn father.

As it turned out Hetty was wrong on almost every count. Edward Mott Robinson never remarried and predeceased his sister-in-law by a month, bequeathing his entire estate to his daughter, while the bulk of Sylvia Ann's fortune eventually went to charity. It was not that Hetty did not try to induce her aunt to abandon that foolish idea of giving money away. During the few years she lived with her mother's sister, she employed every means except violence to make sure Sylvia Ann left her money to no one but her niece. When cajolery, flattery, and humble pleading failed, she used intimidation and constant harassment. She even tried bathos, declaring that if she did not inherit the estate she might well become "a poor, neglected orphan," and "a recipient of public charity." Hetty naturally failed to point out that even then she was worth at least $50,000, a fact surely known to her mother's only sister.

But Sylvia Ann possessed some of the Howland resistance to pressure. Sick as she was and spied upon by Hetty, she still managed to draw a secret will. So that she might enjoy a little peace and comfort in the remaining few years of her life, she kept the news from Hetty, who would have treated this bombshell with cold anger and subjected Aunt Sylvia Ann to a tirade of bitter invective.

In 1863 Hetty left New Bedford for New York, certain that her interests were secured in a will drawn in 1860. According to this document, the entire estate would pass directly to Hetty, with the exception of less than 5 per cent which she could not dissuade her aunt from leaving to charity, old friends, and faithful servants. Taxes, in those golden days, were negligible.

It is hard to imagine what explanation Hetty gave to Aunt Sylvia Ann for joining the father she had so bitterly condemned as a fortune hunter unworthy of any additional Howland money because of his cruelty to his daughter and to his wife, Sylvia Ann's only sister.

Sylvia Ann's undisclosed (to Hetty, at any rate) last will and testament was written on January 11, 1862, with a codicil added November 28, 1864. Because the body of the will was drawn while Hetty was still in New Bedford, Thomas Mandell and Dr. William A. Gordon, the two witnesses and, incidentally, bountiful beneficiaries, must have entered Miss Howland's bedchamber with trepidation. There, dreading Hetty's return from some errand, the trio drew up a document which, in the words of the Boston *Globe,* was to develop into "one of the most remarkable will cases in the history of legal jurisprudence and become a *cause célèbre* throughout the United States."

Sylvia Ann Howland died July 2, 1865, at the age of fifty-nine. Edward Mott Robinson had died on June 14th, that same year. With the exception of pitifully few gifts to charity, totaling less than one half of one per cent of his great wealth, the fortune, nearly $6,000,000 in liquid assets, went to his daughter.

Hetty returned to New Bedford for the funeral of her aunt, comforted by her knowledge of great expectations shortly to be realized. The shock came after Miss Howland's funeral. Then Hetty found that her aunt had disposed of over half her fortune in legacies to other relatives, friends, servants, and to public charities. From the remaining $1,000,000, Hetty was to receive only a life income, the money finally to pass on to various Howland cousins, many then yet unborn.

The twelfth clause of the will and the codicil were the most bitter of all for Hetty. In them she won a Pyrrhic victory and handed the last laugh to Aunt Sylvia Ann. The clause made sure that Howland money stayed in Howland hands just as Hetty always said it should. But it was Hetty's money, the $1,000,000 in which she was bequeathed only a life interest, that would remain with the Howlands.

"After my niece's death," declared Sylvia Ann, "the trustees are ordered to pay over the whole of said Residuary estate to all the lineal descendants of . . . Gideon Howland."

In the codicil Aunt Sylvia Ann gave proof that Hetty's arguments against her father's unworthiness were effective. "After due thought," said Miss Howland, "I hereby revoke my bequest of $100,000 to Edward Mott Robinson." Since the original gift was made to Robinson or "in the event of his death to his heirs or descendants," even this bit of balm was denied to his bereaved daughter.

For a woman who was to spend half the night looking for a two-cent postage stamp she mislaid in a carriage at Bellows Falls, Vermont, a loss of $2,000,000 was not to be taken lying down. Soon after the "secret" document was probated, Hetty, through her attorney, the distinguished New Bedford lawyer William W. Crapo, produced what she claimed to be the true last will and testament of Sylvia Ann Howland. "Hetty's" will, or rather its famous second page, claimed that she, Hetty Howland Robinson, was "sole heir-at-law of Sylvia Ann Howland with whom she had, until within a few years, lived and who performed towards her the duties of mother."

The immediate furor aroused in New Bedford was exceeded only once and that twenty-eight years later when Lizzie Borden went on trial. Scores of Howland cousins were roused to anger along with Sylvia Ann's servants, her nurse, and the City of New Bedford, bequeathed $100,000 in Miss Howland's unbelievably farsighted gesture "for the introduction of water into the city and encouragement of industry or heavy manufactures which requires the use of steam . . . because I believe its prosperity depends upon the establishment of manufactures within New Bedford." Edward Mott Robinson was not the only farsighted one who called the turn on whaling.

26

ended but before Justice Clifford handed down his unexpected and disappointing verdict.

"Miss Robinson," said the *Post*, "now contests her aunt's will in one of the most remarkable cases on record. This is, in itself remarkable enough, seeing that the young lady, already the possessor of millions, is entitled, under it, to an annuity that would add some . . . $70,000 to her annual income. What she wants is the whole of her aunt's estate, worth $2 million.

"The ground upon which she contests the will and codicil is noteworthy. It seems that Miss Howland had quarreled with her brother-in-law, the father of Miss Robinson, and being resolved to exclude him from all share not only of her own property, but of his daughter's also, she proposed, about September, 1860, to her niece, that if she (Miss Robinson) would make a will so that her father should inherit it in no part, she (Miss Howland) would, in return, make a will leaving everything to her niece; the will of each to be posted with the other, and neither to make any other will without notice to the other. Miss Robinson agreed to this and the wills were executed accordingly. But the subsequent will and codicil made by her aunt in 1862 and 1864 were executed without notice to the niece.

"Thus arose a novel question in the courts of this country whether a contract for mutual wills, if proved, can be enforced as being without consideration and against public policy and good morals."

However, it was not a point of law but a question of fact that aroused great interest and curiosity all over this country and even abroad.

"The most singular feature of this strange affair," continued the *Post*, "is an addition to the will sewed on with fine thread to the first page, not changing any provision but a sort of protest by the testator against the validity of any subsequent will which she (Sylvia Ann) under the influence from those around her, might be induced to make.

" 'I implore the judge,' said Miss Howland, 'to decide in favor

29

of this will, as nothing could induce me to make a will unfavorable to my niece, but being ill, and afraid, if any of my caretakers insisted on my making a will, to suffer, as they might leave me or be angry. I give this will to my niece to show, if necessary, to have it appear against any other will found after my death.'"

Hetty admitted that she wrote this appendage to the will albeit at the suggestion of her aunt but swore that her aunt signed it herself in duplicate in her presence.

To this, counselor for the executors, trustees, and heirs replied, "Sylvia Ann Howland's signature was forged!"

This was a serious charge to bring against anybody. But to claim that one of the richest women in America, a descendant of an old, respectable if not distinguished family, had committed two felonies, forgery and perjury, was enough to cause anticipatory shudders of delight in all who loved a scandal and a juicy trial.

The public had a ready-made villain in Hetty Howland Robinson, disliked not only because she was rich and a complete nonconformist, but also because of her reputation among those who had occasion to borrow money from her. There were plenty of heroes—orphans, sailors' widows, old and indigent women, and the New Bedford Public Library, recipient of a $100,000 bequest. No mention was made of the pragmatic Dr. Gordon although there must have been quite a few citizens who would have liked to see this gentleman share the dock with Hetty on the charge of using undue influence.

Hetty fired the first shot. Her witness was a handwriting expert named Crossman who said, "After many months of painstaking research, I am completely convinced that the signatures of Sylvia Ann Howland are genuine." The trustees, et al., countered with their own handwriting expert named Southworth, who said, "After many months of painstaking research, I am completely convinced that the signatures of Sylvia Ann Howland were forged."

To end the stalemate came three big guns, dragged from the

halls of Harvard College, and all aimed at Hetty, her counsel, and her handwriting expert. The awesome trio included Dr. Oliver Wendell Holmes, Professor Louis Agassiz, and Professor Benjamin Peirce. All three unanimously declared that someone had traced Miss Howland's genuine signature and affixed it to both documents in question. If that mysterious someone, they intimated, had taken the trouble to select two different signatures of Miss Howland and affixed one tracing to the first page and the other to the second page of the document, the forgery might never have been discovered. The two signatures, they decared, were exactly alike in every minute detail, too much so to be other than forgeries.

While Dr. Holmes and Professor Agassiz are better remembered today than their colleague, Professor Peirce, a great mathematician and an authority on the incidence of chance, it was Peirce who brought down the house.

"The chance that Sylvia Ann Howland's signatures are genuine," Professor Peirce stated dryly, "is one in 2,666,000,000,000,-000,000,000 times."

It was not until 1870 that the Court handed down its decision and dismissed Hetty's bill in equity on the grounds that there was insufficient evidence of a contract between Miss Howland and her niece to make mutual wills. The matter of forgery was not even considered. This was a blow to all who had hoped to see Miss Robinson, by then Mrs. Edward Henry Green, brought back from England, where she had fled, to appear in the docks of New Bedford's criminal courts.

Chapter Six

To the astonishment of nearly everyone, Miss Robinson became a bride at the age of thirty-three. The groom, forty-six, was a native of Bellows Falls, Vermont, and descended from a family just as old and respectable, although not as wealthy, as Hetty's. The marriage took place in New York on July 18, 1867. It was rumored for years that on the evening of July 17, 1867, Edward Henry Green signed an antenuptial agreement with his bride-to-be, renouncing all his rights to her fortune. Since he predeceased his wife, Hetty was never asked to produce this pact.

At the time of his marriage and for a long while after, Edward H. Green had no need for his wife's money. True, he was not as well situated as his bride, but in those days a million dollars, which he was estimated to have, went far. Unfortunately, as it turned out, it didn't go far enough.

There are many stories of how they met and why they married. One says that Green was a fortune hunter looking over the field for a rich wife when he came upon Hetty. This is not borne out by the Vermonter's character and his million dollars. Other gossip has it that Hetty, fearful of what might happen if proven a forgerer and perjurer, was looking for a husband who would help her escape from the jurisdiction of the criminal courts of the United States. There may be an element of truth in the second.

What seems closest to the facts is the story told by the Bancrofts, Herbert and his wife Molly, of Bellows Falls, who knew Hetty and her husband and were childhood friends of the Colonel and his sister Sylvia. Bancroft's grandfather, Solon Goodridge, was head of the East Indies trading firm of Goodridge and Walker and Edward Henry Green had been its representative in Manila and China for twenty years.

"According to my grandfather," Mr. Bancroft said, "Mr. Green was back in the States, anxious to retire from business and settle down in Bellows Falls, after spending half his life traveling all over the world. He was getting to the age where he felt if he didn't start raising a family he never would. He and my grandfather were having lunch at the Parker House in Boston. That must have been during the Howland will trial. Hetty walked into the hotel dining room and Mr. Green fell for her.

"Grandfather said Hetty was a very handsome woman and Molly and I can verify that even when she was much older. That time when she was on the witness stand her lawyers must have made her dress up in her best, and she looked stunning. At any rate, my grandfather and Hetty were old friends and he introduced them. Well, you know the rest," Bancroft concluded.

Whatever traits of kindness and sympathy the Colonel and Sylvia possessed no doubt were inherited from their father. Despite his sophistication—he knew the East and Far East well, had been in every capital city of Europe, and spoke several languages including Chinese—he was essentially a quiet, understanding gentleman who endured a disillusioning life with Hetty until she brought the marriage to an end.

33

The first of Green's ancestors came to this country from London in 1635, settling in Cambridge, Massachusetts. Edward Henry Green was the eighth in his line of descent. Among his ancestors there were a number of prominent clergymen, a Royal Magistrate, congressmen, a Justice of Common Pleas Court, and a Mayor of Boston—Edward Henry Green's uncle, Dr. Samuel Abbott Green.

Edward Henry Green was born in Bellows Falls, February 6, 1821. His father was a successful merchant of Wendell, Massachusetts, who settled in Bellows Falls because he thought the town had a great commercial future.

Young Edward grew up in this attractive mountain community, one of five villages in the town of Rockingham. Those who recalled him in later years remembered him for his warmth, generosity, and charm. Many stories are told of his returns from his travels, laden with gifts from the Orient. Usually he was attended by a Japanese valet and a hideous English bulldog. Either would have created a stir anywhere; in a conservative New England village the combination must have been devastating.

There are a number of men and women who remember him in his later years and who can recall tales about his earlier life told by their parents.

"My mother was a good friend of Edward Henry Green when they both were young," recollected Mary Nims Bolles, a spry and stimulating nonagenarian, childhood playmate of Green's daughter, Sylvia Ann. "Mother told me once that Edward, that is Sylvia Ann's father, came home from a trip and told his mother he wanted her to have a fine set of furs.

" 'Go down to New York,' he said, 'and pick up something good in furs there and I'll tell my agent to pay for them. You just give him the bill.'

"Well, the next time the Greens went to New York, which was a couple of weeks later, Edward's mother selected some beautiful mink which she was crazy about but when her son saw them he wasn't satisfied.

" 'Give these to my sister,' Edward told his mother. 'They aren't good enough for you.'

"He went down to New York himself and brought his mother the most magnificent set of Russian sables anybody ever saw. That's the way he was.

"One more thing. I know this is true because my father told it to me. Mr. Green's father, Mr. Edward Atkinson Green, I'm referring to, was pretty well fixed financially but his son, Edward Henry, the one my parents knew, kept insisting on having a generous annuity sent to him, which he kept increasing each year. One day his father called on the New York agent and ordered him to cut it down. He said he couldn't possibly spend all that money."

This was the man Hetty married. It would be difficult to find a couple more poorly mated, fiscally at least, than this one. For a short while the newlyweds lived in the groom's Manhattan apartment. Then word reached Hetty that all was not well in New Bedford. Howland cousins and other heirs, furious because Hetty's bill of complaint barred payment of all legacies, were discussing means to bring the bride to court on charges of forgery.

This was enough for Hetty, frightened for once in her life. With her husband she fled to London, there to remain for the next eight years. Since they were spending Edward's money, Hetty apparently had no objection to living well. The couple established residence at the new and exclusive Langham Hotel in London. It was there that Edward Howland Robinson Green was born August 22, 1868, followed by a sister, christened Hetty Sylvia Ann Howland Robinson Green, January 7, 1871, but known as Sylvia.

The panic of 1873, coupled with Hetty's misinformation that the statute of limitations on forgery had run out (since she had fled the jurisdiction of Massachusetts courts this was not true), plus a measure of homesickness, caused the Greens to return to America. Early in 1875 Green concluded the London trading business he had established and the four sailed for the United States.

During the first half-dozen years of their marriage, and while he had money and was willing to spend it, he made all major decisions for his household. The Greens took up residence in Bellows Falls, where Hetty's atavistic tendencies soon broke through the thin shell holding them in check. Expected to take her rightful place as a community leader, Mrs. Green soon gave proof she cared as little for public opinion and society in Vermont as she had for the established conventions of New Bedford and New York in an earlier day.

Soon after her arrival at Bellows Falls Hetty began to get careless about her personal appearance. Her hands were rarely clean, her fingernails were black, and when her dresses tore or grew out of style she neither mended nor replaced them. She shocked her generous, open-handed in-laws constantly by her stinginess, quarreled with their servants and her own, badgered local tradesmen about prices, and bickered with her husband about trivialities. It did not take Mrs. Green long to become as disliked in her adopted village as she had been in New Bedford.

But it was the children, Ned and Sylvia, who bore the brunt of their mother's penny-pinching eccentricities. As a result of the recent panic, their father, whom the children loved deeply and who responded with gentleness and affection, had lost half his fortune. What was far worse from Hetty's point of view, the New York brokerage firm of John J. Cisco, where Mr. and Mrs. Green did business, refused to differentiate between Hetty's money and her husband's. Bonds held in escrow by Hetty were seized by the firm to cover Edward's shortages.

When young Ned was about eight or nine he attended a village day school. Sylvia was sent to a school in the parish house of Immanuel Church, a fortunate circumstance for this Episcopal institution, which seventy years later benefited to the extent of $600,000 by the generosity of its one-time charge. Sylvia's dearest friend at Immanuel was Mary Nims, who never joined in the cruel laughter and scorn that ricocheted from Hetty's tough epidermis onto the thinner skins of her offspring. All through her life, and in the loneliness of her old age, Sylvia cherished the rare affection she felt for Mary and which she received in return.

Mary, now the ninety-one-year-old Mrs. Bolles, vividly recalls their first meeting.

"About 1879, when I was a youngster, the Greens took up residence in the Tucker House," she said. "We heard much gossip about the fabulous Mrs. Green and her peculiar ways of living and when the Greens, in their ancient carriage, drove into our yard it caused some excitement. It was a hot day and the living-room blinds on the south side were closed. From behind this screen a little girl friend and I, with our maid, had a good view of the visitors and made appreciative comments.

"Mr. Green, who was driving, did not get out of the carriage. His wife did and attended to the errand on which they came while the two children, a girl and a very lame boy, played about the yard."

Mrs. Bolles explained that she, too, realized there were many conflicting tales (some of them told in bitter irony by Ned himself) about how and when he had injured his leg, but she *is* sure that whatever caused the damage happened before 1879.

"My father raised tobacco," Mrs. Bolles continued, "and Mrs. Green had heard that tobacco leaves bound on Edward's leg would loosen the contracted ligament. She told my mother that during their first winter there was a snowstorm and they bought Edward a sled so that he might slide with other boys in the park. He had never seen snow before so that his enthusiasm over the sport was so great he injured his knee jumping onto his sled.

"My father furnished Mrs. Green liberally with the dry tobacco leaves and had an interesting talk with Mr. Green about Manila and his experience with earthquakes. Father asked him what he did at such a time and he said, 'I used to go and stand under the stone arches at the entrance to the courtyard (the arches are the last thing to go down) and wonder what the damned thing was going to do next.'

"The following year I attended private school at the Episcopal rectory and Sylvia Green was one of the pupils. The Tucker House, a large square brick mansion with ample ground, was only a little way down Church Street. As I lived outside the village I carried my dinner and Sylvia would come back early in the afternoon with me. Sometimes I went home with her after school and shared the hard candy with which she was supplied.

"Her school dresses were clean and inexpensive and mostly hand-me-downs. She wore glasses, and a stiff sailor hat that was too small for her was perched on her head. When we all dressed for last-day exercises she appeared in a very elaborate dress made with many ruffles of white embroidery that looked like a Godey print. She said it came from England."

Later in life Sylvia frequently spoke of the dress. It was a gift from her father, something her mother would never have considered buying.

Sylvia's eyes were poor from birth, and the detached look about them came, much of the time, not from coldness or disinterest but simply because she had difficulty focusing unless she stared straight ahead. This defect accounted for the bad impression Mrs. Wilks frequently created with the working press. For example, a New York *World-Telegram* reporter, after interviewing Sylvia in 1948, declared, ". . . she has penetrating black eyes which bore into you. She gives the impression of being entirely unemotional. Nothing seems to move her one way or the other."

"She probably couldn't even see that reporter," Mrs. Bolles commented. "Those eyes—they were gray—that seemed to bore into you were a misfortune, not an asset. She had contracted pupils which gave them a concentrated expression. Although she wore glasses, reading was always difficult, which put another limit to her enjoyment of life.

"As a young girl she knew she was watched by her associates and pointed out to strangers as a human curiosity—Hetty Green's daughter. She naturally took refuge in a detached attitude until nothing seemed to move her one way or the other."

There were adequate and frequently occurring reasons why

anyone belonging to Hetty would become an object of curiosity, particularly in a small community. Preston D. Belknap, who publishes the Bellows Falls *Times,* told of an incident that happened long before he was born but which was well remembered by many of his father's friends.

"When the Greens moved out of the Tucker House, this must have been about 1882 or so, and went to New York, Hetty stored some of her furniture in a vacant room over the First National Bank. A cat got into the place, somehow, and was locked in there. The only key to the room was in Mrs. Green's possession and she was away.

"After a day or two the cat got hungry and started to wail. Well, somebody heard it and called the constable. He tried to get in but couldn't. Then they called the fire department and a ladder was raised to the second floor. One of the men broke enough of the glass to get his hand in and on the window hook, raise it, and let the cat out.

"A couple of months later Hetty returned to Bellows Falls. She must have gone right to that room to look over the condition of her furniture. A few minutes later she walked into the bank and laid a cobblestone on the teller's window.

"'There's some glass broken upstairs in my room,' she said. 'Don't expect me to pay for it! Somebody threw this stone in the window. I found it on the floor up there.'

"The teller, accustomed to examining checks, turned it over and noticed that it was damp on the underside. It had just been picked up out on the street."

Chapter Seven

THOSE who remember Ned from Bellows Falls recall him as a shy and rather pathetic child. Lyman S. Hayes, Rockingham Town Clerk and author of *Recollections of Hetty's Neighbors*, has vivid memories of both Ned and Sylvia when they were children.

"For a short while they attended village schools," Hayes wrote. "Sylvia dressed in a cast-off polonaise of her mother's which hung about her ankles, dragging the crippled Ned in a cart. The small boy's insufficient clothing was lined with papers to keep out the cold. Frequently his stockings were minus feet.

"Later at a hotel where the Greens boarded for a time, the woman's economy in soap and water led other boarders to request that the Greens be seated at a remote table in the dining room. Hetty would do her washing in her bedroom. She would tie the

40

wet wash together when it was finished, throw it out of the window to the lawn below. Then she would follow downstairs to spread it to dry."

Hetty's shopping habits must have embarrassed her children dreadfully. To impress upon them that "a penny saved is a penny earned" (a cliché she used most frequently) she would take Ned and his sister with her when she did the weekly marketing.

"In local stores," said Mr. Hayes, "people hated to see Hetty coming, not only because it was her custom to haggle over prices but because her handling of goods with unwashed hands resulted in a distinct financial loss to them. On one occasion where the griminess was more than usually conspicuous Hetty explained this condition by the fact that, in examining old red boards in her barn she had found 'some perfectly good nails' which she salvaged from a sled by pulling them out by hand."

Mrs. Bolles has memories of Ned's inordinate fondness for baseball, which he was unable to play because of his physical handicap.

"He wore some kind of homemade wire contraption on the bottom of his shoe to help him walk although he still limped very badly," she said. "I knew he was crazy about baseball and when the boys had their game he'd stand way out in the field for hours hoping a ball would be knocked to him close enough to catch. Of course he couldn't run for it.

"He was a good organizer, though, and I think once he got a team together that played all around Bellows Falls. They said they played very well, indeed."

Fishing in the Connecticut River just above Bellows Falls was good, and frequently Ned would limp, by himself, to that part of the river where the banks were low and smooth and could easily be reached. Here he would fish for hours. But much of the time he spent with Sylvia. Brother and sister developed a rapport and trust in each other that never was lost. What little they had then they shared equally. When both became rich beyond the dreams of most men, Sylvia never asked Ned for an accounting of her $50

41

or $75 million, the management of which she left completely in his hands.

Once, years after, when Sylvia paid a rare visit to Round Hills after the Colonel's marriage, she complained pettishly about the mosquitoes swarming over the terrace where she and her brother were seated.

"Why, Princess," Ned said, turning to his sister, "you shouldn't feel that way. Half of them are yours, you know."

Ned made only one lasting boyhood friendship at Bellows Falls. This was with John Barrett, later United States Minister to Siam and to the Argentine. Infrequently John's parents, who lived at Grafton, twelve miles north of Bellows Falls, and knew the Greens quite well, would spend a weekend at the Tucker House and take their son with them. The late diplomat recalled those days.

"I was about two years older than Ned," Barrett said. "The first active memory of him I have was soon after his unfortunate accident. My parents used to caution me beforehand when I was with him to be very careful. We didn't play games. We might catch ball on their front lawn but that would stop soon because his mother kept calling out of the window, 'Be careful, Ned!' or 'Don't fall, Ned!' or 'John, don't throw the ball so hard to Ned!'

"So most of the time we just talked and Sylvia would often join us. They were both sweet and shy children, quite close to each other and didn't have friends. We didn't see each other very often as the years went by although once a Washington newspaper ran a story saying I was engaged to be married to Sylvia. There was nothing to it, of course. Even if I'd ever thought seriously about Sylvia, which I didn't, that mother of hers would have scared me off. I liked Ned very much and when he died I felt something good had gone out of my own life."

When his father was home and his mother permitted it, Ned spent a great deal of time with his father. But these occasions were getting rarer. The older Green was finding life with Hetty increasingly distasteful and he was spending less and less time there. An almost complete separation was not far off. In his home

42

town, where he was well liked and respected, Green constantly was subjected to embarrassment by his wife's harsh dealings with local tradesmen and hired help.

On one occasion Green was dining with business acquaintances in the Towns' Hotel. (By that time the quality of food and the service in his own home were unbelievably bad.) Suddenly a female cook emerged from the hotel kitchen and walked to the table where Green and his guests were seated. Green recognized her as "Irish Mary," one of the many servants whom Hetty had fired.

"I hate to bother you, sir," the girl said, "but your wife won't pay me my last month's wages. They're due and coming to me for over a year now. She accused me of stealing her clothing. You know I'd hardly do that, now would I?"

Without a word, Green opened his billfold and counted out not only what Mary asked for but added another month's pay to it.

Sentimentality played little part in Hetty's life, although on at least one occasion she did relax momentarily from her overpowering obsession with the pursuit of money and relive, with Ned and Sylvia, some of the more carefree moments in her own very early life.

The time, which the Colonel never forgot, occurred when he was about fourteen years old and Sylvia eleven. Near the breakup of Hetty's marriage she went to New Bedford for a week, probably to consult with her lawyers there. From Bellows Falls to New Bedford was, in those days, a full night's journey by train. The trio traveled by coach.

When they arrived and were seated in a public hack, Mrs. Green suddenly called out to the driver to turn from Commercial Street.

"Go up Pleasant," she ordered.

"That'll cost you more money, Mrs. Green," answered the driver, who recognized his famous passenger. "It's out of my way."

"Never mind. You do what I tell you to," Hetty replied.

As they moved along Pleasant Street, Hetty kept mentioning various places of interest.

"Here's the house I was born in," and, "Here's where Jane Pierce lived," or, "There's where your Grandpa and I used to walk."

Even this unexpected leap into the past did not end Hetty's sentimental journey. Their cabby was then told to drive south on a narrow road to Round Hills. Halfway there, Hetty stopped the carriage and the three alighted. The trio walked a few feet from the road toward a thicket, with Hetty helping her son over the uneven ground. On the other side of the bush was a swiftly running brook with flat rocks along its banks.

"Here," explained Hetty, "is where Mamma—that's your grandma—used to take us picnicking when she felt well enough."

Then Mrs. Green removed her shoes and stockings, pulled up her long winter underwear, and dipped her feet into the clear water. She told her children to do the same. They stayed by the stream for a little while under a warm sun, and then returned to New Bedford.

By 1881 Edward Henry Green's life with Hetty had become impossible. While the value of Hetty's investments was increasing enormously, that of Green's was not. Hetty was primarily a money-lender who had the foresight to know what men or institutions should be backed by her growing fortune, the merciless drive to collect every cent due her, and the courage to hang on when the market fell. It was when this last happened that Hetty showed her true genius. She knew what and how much to buy. By refusing to sell when others became panicky, eventually she reaped a profit on what looked like a sure loss.

Her husband, on the other hand, was a speculator. He appeared to be a brilliant investor when the market was bullish, but when the bears took over, Edward Henry Green was devoured. After making money for Hetty as well as increasing his own fortune to well over $2,000,000 while they lived in London, Green was down to his last few hundred thousand dollars. His major investments had been in railroads, and the panic of '73 was a delayed disaster for him which he felt most in the early '80s when he could no longer cover short selling.

The Tucker House was closed, to be opened only during the summer months by Hetty and her children. Mrs. Green, Ned, and Sylvia moved into a cheap flat in Brooklyn, not far from the Chemical National Bank in City Hall Square, Manhattan, where Hetty set up headquarters. Green took an attractive apartment in the Cumberland, an expensive residential hotel on Fifth Avenue near 22nd Street. The Cumberland restricted its clientele to men, most of whom were well-to-do bachelors.

At the suggestion of Annie Leary, a bridesmaid at Hetty's wedding, Ned and his sister, raised as Friends in a strict Quaker household, attended a Brooklyn Roman Catholic school for two or three years, for which Hetty had to pay. Miss Leary and Mrs. Green had little in common, yet a strange and lasting friendship developed between these two women. Miss Leary was a devout Roman Catholic. Two years older than Hetty, she was a spinster, generous, kind, public-spirited, and dedicated to bettering the lot of New York's underprivileged, particularly the Italians who lived in poverty on the lower East Side. She was one of the few members of her faith then accepted by New York society. She entertained lavishly in her magnificent Fifth Avenue home and on her country estate at Pelham, New York.

Once Miss Leary actually induced Hetty to move from her dingy $19.00 a month flat at 107 Washington Street, Hoboken, to a $15.00 a day suite in the Hotel Plaza. There Mrs. Green astonished the world by giving an expensive dinner party for her daughter. For the record it should be noted that Hetty returned to an even cheaper flat in the same Hoboken building four weeks later, never failing to mention she had paid sixty cents a plate for hothouse asparagus.

No matter how she tried, however, Miss Leary never was able to persuade her friend Mrs. Green to part with money for "causes." But her influence was felt long afterward when Sylvia bequeathed a completely unexpected $2,400,000 to Fordham University.

It was at St. John's College, now known as Fordham University, that Edward Howland Robinson Green enrolled as a freshman in September of 1885, soon after passing his seventeenth birthday. Despite stories to the contrary, many told by the Colonel himself, who claimed to have got degrees in such assorted disciplines as law, engineering, art, chemistry, and astronomy, he remained only one year.

Green rarely spoke of this unpleasant period in his life when his mother, sister, and he lived together in various cheap flats and furnished rooms scattered over Brooklyn and Hoboken. Their rent during this dismal era was never more than $22.00 a month. According to a story that appeared in the New York *Tribune,* July 17, 1888, "Mrs. Green's table expenses did not exceed $5.00 a week and her others were less than $4.00."

The Greens' mode of life and daily activities were matters of constantly increasing public curiosity. They were dogged by members of the press no matter where they went. Hetty, until well into middle age, made every effort to escape feature writers and others but in later life enjoyed and even encouraged newsmen. The Colonel never shied from reporters; he used to tease them with wild tales, and went out of his way to be kind to them. Sylvia, however, always feared and hated anyone who tried to probe into her affairs, thus becoming a challenge to every city editor. All of this may have proved trying to the Greens at different times in their lives, but it made life easier for their future biographers.

The only Green to be by-passed by the press was Edward Henry, who lived his own quiet, gentlemanly life in his apartment and in his club, the Union, and gradually lost most of his money. Never unfriendly to her husband, Hetty occasionally would visit him and take the children with her. Once, when he became ill, Mrs. Green strode into his strictly male hotel and

46

challenged the clerk to forbid her spending the night there. After a brief skirmish the clerk retired ignominiously.

Hetty stayed with Edward Henry long enough to quarrel with his physician, fire the competent trained nurse attending to his wants, dose him with "squill oil," a homemade panacea, berate him for his incompetence on Wall Street, and leave him just a bit sicker than he was before she came to "cheer him up."

Chapter Eight

SHORTLY before St. John's was scheduled to open in September, 1886, Ned hurt his lame leg again and his school days were over forever. Although he was accustomed to frequent falls and inured to constant pain, this time the injury was more severe and his suffering greater than usual. The three Greens were then living in Mrs. DuChart's boardinghouse at 400 West 23rd Street. Ned was crossing Ninth Avenue on his way home from an errand and was not able to get out of the way of a small boy riding an "express" wagon pulled by a dog.

Ned, tall and heavy, was bowled over. The cart and boy fell on top of him, and the animal, a St. Bernard, dragged driver and Ned for several feet. Ned was unconscious when he was picked up by passers-by. Hetty, only the night before, had returned from a business trip to Chicago. She was deeply disturbed by the accident and troubled by her son's obvious discomfort. She determined she would get medical help for him as soon as possible.

A few days later, when Ned was able to walk again, mother and son began a round of the free clinics in Manhattan and Brooklyn. Ned was dressed appropriately in a secondhand suit, too small for his large frame (he then weighed over a hundred and fifty pounds), and Mamma was attired in her accustomed fashion described by a reporter on the New York *Tribune*, May 27, 1886.

"Mrs. Green," said this journalist, "wore what once had been a black dress, which must have been of practically indestructible material. It turned brown, then green, and still she wore it; and carried an umbrella and handbag of about the same era as her dress."

No need for the pair to go hungry while waiting their turns in the clinics.

"In Mrs. Green's handbag," continued the *Tribune*, "she carried graham crackers—bought in bulk—on which she munched from time to time remarking she was thus saved from paying the 'prohibitive prices' of New York's restaurants."

Unfortunately, Hetty was recognized everywhere. She might be able to deceive social workers and nurses, but she could not escape the keen vision of physicians, who, even in those days, were on the alert for anybody who faked poverty. "Pay up or get out!" they said sternly. Hetty invariably got out. After several days Mrs. Green had exhausted all possibilities of medical charity and was forced to call in a neighborhood physician. This doctor advised an immediate amputation above the knee.

Ned recalled this without apparent bitterness many years afterward.

"Mamma," he told friends in Texas, "still felt there was a chance to save my leg. We both wanted this, of course. We didn't have much faith in doctors and believed, given time, the limb would heal itself."

But neither "oil of squills," rubbed on Ned's bad leg every

49

night by his mother or Sylvia, nor Carter's Little Liver Pills, with which all the Greens were dosed liberally, had any effect as curatives or palliatives.

(A dozen years later, in 1898, Hetty was the subject of a wildly publicized diatribe launched by Dr. J. H. Burtenshaw, a well-known New York physician, who warned his fellow practitioners to "beware of economic abuses tried against them by fakers. Hetty Green," he declared, "was well able to pay for medical treatment but instead worked on the sympathies of my fellow physicians to get free care for herself and her family.")

Ned continued to limp while his leg became progressively worse, and Hetty began a long-lasting feud with railroad magnate Collis Potter Huntington, then in the process of developing a transportation system which when completed would be known as the Southern Pacific. A direct result of this war between the Connecticut Yankee, Huntington, and the Massachusetts Yankee, Green, was Hetty's purchase of a fifty-one-mile-long, broken-down Texas branch line, an offshoot of the Houston & Texas Central which afterward was to become a part of the Southern Pacific.

The New York *World*, December 27, 1887, said, "Hetty Green's great fight has begun. Mrs. Green refused to become party to an agreement entered into between bondholders of the Houston & Texas Central. This road is part of C. P. Huntington's Southern Pacific System. The story is that C. P. Huntington and Associates own the stock of the H. & T. C. which they picked up at a low price, said to be under $10 million. Mrs. Green, however, owns about $1 million of general mortgage bonds besides a large part of the first and second mortgages. . . ."

Financial editors of the day declared that Huntington's move was an effort to squeeze Hetty out of the railroad picture, or at least exclude her from that portion he controlled. He disliked Mrs. Green intensely, a feeling that was mutual. Huntington's expressed reason for wishing to get rid of Hetty was "That woman (Mrs. Green) has no vision of this country's future. She is nothing more than a glorified pawnbroker." The gentleman from Connecticut failed to add another possible cause for his dislike of Mrs. Green. Two years before Hetty had bested him and his associates in a Wall Street mortgage deal.

Hetty, who preferred to take her chances on a long-range loss rather than suffer the acute pain of an immediate financial debacle, decided to hang on and, in fact, try to obtain full control of the branch line. If that could be accomplished she might then sell her holdings at face value and, at the same time, make her tiny railroad a link of the U. P.'s rival, the Santa Fe. The double result of this would be recovery and revenge. While Hetty certainly was a vindictive woman, she never indulged in getting "satisfaction" if it cost her money.

More than four years elapsed before Hetty was able to say she owned her own railroad. An indirect result of her acquisition of this tiny Texas carrier was to provide Ned with the only truly happy period he ever had. Meanwhile the future railroad tycoon stayed close to his mother except for an occasional business trip to Chicago, Cincinnati, or St. Louis, where Mrs. Green was accumulating hundreds of parcels of real estate. Actually Ned was no more than a trusted messenger boy who delivered bonds, other securities, and cash to Hetty's out-of-town brokers. He traveled by coach and was given just enough money to pay for food and lodging in the cheapest hotels. Once in a while his mother's business representatives would feel sorry for this shy, well-mannered young man and invite him to stay in their homes. That several of these had unattached daughters not averse to a marriage with the son of the world's richest woman was no deterrent to their hospitality.

Hetty, Ned, and Sylvia spent the summer of 1888 at Far Rockaway, Hetty going in to her free desk at the Chemical Bank three or four times each week. Through that autumn Ned continued to run intercity errands for his mother, but in January, 1889, he went to Boston to work as a clerk in a brokerage office. Apparently he did not care for either the job or the city because later he rarely referred to those few months in his life. Besides, he didn't make enough money to live decently nor would his mother supplement his income. His father occasionally gave him small sums of cash and that helped him survive.

Ned came back to New York to resume his life with his mother and sister, who had moved to a railroad flat at 502 West 21st Street. Sylvia did the cooking and housework. Meals were irregular, depending upon when Hetty returned from her daily activities on Wall Street. By this time the pain in Ned's leg was so severe that he was unable to run his mother's errands. He had put on considerable weight and the effort of dragging around his two hundred pounds was becoming unendurable. He spent much of his time at home. About once a month he dined with his father at the Union Club.

It was on one of these occasions that Ned, who never complained, suffered such obvious discomfort that his father asked him just what medical help Hetty was getting for him. Usually, during the few brief hours father and son spent together, the only time Hetty's name was mentioned was when the older man would ask, "How's your mother, Ned?" The subject was then dropped and conversation restricted to less controversial topics.

Ned tried to brush off the question of doctors but his father persisted. Finally, he admitted to their many embarrassing rejections at free clinics and the advice given them by their neighborhood physician. It is possible that despite the older Green's rising anger nothing further would have been done. But on their way to the second floor, where they were going to watch a parade from a front window (the date was July 4, 1888), Ned twisted his leg and fell down three or four steps. He was unable to get up by himself.

Porters carried him to a third-floor bedroom and his father notified Hetty, in no uncertain terms, that their son would remain at the Union Club until he had a complete checkup. Meanwhile Green's own doctor arrived. His prognosis, given a few days later, confirmed the local doctor's opinion. Immediate surgery was strongly recommended. Otherwise, he declared, gangrene, traces of which he recognized, would claim the young man's life within a short time.

"It's too bad something wasn't done sooner," he told Green. "Five years ago we could have saved the whole limb. Perhaps as little as two, we might have salvaged the leg below the knee. However, if the operation is successful there is no reason why your son, properly fitted with an artificial limb, can't lead a long and useful life."

Perhaps the best and busiest surgeon in the United States at that time was Dr. Charles McBurney, another Massachusetts Yankee. A graduate of Harvard and Columbia's College of Physicians and Surgeons, McBurney had studied abroad for years under the tutelage of Europe's most brilliant doctors. He returned to the United States in 1873 to open a private practice and to demonstrate operative surgery at his medical alma mater. He gave his time generously to free clinics, but individuals who wanted his services and could afford them squirmed at his fees. His charge for amputating Ned Green's leg would be $5,000, he said.

It would be doing Hetty a serious injustice to say she would not have paid McBurney his fee or whatever fee any other surgeon might have demanded to save her son's life. Undoubtedly she loved both her children deeply in her own peculiar fashion. But Edward Green chose to sell some of his few remaining securities rather than contemplate the dreadful scene he knew would ensue between his wife and the surgeon once Hetty found out the costs. He did not let her know what Dr. McBurney's fee would be.

However, since Ned was technically a minor—he would not be twenty-one for another six weeks—consent for the operation had to be obtained from both parents. Hetty accordingly was advised of Ned's critical condition and warned that his death was imminent if the operation was not performed at once. She agreed. Ned, too, was told the truth about the anticipated extent of the surgery and warned that the amputation would be well above his knee. Although this must have been a tremendous blow, he was convinced that life could be happier on one good leg than it had been on two, one of which was nearly useless.

On July 9th, an ambulance took Ned to New York's Roosevelt Hospital, where two days later Dr. McBurney amputated his leg about seven inches above his knee. The operation was a technical success. Edward Henry Green returned to the somnolence of his club; Hetty, to the bustle of Wall Street; Sylvia, to the drudgery of the West Side flat, while Ned remained in the hospital. His right leg was buried in the Green family plot of Immanuel Church at Bellows Falls, there to be joined by the rest of the Colonel some forty-seven years later. Details of how this final merger was accomplished remain a trade secret, never revealed by the staff of Campbell's, Manhattan's most artistic undertakers, who handled all of Colonel Green's funeral arrangements and performed the synthesis.

Chapter Nine

Iᴛ was more than a year before Ned could be fitted with a cork leg, then the most practical prosthetic device available. Meanwhile, after leaving the hospital, where he spent his twenty-first birthday, he was sent to recuperate at the Tucker House, accompanied by his father and Sylvia. For Sylvia, this was probably the best vacation she had had in years. Freed of her mother's tyranny, even if only temporarily, and in the company of her father whom she respected and her brother whom she adored, what remained of the summer of '88 passed quickly and pleasantly for her. She was even able to renew her girlhood friendship with Mary Nims, known to her friends as Mamie.

"She was not a pretty girl," Mrs. Bolles recalled, "but her complexion was clear pale ivory with a touch of natural color in her cheeks. She was tall, straight, and slender and her features were rather large in a narrow face. Except for myself, most of her

55

friends were limited to middle-aged people whom her mother knew.

"That summer she did give a party, though. It was at the Towns' Hotel, held there, probably, instead of the Tucker House so as not to disturb Ned. No doubt it was paid for by Mr. Green, whom we all loved. We had games and refreshments in the big old-fashioned parlor on the second floor."

Mrs. Bolles paused, smile faintly, then continued.

"It's all so long ago," she said, "but there *was* a certain young man there whom I'll call Billy Smith, although that is *not* his real name. He was of assistance in entertaining and had been one of the boys in the parish school. His family was active in Immanuel Church.

"Sylvia that evening wore a becoming and stylish gown of pale gray crepe trimmed with steel beads on green bands. She looked and, I think, felt like other girls.

"When I met Sylvia the next summer she said, 'I'm told you are engaged.'

"I said, 'That's interesting. I have not heard anything about it myself. To whom am I supposed to be engaged?'

"She replied, 'To Billy Smith.'

"This was a great surprise to me as since early school days I had seen little of him. He had been educated in an academy and we did not attend the same church and had few mutual friends. All of which I explained to Sylvia, adding that I had not seen him since her party, had never been anywhere with him in my life, and did not like him because he was too facetious.

"Sylvia said gravely, 'Never with me.'

"So I concluded Billy Smith had been very nice to Sylvia and liked her very much. I demanded who had told her the news but she adroitly avoided an answer. I could not think of anyone among our friends who could have any object in fabricating the story."

Mrs. Bolles stopped, frowned slightly, pursed her lips, and continued.

life with Mother, Ned could hardly fail to differentiate between "propositions" and legitimate business opportunities.

Hetty's Chicago associates plied him with invitations to dinner parties and weekends at their homes, and they invited him to join their exclusive clubs. Ned, who never lost his earthiness, while polite to his hosts, was as bored by Chicago society as he was later to be indifferent to the proffered inducements of the Four Hundred of New York, Miami, and Dallas.

He had been in Chicago less than two months when he joined the Benevolent and Protective Order of Elks. When he left that city he was a member not of the Chicago Club or the Bachelors and Benedicts, but of the Royal Arcanum, the Odd Fellows, the Red Men, and the Loyal Order of Moose. His initiation into the secret life of a "Brother Elk" was not without publicity.

"An instance of Ned Green's way of doing things was shown when he was inducted into the local lodge of Elks last month," said the Chicago *Sunday Journal* on March 5, 1891. "At the time of his initiation the lodge rooms on Monroe Street had comfortable quarters furnished with no ostentation or luxuriance. No sooner was Ed a full fledged Elk when he decorated, at his own expense, their quarters at a cost of $2500." The decorator was Marshall Field's.

Hetty's wrath was not felt for several months. Then Marshall Field's, unable to collect from Ned, finally sent the bill directly to Mrs. Green.

Rumors of Ned's extracurricular activities began to reach Hetty. While she must have been upset by sight drafts and no doubt grimly ordered him to stop forthwith using this short cut to cash, she took comfort in the fact that as long as he held no power of attorney from her, he could not bind her to any contract, no matter what he said or did.

At this time in her life Hetty included among her pet phobias not only the working press but also those who paid its wages. She had cautioned Ned many times about associating with or even speaking to reporters, editors, and publishers, whom she loathed

61

more or less in that order. So when the news came to Hetty that Ned was contemplating joining the enemy camp Hetty's anger was great. She was then in Mr. Crapo's New Bedford offices boasting about how well Ned was doing in Chicago. Frequently the victim of his client's sarcasm, Crapo, who looked upon Hetty sometimes with disdain but more often with tolerant amusement, quietly handed Mrs. Green a copy of the New Bedford *Standard*, delivered a few hours before Hetty's arrival. The date was July 9, 1891. The headlines alone must have jolted her out of her chair.

A NOVEL NEWSPAPER

HETTY'S SON TO BUY THE CHICAGO TIMES

Suspicion the Young Man Has Fallen Among Philistines

The story followed: "Arrangements have been made for the sale of the Chicago Times to Edward Green, son of Hetty Green, and a trio of prominent newspapermen. An interesting story in connection with this matter is that Joseph Pulitzer is to have a share in the new enterprise. The newspaper is to be called the TIMES WORLD.

"Mr. Green did not seem to be averse to talking about the deal today although he refused to name the gentlemen with whom he is connected. . . . 'My associates are the heads of two powerful New York dailies, while the third has a responsible position on a Chicago paper.

" 'We will probably purchase the Chicago Times and transform it into a triple city paper. That is, we shall devote one page to New York news telegraphed verbatim from one of the principal metropolitan papers, probably the New York World and one page to Boston news, obtained by telegraph in the same manner. There is a demand for New York and Boston news in Chicago but little attention is paid to either of these cities' doings.' "

Considering that Ned had no experience in either publishing or any other business, this was rather casual treatment for a breathtaking venture that might have given pause to such giants as Greeley and Dana.

Hetty dashed out of her lawyer's office and was in Chicago as soon as a combination of the New Haven and the New York Central could get her there. Ned, who protested that there was nothing at all to the story and laughed it off, listened gravely while she informed him that a similar offense would result in a fast return to New York.

The Chicago *Sunday News*, on July 14, 1891, carried a brief item in which Mrs. Hetty Green denied that either she or her son, H. E. R. Green, contemplated buying a newspaper in Chicago or any other place.

Soon afterward, reports of Ned's expanded social life came to his mother's ears. She had frequently, and at great length, warned Ned about predatory women who would marry anyone for money. She was even able to extract a promise (never broken) that there would be no matrimony for him without her consent.

Hetty was no prude. She had spent her childhood among rough, outspoken men and her maturity in association with members of the opposite sex who spoke as frankly in her presence as if she were a man. She probably felt that this was the time for her son to sow his wild oats. When Ned and his lodge brothers visited the cribs in back of Dearborn Street, as she knew they must, they were merely behaving as Nature had intended them to behave.

Many worldly women of Hetty's generation considered prostitutes as evil necessities. They, the respectable ones, reasoned that practitioners of this old profession enabled pure women to remain pure until matrimony unchained them. It was also thought that prostitution prevented upper-class sons from leaping directly from the bed of someone socially or economically unacceptable directly into marriage. With women of the streets there never could be any thought of wedlock.

Ned was sensitive about his physical handicap and believed he was sexually repulsive to women. But his lodge brothers persuaded him on a late evening in September, 1891, to join them in a trip to the red-light district. Perhaps some older member of the fraternity went ahead of the main detachment to be sure that

63

when Ned arrived the madam would have alerted a kind, skillful, and tolerant employee, one who would neither wince at deformity nor laugh at inexperience—for Ned Green, approaching his twenty-second birthday, was still a virgin.

If so, the woman this unknown madam selected was a redhead named Mabel Harlow.

Chapter Eleven

MABEL Harlow's ancestors are not so easy to trace as Ned Green's. As a matter of fact, it is difficult to go beyond one generation. Mabel's mother, a Wilcox, was born in England of Irish extraction. She was one of three orphaned sisters who came to the United States about 1868 and settled near Boston. Soon after their arrival, one girl married Edward O'Connor and lived in Providence, Rhode Island; another became Mrs. George H. Campbell and moved to Highland Park, Illinois; while the third married George Harlow, of Gloucester, Massachusetts.

Mabel was born either in 1870 or in 1871. Texas old-timers tell many versions of Mabel's early life and characteristics, including wild tales about her nymphomania, her use of narcotics, her sexual abberations, and her appearance as a dancer in a traveling side show. But known facts do not bear out any of these allegations except, perhaps, the last one.

Mabel is thought to have made her first appearance in the Lone-Star State about 1889. She went to attend a Dallas convention of the Brotherhood of Locomotive Engineers, although not as a delegate. The session lasted a week. Members of the Brotherhood returned to their wives and families, but Miss Harlow (also known as deVries or Campbell) remained.

She worked in Dallas for a while and moved on to Houston when business became slow. Occasionally she followed the convention circuit, traveling extensively throughout the Southwest and infrequently going as far north as Milwaukee. It is possible that she picked up a husband or two during her meanderings, because she was known variously as Mrs. Staunton, Mrs. Wilson, and Mrs. Kitterage for periods of up to three or four months' duration. In these brief interludes she actually set up housekeeping and shared her bed with only one man—whether with or without benefit of clergy, we do not know.

There were any number of people who remembered her kindly in later years, and not all of them were men. A voluntary subject of an operation that increased her professional efficiency, Mabel could never have children of her own and lavished her boundless affection on countless "nieces" and "nephews." Since her own work started later than that of her neighbors, Miss Harlow was happy to be a "baby sitter," or whatever they were called in those days, so that weary mothers and fathers might have an evening's relaxation in the neighborhood beer parlor. Her young charges remember the presents she frequently gave them and recall that Mabel was always good for a nickel any time they needed one.

After their first meeting Ned Green became one of Mabel's steadiest patrons. He admitted that he tried others in the house but always returned to his first love, and "love," no doubt, is the right word for it. If he had had the money it is likely that young Green would have set Mabel up in a home of their own so that he would not be forced to share her. But Hetty had put a stop to sight drafts.

Early in the spring of 1892 Mabel left Chicago with a free-spending Californian named Pace. Ned was devastated. He lost interest in the city where he had had fun for the first time in his life, and when, that December, Hetty notified him that she was sending him elsewhere, he couldn't have cared less.

Hetty was then in the midst of more concurrent litigation than even she was accustomed to handling. She was suing one New York brokerage firm for what she claimed was the mishandling of her funds and was, in turn, being sued by a Wall Street operator for failure to pay his commissions. The New York law firm of Joseph Choate had subpoenaed Mrs. Green to appear in a suit her erstwhile counsel brought to collect their fees while Hetty was suing her Manhattan attorney for "misrepresentation."

There was also that seemingly endless suit Hetty had begun in 1888 to discharge Henry Barling, last survivor of a trio appointed to administer Aunt Sylvia Ann's fortune. Hetty claimed that the plaintiff had mismanaged the one million dollars in which she held a life interest.

The trusteeship case was being heard by Referee Henry Anderson, a Manhattan attorney. Timothy N. Pfeiffer, a distinguished member of the New York Bar, who later represented Mrs. Wilks, tells the story of how Mrs. Green attempted to make a mockery of the hearing when evidence was going against her.

"This was one of the times," Pfeiffer said, "when Hetty had decided she'd like to have the press with her, and of course, in turn, the public. She had some itch for publicity and ordinarily a small group of reporters watched her cases. I think she wanted to get rid of the Referee.

"Mrs. Green knew he had a choleric temper and that day she bustled into his large room, walked straight across it, flopped down on her knees and began to pray out loud.

"Mr. Anderson quite rose to the occasion. Instead of pounding a gavel or ordering her out, he picked up a large heavy paper cutter from his desk and bowed his great bald head upon it. Profound stillness ensued with Mrs. Green still praying. She finally had to stop. She did not get rid of the Referee."

Hetty did better in Boston. There, the case against her was dismissed, but not before the defendant scared the wits out of the plaintiff, the dignified Joseph Choate, a member of the New York Bar.

Because she claimed to be afraid of robbery, Hetty was granted permission to carry firearms. In her case this meant a small-caliber revolver which usually reposed in her large handbag.

Mr. Choate, a youthful victim of a hunting accident, lived in deathly fear of firearms. The sound of a distant rifle shot could send this lawyer, bold enough in the courtroom, into whimpers. Hetty knew this. She made sure that, soon after the trial opened, Boston newspapers carried stories not only of Hetty's ownership of a pistol but also her prowess in its use.

John McMahon, on the staff of the Boston *Herald* and an expert on the Green family, recalled Hetty's day in court.

"There was a heavy drizzle," he said, "and the session had already begun when Mrs. Green entered, carrying a big umbrella. She went directly in back of Mr. Choate, the enemy, bustled about somewhat, shook her wet jacket on his hair, uttered a stage-whispered threat or two, and sat down loudly.

"With the exception of Mr. Choate, who ignored her completely, everyone in the crowded room, including His Honor, either was grinning or restraining a smile and anticipating a cheerful break in an otherwise dull trial. Hetty did not disappoint them.

"A bit later she was called to the box. There was a moment of silence during which all eyes turned to Mrs. Green. It was then that she raised her umbrella, pushed its point into Mr. Choate's back, and rapidly clicked the spring on it six times in succession as though she were loading her revolver. Mr. Choate gave a cry of terror, leaped out of his chair, and dashed to the comforting presence of a bailiff. Only after the howls of glee had died down and the Judge rapped for order, did Hetty take the stand."

Chapter Twelve

SHORTLY after December 1, 1892, Ned received his mother's orders to close the Owings Building office and come home, there to be briefed on his next assignment and to be Sylvia's escort at her unexpected debut. Home was then at Morristown, New Jersey, where Hetty and her daughter had moved that summer. Their boardinghouse in this suburban community was by far the most pleasant place in which the two women had ever lived together.

The only probable solution to the mystery of Hetty's abrupt departure from her cheap Hoboken flat and her appearance in a decent and comparatively expensive boardinghouse is pressure from Miss Leary, who was desperately sorry for Sylvia. For years this only friend of Mrs. Green had been trying to persuade her to allow Sylvia more freedom and permit her entry into society. But until the summer of 1891 Hetty was adamant. Her daughter was a good housekeeper and cook, society was expensive, and besides, some fortune hunter might make off with her.

But Miss Leary was not to be put off, and finally Hetty granted Sylvia permission to spend some time at the Leary villa in Newport. Her hostess supplied Sylvia with the proper wardrobe. It was not a happy time for the young woman, then twenty, and she later referred to it only infrequently and with some bitterness.

Miss Green was awkward. A so-called hammertoe on her left foot made dancing, and sometimes even walking, difficult if not painful. This was only a minor congenital muscle deformity and, as Sylvia learned later, could have been corrected easily in childhood. But since her mother had been unwilling to spend money on Ned's major injury it would have been unthinkable to ask for the removal of such a slight handicap. After all, as Mrs. Green pointed out, "man was born to suffer." The hammertoe was never mentioned in the Green household.

Although Miss Leary did her best to "bring Sylvia out," it was too late. The girl, by then, had formed characteristics and developed eccentricities that could not be changed or broken by a few weeks in this playground of the very rich. Sylvia was excessively shy and when confronted with young men and women of her own age retreated hastily to the comforting presence of the middle-aged and elderly.

There would have been little point for Miss Leary to prolong Sylvia's obvious unease and no need to give her any further taste of what life might have offered to the socially acceptable daughter of the richest woman in the world. After two or three weeks in Newport Sylvia went home to her mother. Her beautiful new clothes were returned to Miss Leary. This action, in itself, was almost unbelievable considering how little they were used and what long years of service they might have given both mother and daughter.

Sometime that fall, Mrs. Green returned to Vermont to explore the financial potentials of a paper mill that was to be built on the New Hampshire side of the Connecticut River, opposite Bellows Falls. She took Sylvia with her. Since the Tucker House was closed, they stopped at the Towns' Hotel. Their stay was recalled by Mrs. Bolles.

"I was very happy to see Sylvia again," she said, "although we weren't together much that visit. I don't think she got in touch with me right away. Perhaps she thought I'd be too busy with preparations for my wedding and she didn't want to intrude.

"Her only recreation was riding. Her mother would select a horse at a local livery stable, examine the harness, and put her secret mark upon it so that Sylvia might know she was given *that* harness whenever she drove. She always took some older woman with her and kept strictly to main traveled roads."

When her business was concluded, Hetty and Sylvia returned to Morristown, where Mrs. Green soon baffled the local gentry by presenting her daughter to society.

The fact that Sylvia had even a modest coming-out party also may be attributed to the persistence of Miss Leary. Among those who attended the affair and recalled the event many years later were Miss Nina Howland and her sister, the late Mrs. M. Ford, cousins of Sylvia Ann. Another who had vivid memories of that evening of December 7, 1892, when Miss H. Sylvia Ann Howland Robinson Green was presented to society, was Eugene Carroll, a lifelong resident of Morristown. Carrol, too young to attend, stood outside and watched the proceedings.

"Age," said Mr. Carroll with a sigh, "has long since remedied the only obstacle to my presence at Sylvia's debut. But I remember it well.

"First of all, we were completely shocked a couple of months before when Hetty Green moved into the Misses Hunter's rather elegant boardinghouse on Washington Street. I suppose I shouldn't say *I* was shocked since I was too young then to realize what a cataclysmic event *that* was. But my parents were. They, and everybody else in Morristown, talked about it a great deal. You couldn't help being aware of Hetty's miserliness if you read the papers. There was a story about her every other day, it seemed to me.

"Well, the idea of Hetty Green paying forty-four dollars a week for room and board for herself and Sylvia just sounded impossible. But that figure stands out in my mind so strongly that I'm sure it's right.

"Sylvia, as I recall her, was a sad young woman who hung about her mother most of the time. At her party she was 'dressed up,' though ordinarily her clothing was monstrous as could be, long sweeping dresses with myriads of petticoats which had gone out of style ten years before.

"I couldn't possibly remember now who was there but I imagine most of Morristown came, some out of curiosity and others—well, I guess they didn't want to offend Sylvia even if they couldn't stand Hetty.

"We often talked about Sylvia and her one big moment. My mother told me Sylvia wore a long-sleeved dress and looked extremely dowdy. She was quite pathetic and blushed every time Mrs. Green dragged some young man over to meet her. Mother doesn't think Sylvia danced more than once and Ned, naturally, didn't dance at all.

"Mother says the evening was quite dull. Hetty, she remembered, was well dressed and looked handsome. She monopolized the conversation, but Sylvia seemed ill at ease much of the time and guests escaped to a happier atmosphere as soon as they could leave gracefully."

If the result of her debut was to provide Sylvia Green with a husband, the coming-out party was a failure. But if, instead, Hetty wished to demonstrate, at a comparatively small cost, that the world of the young was foolish and cruel and Sylvia would feel rejected there, the affair was a success.

Contemporaries of the Greens said that during the balance of the Greens' stay in Morristown, Sylvia spent most of her hours in the Misses Hunter's parlor or in her room except for an occasional carriage ride with her cousin, Nina Howland, who lived a few doors away on James Street.

Sylvia must have looked forward eagerly to Ned's homecoming. It was a happy reunion for brother and sister. Their week or ten days in Morristown was to be the last time they would ever be together again except for infrequent hours scattered over the next forty years.

Ned remained at home only long enough to take what may well have been the shortest educational course of its kind on record. "How to Become a Railroad President" was the subject. Mrs. Green was the teacher. Her pupil passed with flying colors.

Chapter Thirteen

On December 16, 1892, Hetty organized the Texas Midland Railroad Company. This broken-down branch line was born out of her feud with C. P. Huntington. Its engines were rusty and their boilers leaked. The infrequent passenger trains rarely departed or arrived on schedule. The sky could be seen through the unrepaired roofs of freight cars and grass grew between rotted ties. Yet these fifty-one miles of single track, running from Terrell to Garrett (pop. 1,171), gave President-elect E. H. R. Green the best years of his life and provided him with a chance to show ability and vision far in advance of his time.

In after years, when Ned Green wandered from hobby to hobby and drifted from one brief scientific enthusiasm to another, people belittled his early accomplishments in railroading. But contemporary competitors who felt the sting of business lost by them to the Texas Midland felt that he possessed administrative brilliance. S. G. Reed, a railway authority, claimed that "the success of the T. M. was due in a large measure to the splendid talent with which Green surrounded himself and to his policy of giving heads of various departments full authority and holding them to full responsibility."

Mr. Reed devotes a chapter of *History of the Texas Railroads* to the Texas Midland and Colonel Green. "This railroad," he writes, "grew out of a branch line which the owners of the Houston and Texas Central had begun to build in the early '80s, and which they lost in complicated and long drawn out receiverships of the Houston and Texas Central, the Waco and Northwestern and the Texas Central Railways.

"Mrs. Green was a heavy stockholder in the original H.&T.C. When these railroads went into receivership in 1885 she blamed Huntington and after that fought him in every way she could. She bought the northeastern branch of the Texas Central December 16, 1892, partly to protect her holdings but primarily to give her only son, E. H. R. Green, a chance to show what was in him."

On Christmas morning in 1892 Ned Green arrived in Dallas, Texas, then a railroad center. Here, Hetty's banking agents had made an unsuccessful attempt to pull control of the Waco and Northwestern Railroad from Collis P. Huntington and instead wound up with the Texas Midland. Ned remained in Dallas for a month reading every bit of railroad history he could get his hands on. He pored over countless technical reports and studied dozens of operation manuals.

He stayed in the cheapest room of the old Grand Hotel, which catered to railroad men and was built along the tracks of the Texas and Pacific, within sight and sound of the station, the roundhouse, and repair shops. From his window he could look out and see fast locomotives pull gleaming passenger cars or load freighters west-bound to El Paso or east-bound to St. Louis and intermediate points.

Days and nights were filled with the warning shouts of brakemen and firemen, the dull bops of shifting freight cars, the soft hiss of signaling steam engines, or the mournful whistle of a distant express, its pitch rising gradually to a terrifying shriek before dropping suddenly to the lowest audible note while a locomotive headlight cut a disappearing path through Texas prairies beyond.

Being Mrs. Green's son, he could not keep his identity or purpose in Dallas a secret. Breakfast, dinner, and supper invitations from Hetty's bankers, lawyers, and fellow stockholders came from all over McLennan, Coryell, and Limestone Counties. Nearly every wife had a daughter, sister, or unmarried cousin not averse to becoming a dear friend of Hetty's prospective heir, cork leg and all.

But Ned was not interested. He politely brushed off the many opportunities to become a temporary or permanent part of Dallas' society and spent his evenings and weekends in the hotel lobby. There the friendly, outgoing Ned Green talked to railroaders of every class, from low-caste gandy dancers to the aristocracy of the road, engineers of "Limiteds."

Ned arrived in Terrell just in time to attend the first annual Board of Directors' meeting of the Texas Midland, on January 27, 1893. Since he held Hetty's proxies, accounting for almost all outstanding bonds, there could be little legal opposition to the young man's candidacy for President. The minutes reveal that young Mr. Green was elected to that undesirable office unanimously.

The first public act of the new head of the Texas Midland set Terrell on its fiscal ear. Although extremely short of pocket money (Ned later recalled that he had about eight dollars in cash), he entered the American National Bank of Terrell and, as Mr. Reed declared, "without any preliminary announcement, he presented a certified check for deposit to his personal credit, signed by his mother and calling for $500,000. This was twice the total resources of the bank.

"Fortunately, he did not ask for cash at the time, and after

76

recovering from their shock, officials wired the New York bank on which the check was drawn for some means of identifying Green. The reply was to wait until he removed his hat and if he had a large mole on his forehead the identification should be considered complete. (A simpler method, obvious but more embarrassing, was not suggested.) The mole was there all right and Green was forthwith elected Vice President of the bank."

Although Ned would have felt Hetty's immediate wrath if he dared spend a cent of his "personal" account, this large deposit was no idle gesture. Hetty Green, to use another of her oft-quoted clichés, always believed that "money talked." In a town the size of Terrell, a half-million dollars spoke loudly. Thus Hetty notified Collis P. Huntington that she was firmly behind her son with what counted most to the enemy and to herself and warned him to leave her boy alone. Today no one knows whether Hetty was bluffing. In any event, Huntington did not choose to call her cards and thus engage in a contest that might have damaged both their fortunes. Ned was free to make or break the Texas Midland without Huntington's potentially dangerous interference.

Ned's next act was to move headquarters from Ennis to Terrell. The towns were only a few miles apart but local bankers were happy to give their new colleague a low-cost, long-term lease on a property they held by reason of foreclosure. This was a far better financial deal for the Texas Midland than the one it had in Ennis.

The railroad needed reorganization from top to bottom. It was important for the new President to select men who, in addition to being knowledgeable where their employer was not (and this covered a great deal of territory), also would be loyal to him. Either Ned Green was gifted with remarkable capacity to judge ability and character or else he was extremely lucky in his early choice of men who eventually would help him run the T. M. The two Texans he picked were Frank B. McKay and Lawrence William Wells. Both men remained with the Texas Midland until it was sold and were Ned Green's close friends

77

until he died. Wells, who was only an assistant engineer when Green took office, was elevated to the job of General Manager, while McKay, a freight clerk when he met Ned, later became General Freight and Passenger Agent.

For the balance of his first year in Terrell, the President of the Texas Midland made his home in a narrow hall bedroom of that town's only hotel, the Harris.

"It was about the most miserable place I ever stayed in," Ned told Ed Kiest. "I used to think Hoboken was pretty bad but it was paradise compared to my room at the Harris. The bed wasn't built for us [sic] Texans; it was at least a foot too short. The room was so narrow I could hardly turn around without bumping my shoulders against both walls at the same time.

"Then the heat! The only window faced a blank wall so it wouldn't have mattered if it was open or shut. I was on the top floor with a tin roof about five feet over my head. Well, you know what a Texas sun did to my unventilated cubicle. I bet I sweated off ten pounds every night."

This was shortly before Ned learned to ignore his mother's admonitions about personal expenditures. His past training enabled him to live frugally. He was paid no salary and nothing in Hetty's budget covered entertainment. Food and shelter were charged to railroad operating expenses and, at first, were kept low. The half-million dollars remained untouched in the American National Bank of Terrell.

During his first ten months in Texas it is doubtful if Ned ever had more than a lone five-dollar bill in his pocket at any one time. Supporting evidence of the penury in which he lived is to be found in the following letter sent by the President of the Texas Midland to that railroad's major bondholder. It was written on official stationery and the date is August 22, 1893.

"Dear Mamma:

"I am 25 years old today. I think you might send me money so I could go to the Fair at Chicago in about two weeks before the fall rush comes. It would only cost about $200. I can get passes to Chicago and return. Let me know as soon as you can so I can get ready. I want to see the Fair *so* bad. Please let me go.

"Your affectionate son, Ned."

Chapter Fourteen

Wıтнın a couple of months of his arrival there, Ned became Terrell's first citizen. It was not only because he was white, Protestant, and represented untold millions of dollars, but also because he was affable, democratic, and went out of his way to be friendly. He had a pleasing smile, used frequently, and an infectious laugh.

His physical appearance was outstanding even in a state with a self-promoted reputation for gauging men by mere bulk, physical or financial. Ned then weighed more than two hundred pounds, well distributed over his broad, six-foot four-inch frame. He had been fitted with a cork leg in Pittsburgh, Pennsylvania, where a high accident rate in mines and mills had made that city a center for the manufacture of artificial limbs and eyes.

He had an unexpected flair for publicity and organized a base-ball club which he outfitted with bright red uniforms on the back of which were sewed the words TEXAS MIDLAND. The team's equipment was far better than that of the company it represented. Ned imported a battery of "ringers" from a Fort Worth semiprofessional nine, gave them sinecures on his railroad, and put them on a team that beat every amateur ball club within a fifty-mile radius.

Planters who had had little reverence for the Texas Midland began to regard it in a new light when their local nines always were found on the short end of early Texas League ball games. By the time the railroad was as good as its team, shippers had gained respect for a winner and were ready to do business with a manager who traveled the circuit with his club and doubled as President of the Texas Midland.

Social life in small-town America, during the late nineteenth and the early twentieth century, centered either in its churches or lodges. You went to the church your parents or grandparents attended, which in Texas usually meant Fundamentalist Baptist. If your father was an Elk or a Mason or Moose your chances for joining any of these organizations were enhanced. You treated none of these lodges lightly. Membership was an honor, antici-pated with trepidation for years and, when achieved, enjoyed because it lifted you above the herd. You hoped nothing in your background would be discovered to cause you the ultimate in humiliation, a blackball.

Strangers (white Protestants usually, although exceptions were made for well-behaved Roman Catholics and nonbearded Jews) were welcomed in a man's home for a meal or a night's lodging. This was particularly true in Texas, where hospitality was gen-uine and often overwhelming. But you had to know a citizen and his family for a long time, and trust them well, before you shared the mysticism of the secret ritual, the whispered password, and the cabalistic grip.

Terrell was no exception. Ned attended religious services only infrequently—his excuse was that there was no Quaker meeting-house nearby—but he soon was asked to join every fraternal organization in the community.

In the past, Ned's physical handicap, plus a heritage of life in the shadow of his mother's dominant personality, made him shun the limelight. But in Terrell, which accepted him quickly and openhandedly, and with Hetty fifteen hundred miles away, Ned's ego expanded. During his first six or seven months in Texas he lost so much self-consciousness that he actually took a starring role in a minstrel show. This was given by Terrell's leading citizens for the benefit of the local volunteer fire department.

That year Ned formed a military company named "The Green Guards and Zouaves" in his honor. He paid for the equipment, lent his presence at weekly drills, and was happy to share the lead carriage with Mayor Headly at all parades.

One of Ned's sponsors for membership in Terrell's many lodges was W. P. Allen, the local banker who, with four or five others, became Ned's loyal cohort. These few friends were the only ones whose lifelong association with him was untainted by any thought of personal gain. Allen became "Dear Walter" in hundreds of Ned's letters, written throughout the next forty years.

Allen, three months older than Ned, had been married for several years before Ned made Terrell his residence. As most happily married women would have done, Allen's wife, Betty, did her best to "match" the young railroader with Kate Schneider, an attractive young Dallas girl. Kate became a frequent weekend house guest of the Allens, where Ned spent much of his spare time.

It was a warm, easygoing household, totally unlike anything Ned had been used to in childhood, and it provided a good backdrop for Betty's intended matrimonial production. Although the romance between Miss Schneider and Mr. Green was slow in flowering, it might well have developed into marriage. Kate was getting used to Ned's physical handicap and he was beginning to forget Mabel.

Until he had met Mabel, Ned had sublimated his normal sexual appetites. Without her, he was timid, afraid to make advances, and shy of having relations even with professionals who might show revulsion. In the winter of 1894 Ned wearied of his dingy hotel room, his self-imposed celibacy, and his rigid economy. With total disregard for the consequences he cashed a check for $2500. Then he and two fellow bachelors rented quarters above the recently abandoned Harris Opera House. Their apartment soon became notorious as "The Green Flats," headquarters for Terrell's young men about town and a trysting place for their unescorted ladies. Beds were occupied as often doubly as singly.

One of Ned's roommates was Joseph B. Tartt, the Texas Midland's first auditor, and the other, Thomas E. Corley, who began his business career as a clerk in Allen's bank but wound up as the railroad's treasurer.

Ned paid the major share of all expenses in the Green Flats. He even hired a cook and two young Negro houseboys, one to act as his valet and the other to perform general chores about the apartment. The fame of this ménage soon spread over much of central Texas, and President Green's lucky roommates basked in reflected glory. Many years later, Corley recalled their apartment in the Harris Opera House.

"I'm not likely to forget that setup," Corley said. "I was nineteen years old and it was pretty wild. I don't remember the cook's name any more but the colored boys were twins, Elijah and Isaiah Cooper, and if this sounds like fiction—well, it isn't.

"Lige had been a porter for the traffic department of the T. M. and I don't know what Ike did before. Lige became Ned's personal servant, a kind of 'gentleman's gentleman.' He pressed and cleaned the Colonel's clothes; heated the water for his bath; dressed him, and helped him put on his cork leg. They made more money and they ate better than ever before in their lives. I guess we all did.

"Ned had kind of an office with an extra cot in it and his secretary used to come up there a lot. This was next to his own bedroom and there was a bath between it and a smaller bedroom which Joe and I shared. Ned had the tub fixed so Lige could lower one side and let the Colonel get in and out easier. He was a hell of a big man and had a lot of trouble dragging his cork leg around.

"We also had a dining room, a kitchen, and a good-sized parlor. There was nothing elaborate about the furnishings; they were just comfortable. We did lots of partying and some drinking, not too much although we usually had a couple of jugs of pretty good corn liquor around. I don't think Ned touched it. The girls those days drank more than the men, or at any rate the girls we brought up there did."

Reproductions of early gaiety in the Green Flats were preserved for many years by the actions of a skilled amateur photographer whose hidden equipment, slow though it was, caught scenes of these carefree bachelors in *flagrante delicto*. Memories of the fun these unexpected snapshots gave even to unknowing participants may have been the reason for Colonel Green's delight in pornography when his sexual pleasures became vicarious.

Infrequently, real professional talent was brought in from Dallas, only twenty-two miles away. These special party arrangements usually were made well in advance and local gentlemen, married or single, who participated in them, let it be known there would be no "open house" in the Green Flats these expensive weekends. One particular Saturday night was recalled in 1936 by Mr. J. W. Cummings, a retired railroader in his seventies whose memory of the Green Flats girls was sharp.

"I lived at my parents' home in Terrell but I used to go up to the Green Flats occasionally," Mr. Cummings said. "There was a salesman from Terrell who was on the road a lot and used to hit Dallas every couple of weeks. He knew all the high-steppers there and he'd make the arrangements but somebody else had to meet the girls when they got to Terrell because he was married.

"They [Mr. Cummings still careful in his use of the third person plural] were waiting around one Saturday night for four hookers who'd been paid half their fees in advance and given round-trip railroad tickets. I happened to be there about eight o'clock when three of them came in off Number Eighty-six, that was the Ennis Local. They were all good-lookers.

"The fourth one wasn't there. One of the girls said she was busy and couldn't get away until the ten eight. So the salesman said he wouldn't mind waiting and they should go ahead. Well, Ned picked out one for himself and took her to his room. The others did the same.

"Late the next morning everybody who was left got together in the dining room. The only two missing was the salesman and his girl. He had to leave the Green Flats about midnight so he could go home and get to church the next morning with his family. The lady was still asleep.

"Well, they were all eating and maybe having a few drinks when the door to a bedroom opens and out walks this beautiful redhead. Ned took one look at her and yelled 'Mabel!' At first she looked puzzled but when she saw him limp over she recognized him and said, 'Hiya, Eddie.' They threw their arms around each other like they were long-lost lovers."

Thus Mabel re-entered Ned's life. After cleaning up unfinished business in Dallas, she returned to Terrell a few weeks later. It was perfect timing. Tartt was getting ready to be married and Corley was due for a transfer to Waco. The boys moved out and Mabel moved in.

To the embarrassment of respectable Terrell gentlemen, friends of the President of the Texas Midland, and to the disappointment of most of the community's matrons, Mabel was openly installed in the Green Flats. Mr. Green called her his "housekeeper" but nobody was fooled. Miss Schneider, who no longer found Terrell interesting, took off for weekends in Fort Worth, and shortly after became Mrs. William D. Anderson. The secretary was replaced by a young man who seemed able to handle all of his employer's requirements between the hours of 8 A.M. and 5 P.M.

The most deeply offended by Ned's defection were the Allens.

Although young Green was still welcomed in their home, Mabel was not. Other Terrell doors were closed tightly. Plans Ned may have had to take higher degrees in local lodges were dropped because instruction teams never could find the time to teach him. Brothers who didn't care what he did under a sheet, political or social, as long as it was done in secret, were chagrined by his open defiance of "the code."

His New England forebears must have been responsible for a measure of caution Ned took in his financial arrangements with the new "housekeeper." Even before Mabel moved into the Green Flats, the President of the Texas Midland consulted L. C. Alexander, counsel for the railroad. Mr. Alexander (later Circuit Judge Alexander) drew up an agreement between Ned and Mabel in which the latter's duties were clearly (if not completely) defined and the former's obligations limited to a monthly salary not to exceed $150. The party of the first part was given the right to abrogate the contract at any time by giving thirty days' written notice to the party of the second part. Parties of both parts seemed satisfied and the agreement was duly executed.

Although Ned had been given a free hand to run the Texas Midland, all railroad expenses were cleared through Hetty's New York Westminster Company, a holding company for her widespread operations. Consequently, with the exception of the first daring withdrawal of $2,500, the balance of the $500,000 in Ned's "personal" account remained intact. There is no record of what Hetty said when she saw the bank statement, a copy of which was sent to her, but no matter how much Mrs. Green remonstrated, her son ignored her. The money was in his name and he alone could write checks on it.

However, Ned did display a certain amount of caution, and in order to keep his mother in ignorance of Mabel as long as possible he withdrew another $10,000 and set up a special account in the American National Bank. Checks drawn on this account, he told Allen, were to be sent only to himself.

"When Mabel first came to Terrell," the President of the

American Bank recalled, "we used to honor checks Ned had made out to 'cash' and endorsed by a 'Mrs. M. E. Staunton,' who presented them for payment. Later on this same woman began to bring in monthly checks for one hundred and fifty dollars each made out to 'Mabel Harlow.' We questioned her politely about this and she told us 'Staunton' was her married name but because her husband recently had died she intended to go back to her maiden name. There was no reason for us to disbelieve her."

Despite his preoccupation with Mabel, Ned was not neglecting his duties as President of the Texas Midland. His first move there was to find out what was needed to transform this inadequate carrier into a first-class railroad. He told Wells and McKay to hire as much additional staff as they required and make a complete survey of the T. M. He gave them six months to complete the job.

"We figured," McKay said, "the boss was trying to make some kind of show for Mrs. Green. He'll send Larry and me out and we'll turn in our report. He'll bury it, stall around for a while, and the Texas Midland will go on as usual, with everybody who worked for the railroad ashamed to admit it.

"When we finished the survey we only confirmed what was our and the rest's idea that the Texas Midland was a very decrepit piece of railroad. We knew what had to be done but we never figured the boss would do it. This was going to cost a lot of dough because we wrote down every damned thing we knew we had to have. We didn't go out of line, just kept to the facts."

But the Wells-McKay report, a voluminous, detailed statement, was the basis for improvements Ned ordered almost as soon as he had read it.

"It was like a dream," McKay continued. "He really had confidence in our judgment and did everything we suggested and then some. I don't want to be technical but we were using sixty-pound rails and they were way too light. We recommended eighty and we got 'em. We needed new ties and we got those, too. There was a new kind of ballast we checked on, burned gum board it was called. It was some claylike material, made out of white cedar; expensive to start out with, but guaranteed to outlast anything else, and besides it gave the cars a smoother ride.

"Our bridges were in terrible condition. They were wood and had to be repaired and jacked up all the time. Ned replaced them with steel and while he was at it he tore down most of the stations and built new ones. I remember one station where maybe some farmer who lived miles off used to load his crops. It never had a real name but the boss put up a nice little building there. He called the stop 'Harlow' and it showed on our timetables, too. He used to kid about it and when we got an express going through, it had orders to stop there. Passengers would wonder why the hell a through train would pull up at a place with the population listed after its name as (pop. 1). And nobody around you could see for ten miles."

One recommendation was to extend the Texas Midland's fifty-one-mile right of way to connect with a through east-west carrier on each end of the line. This would speed freight shipments as well as give the T. M. a chance to create a fast "name train" for prestige. Wells reported the total cost of these improvements would run considerably more than $2,000,000.

"We thought the boss would balk at this but he didn't," Wells recollected. "He first got trackage rights with the Cotton Belt from Greenville to Commerce and covered us on the south end by a deal he made there. We had to build our own connecting lines and before we got finished the T. M. had a hundred and twenty-five miles of track."

According to S. G. Reed, Green first connected his railroad with the H. & T. C. at Ennis. Then he started construction of fourteen miles of rail north from Roberts, which was the northern terminal, to Greenville, reached in 1894. This gave Ned a connection with the Cotton Belt and the Sherman, Shreveport and Southern, which later became the M. K. T. (Katy). Then he built thirty-seven more miles of trackage beyond Commerce to Paris.

Wells continued, "I was sent out to Commerce, headquarters for construction from there to a little station at the end of the line called Klondike. Once a week or so Ned used to come over from Terrell to watch us extending the tracks farther and farther. Sometimes he'd be riding in a gondola—that's a freight car with sides, a front, and a back but no roof—fixed up as good as they could to make it comfortable for him. But more often he'd be up in the cab with the engineer. I can remember how he'd have a big grin on his face like a kid whose dreams came true.

"They'd help him down and he'd stand there asking me how it was going and if I needed anything but he never interfered. He seemed real happy and he'd stay for an hour or so. Then he'd wave good-by to all the gandy dancers, the navvy gang, and the water boys. And they'd take off their old hats and wave and yell back. Even in that stinkin' hot sun I guess they were glad to be working for a railroad president who recognized them although they were only Spicks, Greasers, and Indians."

By the time construction work on stations was completed and Green's agreements with connecting railroads were signed, larger passenger cars he had ordered were delivered. He was then able to make up his crack name train, called the Lone-Star Special.

"It was a beauty," McKay said. "The first train operating in the South, I guess, with an observation-sleeping car and a café lounge. It was part of a through passenger equipment train, operating between St. Louis and Galveston over the Frisco to Paris (Texas), the Texas Midland to Ennis, and the Houston and Texas Central to Galveston. Everybody who worked for the T. M. was damned proud of the Lone-Star Special. And by God, we ran *on time!*"

Only once in his career as railroad President did Ned seek help from his mother and this was almost at the start of the venture. Against the advice of his more experienced colleagues Ned, anxious for new business, invaded the territory of another carrier. Wells recalled this incident.

"Ned made a deal with some farmers to bring in their cotton

by wagon to Garrett from Ennis," he said. "At that time Garrett was the point of our connection with the Houston and Texas Central. This was called 'scalping,' invasion of another railroad's territory, and the H. & T. got sore as hell. They canceled through rates with the Texas Midland, and unless something could be done about that we were finished.

"Well, Ned sent a wire to Mrs. Green telling her what had happened and asked her to see what she could do. The tough part was that the H. & T. was Huntington's property. I'm not exactly sure what she did. Somebody told me later she put a squeeze on Huntington for a property he was trying to buy from her in St. Louis. Maybe so. All I know for certain is that a couple days later we got our through rates back again."

A big surprise was in store for the Texas Midland, for Ned's adopted city, and for his new housekeeper. Early one spring morning the Lone-Star Special pulled into its terminus and unhooked a magnificent new private car, painted deep maroon. On the sides were the numerals 999. Below these, to the astonishment of Terrell's citizens, who gathered every day to watch the arrival of the Special, was embossed, in foot-high letters, the name MABEL.

The President himself, assisted by Lige, then limped down from the richly upholstered vestibule, smiled broadly at the gaping audience, and entered his office in the station.

The *Mabel* was designed by George Mortimer Pullman himself and built under his direct supervision at the Pullman shops in suburban Chicago. The cost was about $75,000 and nobody knows what Hetty's reaction must have been.

Tom Corley, who was one of the *Mabel*'s first official passengers, recalled the private car vividly.

"Unless you're talking about palace cars, 999 was the most elegant private car I ever saw. The fittings were beautiful and everything done in the best of taste. It had extra-heavy suspension springs and the newest type of shock absorbers. You could hardly feel a bump.

"There was an observation end, deeper than the usual ones, with real easy chairs you could turn in every direction. There were three staterooms, one very large for the Boss and Mabel. It had a huge brass bed. A lavatory connected with it, in fact the car had three toilets for Ned and his guests and one for servants. There was a good-sized dining room and a modern kitchen equipped with a couple of iceboxes. In the back of the dining room were quarters for the cook and Lige. There also was an office separated from the observation end by a partition you could move to one side, kind of like the louver doors they have today."

It would have been interesting to witness Miss Harlow's reaction to her first view of the *Mabel*. She must have been aware that she had already come a long way in a short time. Her first trip on the *Mabel* with Ned was to St. Louis, where they were joined by John Ringling and another Mabel, Mabel Burton, a telegraph operator who married the circus owner. After comparing each other's private cars, attending a performance under the big top, and dining in the *Mabel*, Ned and his housekeeper returned to Terrell. There an unpleasant surprise was in store for them.

When President Green arrived at his office the following morning a delegation of irate Terrellians was awaiting him. The committee was headed by Joe Keller, City Marshal, reinforced by the Reverend Wilfred Mutch, pastor of Shiloh Baptist Church, and another member of the cloth. Tom B. Griffith, an infrequent Green Flats visitor, recalled Ned's discomfiture at the mission of these solid citizens.

"The Marshal was about three times Ned's age," Griffith said. "And even though they were lodge brothers and Green was President of the railroad he didn't hesitate to let him have it. He told him the people of Terrell were offended by his open squiring of a 'whore'—and that's exactly what he called Miss Harlow—and that she'd have to get out of town. Otherwise, Joe warned Ned, he'd be forced to place the 'housekeeper' under arrest.

"Joe made no threats against Ned, personally. He liked him a lot. We all did for that matter and Ned was putting Terrell on the

91

map. We figured this woman was taking Ned and the sooner the affair was broken up the better it would be for everybody concerned.

"Ned said little. He was polite and listened while they talked. Nobody knows what he thought. Maybe he figured what he did in his spare time was nobody's business but his own, or deep down they were right. He didn't promise anything but the next week the Green Flats was closed.

"Ned moved back to the Harris, where he took half a floor, and Mabel left town. We didn't know it at the time but we found out later Ned had fixed her up with a housekeeping suite in the Grand Windsor Hotel in Dallas. That's where he spent his weekends from then on until he lived there himself."

Chapter Fifteen

Nᴇᴅ's father was the first member of the family to hear about Miss Harlow. Word apparently reached him at the Union Club, probably via some railroad official who had been entertained on the *Mabel* during a trip to the Southwest. With Hetty's connections everywhere and her acquaintance with scores of people who would be delighted to give Mrs. Green all bad news, true or false, it seems impossible that she was long in ignorance of her son's affair of the heart.

She surely watched his personal expenses mount and was hardly the type to forget about that half-million dollars placed in Ned's name. But the miracle is that she said nothing, and for a long while never even acknowledged Mabel's existence. When at last she did, she referred to her coldly only as "Miss Harlot." Hetty lived in fear that someday Ned would get married; since it was hardly likely that he would marry Mabel, she may have considered this the lesser of two great evils.

Sylvia, at her father's request, wrote Ned a letter asking him to join them at Bellows Falls, where they intended to spend the summer in the Tucker House. Edward Green was beginning to suffer from the kidney complaint that finally killed him and Hetty thought a few months in Vermont might help him get well. The older Green may have believed a "man-to-man" talk with his son would produce desirable results. But Ned was too busy to be with his father again until the latter was on his deathbed.

With no prospect of a reunion with her brother, whom she had not seen for more than a year, Sylvia returned to Vermont to act as her father's nurse. She hardly ever left the Tucker House, but it is obvious from the correspondence between her and Mamie Nims that Sylvia was longing for company.

"Even though we lived in the small town, separated from each other by less than a mile, the only way we kept in touch was by mail," Mamie recollected.

"Once I wrote Sylvia a note asking her and a distant cousin who was visiting her father to join a party of young people picnicking at Table Rock on the summit of Mt. Kilburn where there is a wonderful view of the Connecticut valley. The cousin was considerably older, a woman in her sixties I would suppose, and I included her only out of courtesy, thinking she would refuse. This would give Sylvia a chance to get out with girls and boys her own age. Sylvia was then twenty-three.

"It would have been the event of a lifetime but Sylvia could not go. She answered me at once.

" 'Tucker House
" 'July 10/94

" 'Dear Mamie,

" 'It was so kind of you to invite my cousin and myself to go up the Mountain with you. But my cousin said she would not go unless my father would go, but he is not able to so that ends the first lesson.

" 'My father don't think it would be right for me to go and

94

leave them when they are my guests and are only to be here such a short time. I don't think I shall ever go up the mountain as something always prevents my so doing, but I hope you all will have a lovely time and I shall try and see you from a distance. With many thanks for your kind remembrance of one who wants to *go so bad*. [The emphasis is Sylvia's but the phrasing is reminiscent of Ned's letter to his mother requesting permission to attend the Fair.]

" 'With kind regards to your Mother.

" 'I remain your loving friend,
" 'Sylvia.' "

Later Hetty joined her husband and daughter for a week at the Tucker House and Sylvia was granted permission to give a party.

"Dear Mamie," she wrote. "I have invited several friends to spend Monday evening, August 19, and would like to have you, and would be pleased to have you stay all night with us.

"I thought it would be pleasant to play games and enjoy ourselves.

"Hoping this will find you all well, with love to your mother and self.

"I remain your loving friend,
"Sylvia Green.

"P.S. Can you come by seven (7) o'clock so as to be here when the rest come?

"S. G."

Mamie Nims accepted and remembers Sylvia's party very well.

"As soon as I arrived," she said, "Sylvia took me into the parlor. It was well furnished in Colonial style. Looking about, I saw on the mantel a portrait of a handsome young woman painted on ivory. I asked her who it was and she said, 'My mother.' On the wall were framed tapestries which she said were embroidered by an aunt.

"We played cards by the inadequate light of a single kerosene lamp and were served cake and lemonade.

"During the evening two gentlemen called on Mrs. Green. They were a local deacon and an organizer who was trying to establish a Y.M.C.A. in Bellows Falls. Of course, they were soliciting funds for the undertaking."

Sylvia's guests were privileged to witness Mrs. Green in action.

"Her technique in dealing with those who asked financial aid was wonderful," Mamie continued. "She was very polite and evidenced much interest in the project. In fact, she asked so many questions and talked so much the two gentlemen departed in amicable mood but empty-handed.

"This was the only time I remember seeing Mrs. Green well dressed. She wore black brocade trimmed with jet which, although not of the latest style, became her. With her gray hair arranged high on her head and with her animated face, she bore some resemblance to the young lady in the portrait on the mantel.

"Sylvia sat on the arm of her chair while she was talking. She seemed proud of her mother and happy. She never intimated by word or act that her mother's peculiarities were trying and she cheerfully submitted to all the restrictions imposed upon her.

"I stayed at the Tucker House that night. We had breakfast in the room across the hall from the parlor, the one farthest from the kitchen. It contained a table, some plain chairs, and a whatnot with nothing on it. I met Dewey, the Skye terrier, whose name later adorned their doorplate in Hoboken. Someone had given him to them and Mrs. Green told me in an impressive whisper that he was worth three hundred dollars. Having been brought up with a St. Bernard, I failed to be impressed."

Hetty had acquired Dewey some time before 1890. Unless we are to believe he was substituted for another black, bewhiskered little animal, he must have lived to an age well beyond canine actuarial probabilities. New Bedforders recollect seeing this high-strung, ill-tempered beast in 1891, by then not a puppy. Mamie Nims refers to him in 1894, and a picture of Hetty, holding Dewey in her arms, appears in the June, 1910, issue of *Cosmopolitan*.

Dewey was more than a household pet. Often he was a property owner, at least for those brief periods when as "straw man" (if this phrase may be used to include canines) he held title to real estate being transferred from Mrs. Green to a buyer. Other times, by becoming Mrs. Green's host, this much-traveled terrier was of incalculable value to Hetty in her ceaseless battle with the tax collectors of New York, New Jersey, and Massachusetts. Then Dewey was listed as lessor on residential leases; his name was affixed to doorplates and mailboxes, and consequently Hetty became her dog's guest. In Mrs. Green's devious hands, the art of obfuscation was developed to near-perfection.

Dewey had an unfair advantage over all other dogs: nature had endowed him with a full complement of extra fangs. Another of his distinctions was that while he may not have been the only dog to be a registered hotel guest, at least he was the only one in the history of Brooklyn's Hotel St. George. The daybook for Tuesday, December 4, 1894, shows the following entries:

> D. Gray, City
> H. Gray, "
> S. Gray, "

As pursuing reporters discovered, but only when their prey had fled, "H. Gray" stood for Hetty Green, and "S. Gray" for her daughter. But the identity of "D. Gray" remained a secret for some time although rumors soon spread that this was a subterfuge to conceal the name of a man who had eloped with Sylvia. Soon after, in order to contradict that gossip, Hetty, herself, introduced "D. Gray" to the press. She did not disclose her reason for the use of his alias. However, it was obvious to those who followed Mrs. Green's career that she was again attempting to avoid the service of a subpoena. This time the plaintiff was Miss Mary Irene Hoyt, who was seeking to recover $100,000 in damages from the defendant for the use of "false and defamatory language."

Hetty appeared astonished that anyone should take offense at a few innocent comments.

"All I said," she averred, "was that lawyers were strange birds and that Miss Hoyt was ill perhaps, because of the pressure of unnecessary lawsuits."

The following excerpt from a story that appeared in the New Bedford *Times*, June 6, 1894, suggests a different interpretation of Hetty's innocuous remarks.

"'Oh! Did you ever see such a set of buzzards!' Mrs. Green shouted. 'It is sad to think of poor Irene Hoyt! Joe Choate and the other buzzards got hold of her and she is in an asylum now.' . . ."

Hetty was not without defenders. A story by one unknown champion appeared in the Boston *Herald* on July 14, 1896.

"She has a weakness for children and is always trying, and with success, to make friends with them. The people who know her well . . . will tell you that Hetty is eccentric and whimsical but after all, they like her. She is interesting. She is kindly.

" 'The poor in this country have no chance,' she once said. 'No wonder Anarchists and Socialists are so numerous. . . .' "

There is still one more journalistic apologist for Mrs. Green. This one appeared regularly in *Putnam's Monthly* under the *nom de plume* of "The Lounger." He sets forth his opinion of Hetty in a caption that appears below the lady's likeness and admits his adulation is based solely upon this photograph.

"I have never had the pleasure of meeting Mrs. Green," wrote the Lounger, "and until I saw this picture I imagined her to be a very different looking woman. But now she looks to me like a woman who would hand .out a few hundred (dollars) . . . to help a scapegrace nephew. There is nothing sharp or shrewd in this face. It is the face of a motherly soul. . . ."

Others who viewed this picture of Hetty recently expressed amazement at the Lounger's interpretation. To them, Hetty, who appeared on page 125 of the 1900 issue of *Putnam's*, looks just as they had always pictured her. Her lips are thin; her jaw juts out firmly from a rocky face, and she stares directly at you with cold, unyielding, blue eyes.

Chapter Sixteen

For almost a year after Miss Harlow's departure from Terrell, Green continued to live at the Harris, spending only weekends in Dallas with Mabel at the Grand Windsor. On the same floor of the Grand Windsor as the Green-Harlow establishment lived a family named Cammack, with three children.

"My father was a railroader," Mary Cammack, the youngest child, recalled. "He was working in St. Louis for the Katy when he was transferred to Dallas. Until he and my mother found out if we'd be there long enough to make it pay to buy a house, they rented rooms in the hotel. Lots of railroad men did this and the Grand Windsor catered to them.

"We first knew Mabel as Mrs. M. E. Staunton, the name she was registered under at the hotel. We never met Mr. Staunton.

Mabel was beautiful and had long, wavy, red hair which she could let down to her hips. She used to allow my older sister to comb it out for her. She used lots of make-up but on her it looked good.

"She was kind to us Cammack kids and gave us candy or a penny if we needed it, which was always. Sometimes, when my parents wanted to go out for the evening, she told them she'd keep an eye on us. We'd sneak out of our beds and come over to her place, at least my sister and I would, and she'd let us try on her fancy clothes. She had a closet full of them and her bureau was covered with a million jars of cosmetics, powder, rouge, and whatever else they had in those days.

"We thought she lived in the one room where we used to visit her. We didn't realize, and my father didn't either for a while, that a door between it and another couple of adjoining rooms could be opened. We didn't know where she cooked—I guess we didn't think about it—and imagined she ate in the dining room like we all did. Every weekend this tall, lame man would come to visit her and usually we wouldn't see Mabel again until Sunday night."

Mary Cammack remembers the first time they met the "tall, lame man."

"I didn't think he even knew we existed," she said, "but Mabel must have told him. He was simply crazy about children. One Sunday afternoon he knocked on our door and introduced himself to my parents. He told them he was a friend of Mrs. Staunton and he wondered whether they'd mind if he and Mabel took us for a ride in a carriage he'd hired from the hotel livery stable.

" 'It holds five,' he said, 'and it would be a shame to let all that space go to waste on this nice spring day. Charlie (that was my brother, who was six years older than me) can sit up front and help me handle the reins.'

"My father knew who he was, of course—everybody in that part of Texas did—and when we came back from our ride, the

100

two of them had a nice talk about railroading. Although my father was only a brakeman and Ned was the President of the T. M., he was very nice to him. I remember he asked my father all kinds of questions about the business and listened attentively to his answers.

"Later on, when my dad found out about the relationship between Ned and Mabel, he tried to break up our friendship through my Sunday-school teacher. But that didn't work out and we still sneaked over to see Mrs. Staunton and Mr. Green. By that time I guess my father liked Ned so well he didn't say anything more to stop us from visiting them. Besides, my father lost his job with the Katy and Ned gave him a better one working under Mr. Corley on the T. M."

Soon after Mabel was established in Dallas, Ned voluntarily raised her salary to $200 a month. This unexpected increase convinced her that devotion to duty could offer more than the mere pleasure of doing a job well and that by remaining faithful to Ned and conforming to his mores she might be able to stretch a temporary engagement into a lifelong career.

Naturally, Mabel was aware that Ned, the only son of the world's richest woman, had considerably better than average prospects. But she also realized that her position as housekeeper, or even mistress, held no guarantee of permanence, particularly when viewed in the light of her employer's escape clause.

It would not be in keeping with Mabel's character to assume she made a sudden decision to get what she could out of Ned Green. Although a professional, and as such accustomed to cash in advance, Miss Harlow was not avaricious and often had permitted love to interfere with business. In the past she had been generous with her favors and frequently refused to accept the usual honorarium simply because she liked the man she went to bed with. Several times she had spent romantic, but unprofitable, months with a lover, and returned to duty penniless.

Mabel liked corn liquor, but Ned hated to see a woman drink. So she became a model of sobriety, accepting only an occasional

101

highball, sipped slowly in ladylike fashion, or succumbing very rarely to an impulsive three-day spree.

Ned was intelligent and enjoyed talking about his work and his hobbies. Although it is doubtful if Mabel went beyond the fifth grade or ever read a book in her life, she was far from stupid. Skilled in the art of pleasing the opposite sex, she had long been aware that all a woman needs to seem intelligent to most men is to be a good listener. No wife ever laughed more heartily at her husband's stale jokes or listened more attentively to his daily business triumphs than Mabel did for Ned.

Until their romance wore thin, Mabel and Ned were as happy as any couple could be with such opposite tastes, backgrounds, and mental capacities. The further handicap of society's long refusal to accept Mabel was overcome in part by her willingness to recognize her limitations and in part by Ned's contempt for the world of society, which held out open arms to him.

One not-to-be forgotten lesson that Mabel learned from her first salary increase was thrift. In her recent insecure past, money was something to be spent almost as quickly as it was earned. But when she achieved the measure of security her association with Ned gave her, she made sure that she saved or invested some portion of her earnings. Her first bank deposit was for $15.00.

Mabel had as much trouble cashing her first check in Dallas as she had had in Terrell. In Terrell she had been known as Mrs. M. E. Staunton and then as Mabel Harlow, but for some strange reason the process was reversed in the former city.

"We all knew Mabel," recalled Sam Turner, who used to be a teller in the National Exchange Bank of Dallas. "She and the other girls liked the feel of new money and used to turn in their old two-dollar bills for fresh paper. I was teller at the ladies' window when she brought a check in for me to cash. First of all I was surprised anybody had given her a check. I'd never heard of anything but cash payments in her line of business.

"I suppose if this one had been made out to 'Mabel Harlow' I wouldn't have questioned anything but the size of it, but I simply couldn't figure out where the hell she got one for 'Mrs. M. E. Staunton.' Well, we all recognized the signer of that check, so we asked him to clear up the question of identity, which he did. Thereafter our bank knew this woman by two names."

This design for living might have continued indefinitely had it not been for the interference of well-meaning friends or, as Ned called them, and without rancor, "interfering old women." Led by a retired army career officer, Major Briner, who knew Ned's father, a delegation of Terrellians, still trying to separate the lovers, harassed the hotel management until Mabel was asked to leave.

After an embarrassed management of the Grand Windsor finally yielded to purity, Ned Green moved his establishment to the Oriental Hotel, a few blocks away. Here, Ned's willingness to lease an expensive six-room suite and pay for its refurbishing seems to have overcome any squeamishness that operators of the hotel may have felt about granting space for Mr. Green's lady.

About this time Ned decided to leave the Harris and spend all his nights with Mabel. He still used Terrell as his T. M. headquarters and arrived there each morning in his private railroad car. To maintain the fiction of a Terrell residence, Ned rented a room in the home of Oscar Price, a lodge brother. He paid rent for this room and another in the Bondurant N. Jarvis home when Oscar died, for the next twenty-three years. He never slept in the first room, never even saw the second one, and kept no more than a moth-eaten pair of trousers and an old cork leg in either.

For the rest of Ned's life he claimed this little town as his home. In whatever hotel he registered, whether it was the Waldorf-Astoria, the Planters' in St. Louis, or Denver's Brown Palace, on the line where a guest declares his residence he unfailingly wrote, "Terrell, Texas." Affection played a minor role in the love affair between Mr. Green and the Lone-Star State. A highly favorable tax structure starred.

This is not to deny that Ned was happy in his adopted home or that he made many warm and lasting friendships in Texas.

103

Undoubtedly these were the best years of his life. But one characteristic Ned retained from his long line of Howland ancestry was a strong dislike for public levies. When he first learned that Texas was almost unique in providing its baronial landowners and others who were very rich with practically painless taxation, Ned Green decided that a home in the Lone-Star State was just what he needed.

Unaware that merely because a man continuously says he is a Texan (or a Pennsylvanian or a New Yorker) he is not necessarily a legal resident of that state, Ned went through life firmly convinced that he, like Hetty before him, had successfully confused varied assortments of revenue agents.

One levy Ned never refused to pay was his poll tax, which he might legally have avoided since the Texas Legislature, in its desire to be equitable, permitted a man with a single leg or similar handicap, or male citizens past the age of sixty, to escape this twenty-five-cent impost.

As long as he actually lived in the state or was able to get there on Election Day, Ned voted from "The Fifth District, in the Town of Terrell, in the County of Kaufman, in the State of Texas." After it was physically impossible for him to be there in person, he cast an absentee ballot. In later life this was all part of Ned's design to avoid tax assessments, but when he first arrived in Terrell and was convinced he would live in Texas for the rest of his days, he voted because he wanted to exercise his franchise. He even ventured into the bewildering maze of Southern politics, through which he was led by a Negro, known widely as "Gooseneck Bill" McDonald.

Chapter Seventeen

HE was baptized "William Madison McDonald," but with the exception of close relatives, most of whom he supported, he was known from Texas to Maine as "Gooseneck Bill." The Deep South customarily added a qualifying phrase, "that uppity nigger." To all who ever saw him, the origin of his nickname was obvious. A contemporary described Bill as a "tall, gaunt, colored man with thin, hawklike features, a tufted crop of jet-black hair, and a narrow head, mounted on a scrawny neck hardly wide enough to contain an enormous Adam's apple which bobbed up and down wildly every time he talked."

For more than half a century McDonald was a force in Texas politics, controlling a small but potent block of votes sometimes used to swing the balance of power between embattled white leaders, not only in Kaufman County, his bailiwick, but also at Presidential conventions wherever they were held. Bill, of course, was a Republican, the only party he was permitted to join in his native state.

Because the Republicans had not won a state-wide contest since the days of the carpetbaggers, Bill's power lay in his ability to help elect national committeemen who in turn designated the party's Presidential ticket. For this reason McDonald was cultivated by white politicians, from Senator Matthew Quay, of Pennsylvania, up to Senator John Sherman, of antitrust fame.

Bill was one of eleven children. His maternal grandfather was a Choctaw Indian, and that's as far back as his ancestors can be traced. He had innumerable aunts, uncles, and cousins but since each one customarily bore the name of his owner, McDonald never knew who they were. His own surname came from that of his father's Georgia master.

Both of Bill's parents had been slaves, but when he was born Lee had already surrendered at Appomattox and the McDonalds were free to raise their family on what could be gleaned from sharecropping twenty acres of cotton. Bill's father occasionally supplemented the family income as an itinerant blacksmith.

Gooseneck was born June 22, 1865. His parents were then living in rural Kaufman County, about sixteen miles southeast of Terrell. Schools were segregated, wretchedly inferior, and the term lasted three months. Children spent the nine months of "vacation" working on the farm. Young McDonald was lucky to have a fine teacher all seven of the years he spent in the one-room schoolhouse. She was perceptive and recognized this pupil's intelligence and encouraged him to continue his education elsewhere.

Despite his parents' need for him on the farm, where there was no letup in the daily grind for existence, they were persuaded to allow Bill to go to college. Naturally, they could not give him money, but by cutting down their own meals they managed to pack enough food to last at least part of the three weeks it took

Bill to walk to Nashville, Tennessee, seven hundred miles away.

This was the summer of 1880 and Bill was fifteen years old. He carried a letter of recommendation from his teacher to the President of Roger Williams College, now part of Fisk University. Young McDonald's credits were sketchy but no more so than those of most of the undergraduates at this school, and Bill was accepted.

By limiting sleep to four hours a day, and food to a bare minimum, Bill was able to return to Kaufman County in 1884 with a paper that entitled him to add "B.A." after his name and to accept a job teaching school at a salary of $200 per annum.

"I spent the next five or six years in broken-down one-room schoolhouses all over the county—Brayville, Elmore, and Baylor," Bill recalled. "It was bitterly discouraging. We had so little to work with in human and physical equipment. My people were disorganized, and even those who were allowed to vote didn't bother. They were too busy trying to keep alive and if they ever scraped up the twenty-five-cent poll tax, they found that two bits could be put to more immediate needs.

"Nobody who wasn't a part of this continuous struggle to get enough food into his belly could possibly understand what life down here meant for us Negroes. When we were fortunate we went to bed only a little bit hungry, but most of the time we weren't fortunate.

"I know I got exceptionally good breaks. Many of the whites I came in contact with in the county and elsewhere were extremely kind and I, for one, don't believe every Southerner is a 'redneck.' In fact, if it hadn't been for their help, I wouldn't have gotten anywhere.

"My people needed leadership and the recognition that goes with it. I felt that with my education I was in a position to guide them. I first got interested in fraternal work. This took me all over the state—conventions, conferences, all kinds of meetings. I used to do this in my spare time and I paid my own way. But in 1890 the Masons offered me a small salary and modest traveling expenses so I quit teaching and gave all my time to lodge duties."

From fraternal activities Bill slid into politics. By 1895, when he was just thirty years old, he had become the best-known Negro in Texas. Using every possible means, even if it meant depleting the treasury of some local lodge, he saw to it that poll taxes were paid and that members of his race voted.

Village, town, county, and state leadership, with the exception of certain West Texas areas, was overwhelmingly in the hands of the Democrats, who admitted no Negro to their ranks. Members of this dominant group cared not a whit how many Negroes were Republicans and scorned any Southern white man low enough to join the party of Abraham Lincoln, even if it meant appointment to a Federal job.

Bill was then married and living in Forney, a small farming community eight or nine miles east of Terrell, on the T. M. right of way. This was the heart of what is now the Fifth Congressional District, which included Dallas, Henderson, Ellis, Johnson, and Kaufman Counties. Here, McDonald had welded together over three thousand Negroes into a single political unit called "The Black and Tans." There actually was a rival all-Caucasian Republican organization labeled "The Lily Whites," beneficiaries of Federal patronage doled out from Washington to registered Republicans.

The Lily Whites were far outnumbered by the Black and Tans. Through control of this latter organization Bill had climbed to a position of considerable influence in the Republican Party and had to be recognized by Northern leaders. While privately some of these white gentlemen agreed with the Southern corollaries about "keeping the Nigger in his place," publicly they did not dare to repudiate the policy that had kept their party and themselves in office.

In addition to his ability to lead and his educational superiority over his brethren, who respected the book learning they themselves did not possess, Gooseneck Bill was aided by strict

108

adherence to one rule, basic to the continuing success of any political boss—"Never promise more than you can produce."

That McDonald happened to be honest presumably was not a political asset; in fact, by some it was considered a liability. Men accustomed to behind-the-scenes pay-offs to precinct, county, or state chairmen were frequently at a loss when they tried to do business with this leader who refused to line his own pockets.

Soon after his first meeting with Gooseneck Bill, Ned Green was offered a concrete example of the former's odd code of ethics.

"I'd just joined the Black and Tans," Green said. "I was one of a half-dozen whites who belonged. We were all transplanted New England and Pennsylvania Quakers, Republicans by principle and probably birth. We couldn't tolerate the Lily Whites and there was no place else to go. I certainly didn't give a damn what my Texas acquaintances said. They called me everything from a 'nut' to a 'nigger lover.' My close friends merely smiled and attributed it to Northern eccentricities.

"I was replacing a Negro delegate to the Presidential Convention in St. Louis. I knew the fellow'd had some travel and incidental expenses, plus his loss of prestige, when I took over. I wanted to compensate him for everything. I told McDonald, who was to be the other National Committeeman from our district, to find out how much money it would take to make this boy happy again.

"He came back in a couple of days with the answer, 'Seventy-five.' It sounded pretty high to me. I didn't believe he'd spent much on out-of-pocket expenses and I didn't think his 'pride' was worth all of that. But I'd asked for his job; I'd offered to pay him, so I was hardly in any position to renege."

This incident occurred in Green's rooms in the Oriental Hotel, and Gooseneck Bill recalled that when Ned was told what his gesture would cost him, he paused for a minute, raised his eyebrows, then walked slowly over to his desk.

" 'I'll make the check out to you, Bill,' he said, 'and you can

109

take care of Canon.' That was the colored fellow he was replacing.

"He handed me the check. I took one look at it and I almost hit the ceiling.

" 'Mr. Green,' I said, 'I told you seventy-five *dollars.*'

"He gave me a real broad smile, tore up the old one, and handed me a new one.

" 'You're O.K., Bill,' he said. 'I think you and I are going to be able to do business together. Why, I do believe even my mother would have trusted you.'

"I didn't want to cross Ned Green but I almost felt like telling him I was damned sure his *mother* never would have handed me a check for *seventy-five hundred dollars.*"

Chapter Eighteen

Aᴌᴛʜᴏᴜɢʜ Ned's reasons for entering the political arena via a back-door entrance apparently were sound, it is still difficult to understand why he went into the field at all. In the first place, since salary certainly was no object, it would have been a simple matter for Ned to receive a nice-sounding appointment from the state's chief executive. For that, all Green's influential friends would have had to do would have been to request the Governor to appoint the President of the T. M. to membership on a committee or commission carrying heavy prestige and light duties. There was ample precedent for this action.

Ned often used to tell his long-time secretary, Walter P. Marshall, "I got into the game because I wanted to clean up the Texas political mess," but it is extremely doubtful if Green realized there was a "political mess." Besides, his initial demonstration of willingness to buy his first political job, and his later successful attempt to oust a progressive Mayor of Dallas because this gentleman didn't like Mabel, clearly proved Ned was no reformer.

Once Ned told his close friend, Joe Epstein, a New Bedford reporter, that he went into politics "to see that the colored man got a better shake." But this was nonsense because even when Green became one of the richest men in the country, he never displayed the slightest bit of social-consciousness; he never joined a "do good" organization and never contributed a cent to any group formed to combat social injustice.

While it is true that among his friends Ned included Negroes, Jews, and Roman Catholics and never by word offended their race or religion, it is also a fact that with the exception of Gooseneck Bill, he hired Negroes solely for menial jobs; he retained his membership in highly restricted clubs and kept silent when party members denounced the Church of Rome.

Ned's initial venture into politics was made shortly before the Republican National Presidential Convention met in St. Louis in June, 1896, when Governor William McKinley of Ohio was chosen as standard bearer. While it would seem impossible to dredge up a more typical representative of his party's Neanderthal wing, several high-ranking Republicans, prior to the convention, were not sure that McKinley was "solid" enough on tariffs. The man these statesmen had in mind was "Uncle Joe" Cannon, the Illinois Congressman whose forty-six-year voting record in the United States House of Representatives was not tainted, in a single instance, by the slightest tinge of altruism.

Should "Uncle Joe" either be "unavailable" (an idiotic adjective descriptive of practically no politician in history) or "unacceptable," then McKinley's opponents would settle for Thomas ("Czar") Reed of Maine, Speaker of the House. The anti-McKinley faction was headed by a trio of rascals and political opportunists rarely matched in a long saga of opportunism. These

112

stalwarts included two Pennsylvanians, the Honorable Boies Penrose and the Honorable Matthew Quay, and the distinguished New Yorker, the Honorable Charles Platt.

A telegram signed by Senator Quay, dated May 1, 1896, summoned Gooseneck Bill to Washington. There he met with a committee consisting of the previously mentioned trio augmented by Stephen Elkins, a Republican of West Virginia, and "Uncle Joe" himself.

"The meeting was short," Bill recalled. "I was notified that our candidate was going to be Tom Reed and they appointed me his Texas campaign manager. They gave me the money to organize and told me to go ahead and get my delegates lined up for the convention.

"I went back to Texas and started in to work. A couple days after, I got a message that Mr. Edward Green wanted to see me at the Oriental. I knew who he was but I didn't know what he wanted. I called on him at his hotel but they wouldn't allow me to go upstairs or sit in the lobby so I politely told them to let Mr. Green know I'd been there. Then I walked back to my headquarters down on Commerce Street.

"About a half-hour later in walked this great big, powerful gentleman. He stuck out his hand and said, 'I'm Ned Green and I apologize for the treatment you got at the Oriental. It won't happen again.' He called me 'Mr.' McDonald but I wasn't used to that and I told him to call me 'Bill.' But I never called him anything but 'Mr.' or 'Colonel' Green during all our years together, and I guess I was as close to him as a Negro ever can be to a white man."

Green wanted to make his political bow as a delegate to the St. Louis Convention. Actually all the President of the T. M. had to do to eliminate Bill's previously selected partner in the team that would represent the pro-Reed faction at St. Louis was to pay him off. But McDonald, in order to maintain the fiction of democratic rule, insisted that his new, self-imposed partner be "elected" at a convention of the Black and Tans.

113

"I'd already bought off the guy Mr. Green was replacing," McDonald admitted, "but I wanted him to see how politics worked. He didn't even know who our man Reed was and he'd never heard of Matt Quay. Mr. Green gave instructions and I brought down my delegates, two thousand strong, in flatcars on the T. M. right into Terrell.

"We had banners, REPUBLICANS FOR REED, and we marched along the street, singing and shouting. The sidewalks were lined up with white men, cheering and laughing at us. I led the parade. In the middle of it, riding in an open carriage, was Mr. Green and two other white men, the Terrell postmaster and a Port Collector. We all marched out to an open field where we'd put up a big camp meeting tent. We elected Mr. Green and me.

"I wired Walter Kaufman, he was the Republican Chairman of Kaufman County, what we had done and Mr. Green told me to invite him over to the Oriental Hotel for a celebration. He told me to come along, too. We had a big party up there. That was the first time I ever was a guest in the hotel and, except for the waiters and Mr. Green's valet, Lige Cooper, I was the only colored man. I felt uncomfortable and no matter how much Mr. Green urged me I wouldn't eat or drink anything. I didn't want any incident to spoil everything for him.

"Well, there was feasting nearly all night, everybody but me was drinking whisky and champagne, smoking Mr. Green's special twenty-five-cent cigars, and we 'elected' Reed President of the United States."

Unfortunately, Ned's first try at politics was a failure and the "election" held in the Oriental was not confirmed at St. Louis. There, the McKinley supporters, masterminded by the wily Marcus Hanna of Ohio, refused to recognize the Green-McDonald faction and instead seated a delegation headed by Myron T. Herrick.

Gooseneck Bill determined to salvage what he could from the convention for both Ned and himself. It was obvious from favorable reactions, even from opponents, that Green, under proper guidance (Bill's), could become a factor in Texas politics. First of all, Ned was Hetty Green's son and this made everyone curious to find out for himself what sort of offspring that detested woman could produce. Their astonishment at her son's size, affability, and charm was apparent the moment they shook his hand.

He was a gracious host and spent plenty of money for entertainment. With Bill behind the scenes, the headquarters they had set up in the Planters' Hotel became the most popular at the convention. The rooms were constantly filled with delegates not only from Texas but from all over the United States. The food was excellent and the supply of liquor more than ample. In other and crowded gathering spots delegates had to serve themselves, but in Ned Green's spacious apartment there were a dozen colored waiters, whom Bill had garnered from the best restaurants in St. Louis, happy to serve the white gentlemen whatever they wanted.

While Bill did not know every delegate personally, at least he knew something about him. He briefed his protégé beforehand so that when Ned met the Senator from Indiana, or the Congressman from New Jersey, Green usually was able to ask the right questions. McDonald concentrated on Texans, however, and pulled Ned into many an impromptu meeting with them. Ned was having the time of his life, and if this was not the reason he entered the political arena, at least it was a good excuse for him to stay there for a while.

After sounding out Republicans of every faction and getting the proper responses, Bill decided to take a gamble and run Ned Green for the Chairmanship of the State Republican Executive Committee. This was the most powerful position a Republican could hold in Texas. As long as that party was in power at Washington, control of all Federal patronage in Texas was in his hands: no postmaster could be appointed or reconfirmed and no U. S. Revenue Agent, U. S. Marshal, Port Collector, or Federal assessor, surveyor, clerk, etc. could hold his job without the endorsement of the Chairman. In addition to this authority, the

Chairman held a meaningful voice in the party's choice of Presidential nominees. At St. Louis, Hanna had demonstrated this and, by recognizing only the dispenser of patronage, McKinley's man, obliterated the opposition.

The State Republican Convention was scheduled for the following month in Fort Worth. Ned would not be without opposition. Herrick's man was the incumbent and much would depend on who was named temporary chairman with authority to recognize anyone he wished. Gooseneck Bill was Ned's floor manager.

"We ran Cane for the temporary chairmanship," McDonald said. "They always gave a Negro this job and a white man the permanent spot. Cane was a colored man and Collector for the Port of Galveston. He'd had a scrap with Mr. Herrick, who put up Charlie Ferguson, another Negro, who was the Chief Clerk for Mr. Dickinson, the U. S. Marshal. Well, they got Ferguson elected over Cane as temporary chairman.

"This didn't faze me. I went and worked on the delegates and put all the Green badges on them and I had them mill around there from Tuesday to Saturday morning. That was when the voting was to be."

McDonald had no qualms about revealing his simple method of winning the election for Mr. E. H. R. Green.

"We had plenty of money to spend—Mr. Green gave me thirty thousand dollars to start with, and we just bought the delegates. We sort of ran a commissary, fed them and kept them there. They couldn't get away from us and the longer they stayed the more Green delegates there were, because we were giving them everything.

"When we walked into that convention Saturday morning even Mr. Herrick knew the jig was up. Everybody wore a Green button and carried Green banners. The 'Green Zouaves' came up from Terrell and we hired five more bands, colored and white, from Fort Worth. We buried Mr. Herrick's man and put Ned in. We had a majority of more than eleven to one."

Ned Green took office September 1, 1896, and Gooseneck Bill

went on his protégé's payroll at a monthly salary of $575, which was $275 more than he had asked for. This put McDonald in the highest salary bracket of any Texas Negro. Bill bought a house in Dallas; made an avocation out of lodge activities, accepting political fealty instead of cash; spent a large portion of his time in Mr. Green's behalf, and opened his own private bank.

Mabel was kept in the background. Ned suspected and McDonald knew that the presence of Miss Harlow, who had worked many a convention, might embarrass more than one delegate.

Ned still continued as operating head of the Texas Midland, but he began to depend more and more upon Wells, McKay, and Corley and went to Terrell only two or three days a week. The three had more than proven themselves, and each man's salary was raised accordingly.

Almost one-third of the T. M.'s freight cargo was cotton, and when the boll weevil crossed into Texas from Mexico in the late 1890s and devastated crops, railroad revenue dropped in proportion. All railroad officials were deeply concerned, but Green was the only one to take positive action. He sent McKay out to buy land where weevil control could be tested.

"I picked up a thousand acres in eastern Kaufman County," McKay said, "but since none of us knew a damned thing about farming we told Ned he'd better get an expert. He did. At his own expense he hired Dr. Seaman A. Knapp, President of Iowa Agriculture College, who was supposed to be the best man in the business, and brought him down to Texas. He put Knapp in charge and gave him plenty of cash to operate with.

"Dr. Knapp formed a team of scientists from Texas A. and M. and set up an experimental farm. Washington sent down a couple of bright boys from the Department of Agriculture. Well, they all worked together on this project for the next three years, and Ned Green footed every cent of expense except the Federal Agents and one of these fellows was from Texas and came under Republican patronage.

"When Knapp's men were finished they had the problem licked. They recommended something pretty simple but only after they'd tested about everything else. They said to plant early-maturing North Carolina cotton seed, which developed in August before weevil eggs were hatched. Ned sent men all along the T. M.'s right of way to show farmers what to do. Before long we had our cotton business back.

"This was the biggest achievement in Ned's life. It was the start of the U. S. Department of Agriculture's County Agent system used today in every state of the Union. His active moral and financial support on weevil control was directly responsible for this. Every farmer in the country today owes a debt of gratitude to Mr. E. H. R. Green."

Chapter Nineteen

Ned tired of hotel life and in 1897, without consulting his mother, he bought a three-story brick building in the heart of the business district in downtown Dallas. His offices were on the street level, and he installed Mabel in living quarters on the upper floors. Ned's friends were not happy about these arrangements. They liked young Green and were glad to have him in their homes and clubs, but wives did not appreciate his housekeeper.

He could understand why Dallas ladies were not anxious to be hostesses to Mabel and was not offended by their rejection of her. However, for the first few years of their life together, Ned accepted few invitations that did not include his housekeeper. What entertaining he did was in hotel dining rooms or in his private railroad car, and he saw to it that Mabel remained in their apartment during these times.

Ned still loved Mabel and remained faithful to her as long as she passed her favors on to no one else. But Mabel was bored. She had few inner resources and no friends except former colleagues still working the red-light districts. Occasionally they dropped in to see her when they were off duty. But while Mabel was not ashamed of her erstwhile associates, the memory of her ejection from the Green Flats was still painful. She did not want a recurrence of this unpleasant experience and was afraid that a trek of prostitutes in and out of her new apartment would give ideas to the Dallas police.

Mabel's former clients would have been delighted to renew old acquaintance with their voluptuous friend but were unwilling to take chances except on rare occasions. Lige and Bill, who were completely devoted to their employer, were around too much of the time for many side excursions. Nobody wanted to incur the ire of a man reputed able to apply $100,000,000 worth of anger to the object of his wrath.

Mabel had the misfortune to be caught on two of the few times she wandered from the paths of conformity and virtue during the early phases of her liaison with Ned. The first occasion took place soon after she and Ned left the Oriental. Lige that day was with his master in Terrell and Bill was in Fort Worth performing some task for one of his lodges. Even the Cammack children, who had been company for "Aunt Mabel" all afternoon, had gone home for supper. The housekeeper was entirely alone.

When Ned returned later, his mistress was gone and so were the contents of a bottle of whisky she had left on her dressing table. The week before she had told Ned a "lady friend" was coming to town with a carnival. Green suspected that Mabel once had been a performer in this tent show and sent Bill to find her.

McDonald circled the midway several times. He was ready to return without Mabel when he glanced up at a platform just in time to observe a familiar, attractive, and scantily clad rear end swaying gaily to the exotic sounds of a flageolet and bass drum. The show was about to begin and the alluring buttocks could have belonged to no one but Miss Harlow, a guest star, and the last of the line to dip down the steps into the tent below.

How to get Miss Harlow away from the show without creating a scene was a serious problem for McDonald. He was afraid to enter the tent. Even though he would be standing far off in the colored section, Miss Harlow still might recognize him and then disaster would strike. In the eyes of the shouting Southern sports who crowded eagerly around the arena where the now completely disrobed girls (including Miss Harlow) were gyrating bumping and grinding, Bill would not be considered a proper escort for any white lady, drunk or sober.

A lodge brother, dressed in police blue and hired to keep order among the carnival's colored customers, came to the rescue. The distress signal was passed and recognized. A white officer was apprised of the situation and Miss Harlow was requested to leave. Regretfully, she returned to Ned, reasonably sober, and was quickly forgiven. Ned could appreciate boredom.

Mabel's second infraction was more serious. One day the impulse to escape from the confinement of their home, where she spent most of her long hours, was irresistible. Ned was in New Orleans with Wells and McKay to attend a conference of railroad officials. Mabel was alone. She had a few drinks, then wandered down to the station. There she ran into one of Ned's acquaintances, R. G. Robinson, Superintendent of the M. K. T. Railway, who had stopped off at Dallas to ice his private car, replenish the commissary, and see if he could pick up interesting company for the two-day ride.

The Katy official, in an offhand way, asked Mabel if she wouldn't like to accompany him. On the impulse of the moment Ned's lady accepted. When the pair arrived in New Orleans, Mabel, still drunk, raised the blinds of the bedroom she had been sharing with Robinson. She squinted at the outside world trying to orient herself. There, to her horror, on an adjacent track directly opposite and not six feet away was her namesake, the *Mabel*. The wanderer sobered quickly and a frightened, remorseful, and hung-over housekeeper tried to sneak into New Orleans.

She had no money but knew she would find friends on Basin Street where she could borrow enough cash to return home. She might have got away with the escapade and reached Dallas before Ned but for an unfortunate circumstance. Robinson's porter was a member of Lige Cooper's own Masonic chapter and within hours he told Mr. Green's valet the entire story, repeated at once to the master.

Ned, normally good-natured and slow to anger, was furious. Before the day was over he used his influence to have Robinson fired, no mean display of power in itself since the Superintendent was third in command of one of the largest railroads in the world. Green, knowing where his housekeeper could be found, had the New Orleans police quietly pick her up, take her into custody, and hold her until the conference ended.

Green was not sure he still wanted her, but when Mabel, alluring despite forty-eight hours in jail, promised to behave, he told her she would have another chance. Miss Harlow, or Miss deVries, as she was known in New Orleans, was released in Ned's custody. While the pair went back to Dallas together, sharing the master bedroom on the *Mabel*, their relationship was never again quite the same.

Having been a paying client himself, Ned was thoroughly familiar with Mabel's background and he realized he should not expect too much from his amoral mistress. But his pride was wounded deeply and he listened to so many "I told you sos" from friends that for the first time since his impetuous action in setting up a permanent relationship with a prostitute he considered breaking up the affair and sending Mabel back to her former life.

He began to take stock of a future with his housekeeper. He was past thirty and not as naïve as he had been in Chicago. He knew Mabel could do nothing but damage to his career and that

122

he would have to abandon all pretenses of a decent social life as long as she was his acknowledged mistress. He would be coming into a vast fortune someday and, with a proper spouse, he might enjoy a world open only to a limited group of those with unlimited means, a land beyond the dreams of most men. But as Stanley Chipman phrased it in the New Bedford *Standard*, "Mr. Green was diverted by the entrancing business of living." Unfortunately, he did not quite know how to go about it. His mother's early training had cursed him with a confused approach to the disposition of wealth. Because he had never been taught how to spend money wisely, he lost the great satisfaction it might have given him. If he had left Mabel then it would not have been too late to undo this harm.

Ned made a few unsuccessful attempts to break Mabel's hold on him. After his housekeeper's recent defection he was in the proper mood to accept an invitation to the big Dallas social event of the year, the Winter Ball. There he was introduced to Miss Tully Carter, of Sulphur Springs, a town eighteen miles east of Terrell. Miss Carter was a recent graduate of North Texas Female College and was in town for the season. She was tall and attractive and got along well with Ned almost immediately. She came from an "old" Texas family, which meant that her parents had been in the state for perhaps thirty years. Her father was a successful planter and Miss Carter was not seeking a rich husband.

Green was interested. Miss Carter's escort was her brother, who happily relinquished his charge. Tully's dance card was filled but she managed to sit out several numbers with Ned. Tully put him at his ease. He talked about his mother and made his life in New England seem funny. He discussed his plans for the future, railroading and his experimental farm. Ned had an enjoyable evening. He saw Miss Carter several times during the next few weeks, and when she was ready to leave Dallas he took her and her brother home to Sulpur Springs on the *Mabel*.

Tully had mentioned that she liked sailing on the Gulf and that with classmates and her parents she had gone to the Tarpon Inn on Mustang Island. Ned disliked the sea. He was uncomfortable when he tried to walk on anything that was not level. However, he wanted to please Tully. The Tarpon Inn wasn't for sale and neither was Mustang Island. But for $100,000 he could buy a sizable piece of Gulf-front land on nearby St. Joseph's Island, below Aransas Pass. He bought it. For another $25,000 he obtained title to a large home there and converted this to a private club. He called it the "Tarpon" and invited his Dallas friends and their families to join.

Ned furnished transportation on his car, from which the name "Mabel" had been deleted, with only the numerals "999" remaining. Convinced that the President of the T. M. had at last relegated his housekeeper to her proper place, the ladies of Dallas accompanied their husbands on weekend trips to the Tarpon. Miss Carter and her family were frequent guests. Mabel stayed at home.

By the end of the summer of 1899 Tully and Ned were reported engaged. No official announcement was made but there was an "understanding" between them. The Carters liked Ned and he in turn was fond of them. The next problem was to let his mother in on the secret. By this time, however, it was not a secret from Hetty. In no uncertain terms she summoned him to New York. Apparently the umbilical cord had merely been stretched, not severed, and Mrs. Green's boy hurried home to Mamma. Whatever this forceful lady said was effective, and when Ned returned to Dallas his ardor for Tully had been cooled off; the affair ended abruptly. Chances for a recurrence or the development of a similar situation were slight. Ned had promised his mother he would never marry without her consent. Mabel's position, certainly known to the omniscient Hetty, became less ambiguous.

Ned's belief in his complete emancipation was shattered. He was astonished by his immediate surrender to this demonstration of his mother's power and became aware that no matter how loosely Hetty held the reins, any time she tightened her grip, her son geed, hawed, trotted, ran, or stopped.

124

A conservative estimate of Hetty Green's yearly income in 1900 was $7,000,000. At the same time the national average individual income was $490. Today, most of Hetty's intake would go to the United States Collector of Internal Revenue. But· when Ned was dipping fearlessly into the till, and without audible cries from Hetty, there were no comparable taxes. Even the minuscule 3 per cent she should have paid, Hetty managed to dodge.

These figures reveal only a partial glimpse into the potency of a hundred million dollars at the turn of the century. A fine saddle horse could be bought for forty dollars; the tab for a nine-course meal at Delmonico's didn't exceed seventy-five cents, and the best bottled-in-bond rye whisky, aged in the vat for eleven years, retailed at one dollar a quart. Nobody ever heard of "fifths"!

As a kind of consolation prize, Ned bought himself an automobile, the first one in the entire State of Texas.

Chapter Twenty

In the summer of 1901 Sylvia and her father got their first and last ride on Ned's private railroad car, by then rechristened the *Lone Star*. It was not a happy trip. The older Green was going home to Vermont to die and he wanted his daughter with him during his last days. For the preceding months he had been in constant pain and, though he was ambulatory, his physician advised him to stay in bed as much as he could.

Hetty agreed to reopen the Tucker House. She, herself, was too busy on Wall Street to go with him to Bellows Falls but was not unwilling to grant Sylvia permission to act as her ailing husband's attendant. As a matter of fact, Hetty was glad to get Sylvia away from New York.

Hetty, always fearful that Sylvia someday would marry and

leave her, had received two recent frights, both at the hands of her friend, Annie Leary, now a Papal Countess. The Countess, who apparently never gave up, invited Hetty and Sylvia to a small party at her country estate. Hetty either didn't want to go or couldn't accept and sent Sylvia. The guest of honor was the Spanish Duke de La Torre. Miss Green was his dinner partner. The following day several New York papers carried brief items hinting that Mrs. Green's daughter and the Duke were engaged. Hetty didn't even bother to issue a denial.

A few weeks later, at another of the Countess' affairs, Sylvia's escort was Eric Hope, the Earl of Yarmouth. This Britisher was a charming, handsome young gentleman who certainly was not unaware of Miss Green's prospects. Sylvia had one of the most pleasant evenings in her life. Again the press reported an engagement. But the New York *Daily Telegraph* went further. It called the Earl a fortune hunter and accused him of trying to make off with any American girl rich enough to support him in the luxury to which neither he nor his ancestors had been accustomed for the preceding five generations.

The Earl promptly sued the *Telegraph* for $25,000, a sum modest enough considering the extent of the libel. To the astonishment of everyone, Sylvia, despite her mother's violent protests and in a rare state of rebellion, appeared for the prosecution. She was an excellent witness and told the Court the Earl had not even hinted he was considering matrimony with her.

Edward Henry Green had only a few business interests remaining. In order to put his final affairs in order, this neat, unobtrusive gentleman, whose life with Hetty had been so different from the one he had hoped for, needed his wife's signature on several papers. William Crapo was his lawyer as well as Hetty's, and he asked this attorney to help him get Mrs. Green to affix her signature where it was required. No money was involved but Edward was afraid his wife would find some reason to refuse. He needed moral support.

Crapo was glad to oblige his client and came down from New

127

Bedford to see what he could do. It did not take long to persuade Hetty to scrawl her name once she realized she had nothing to lose. She then bade good-by to the pair who had come to see her.

"It was a cold, rainy night," Crapo recalled. "Hetty was living in some cheap boardinghouse in Brooklyn. We spent about an hour with her and that was enough. The room was bitter cold. I was chilled to the bone and so was Ed. He looked sick, too. It was ridiculous for me to expect it but I was hoping Mrs. Green would at least offer us a cup of tea but she didn't and hinted we ought to leave.

"I rode back with Green to his hotel room in a cab. When we got out of his wife's roominghouse I said, sort of consolingly, 'Well, Ed, women are strange creatures, aren't they?'

"He turned to me and with a sigh answered, 'Ah, yes, Bill. Some are!'"

Sylvia wrote to her brother telling him how ill their father was. Ned replied, saying that while he would not be able to join them (he did not say why), he was dispatching the *Lone Star* to New York. The car would be at their disposal. He sent along a young T. M. clerk with authority to make all travel arrangements on other carriers and included Lige to act as his father's body servant as far as Vermont.

A few days later the *Lone Star* delivered its passengers at Bellows Falls. Station attendants helped Lige carry hundreds of pounds of ice-packed delicacies into the Tucker House. Since there were limited facilities there, neighbors, glad to oblige an old friend, stored these gifts from Ned in their springhouses. Lige gave the Tucker House a thorough cleaning and airing and, before returning to Texas, saw that his master's father was made comfortable in the second floor front bedroom overlooking the Connecticut River.

Green's last days were recalled by Miss Blanche Webb, who, as a little girl, frequently called on her ailing neighbor with a playmate, Marian Hadley.

"We felt so sorry for Mr. Green," she said. "He was such a

128

very sweet old man and he seemed quite pleased with our visits. He was very fond of children and when my companions and I came to call while he was still in bed he was extremely old-worldly and would shake hands with us Chinese fashion.

"For weeks and weeks he lay on his bed where he could see the Vermont hills and the river he loved. He used to tell us stories about his childhood, about Jack Adams, the great riverman who fished him out of the Connecticut when he fell in one day. He talked about the little Chinese and Filipino boys and girls he used to know when he lived in the East. He never complained about himself and I never heard him say a word against Hetty even to his best friend, Henry Wells, who was with him every day.

"Once in a while he did mention Ned and would ask Sylvia if she'd heard from her brother. I suppose he was hoping Ned would come to pay him a visit."

Ned got to Bellows Falls once before his father died. He stayed at the Tucker House for a few days and promised he would go back as soon as he could. But Green died before his son found the time to return. The old man's modest obituary was carried in the Boston *Herald* under a Bellows Falls dateline, March 19, 1902.

"Edward H. Green, husband of Hetty Green, richest woman in the world, died at the old Green homestead this morning," reported this newspaper. "He had been confined to his bed since last September with kidney trouble. Mrs. Green and their daughter, Sylvia, were with him to the end, but Edward, their son, was in Texas unable to reach here before his father's death.

"Mr. Green had passed his 80th year. For years he lived in Manila but after his retirement, he lost his fortune in Wall Street. He spent most of his time in the Cumberland Hotel and the Union League Club, visiting the old homestead at Bellows Falls occasionally."

Edward H. Green was laid to rest in the family plot at Immanuel. The Rector, the Reverend David L. Sanford, conducted

129

services in the beautiful old church designed by Richard Upjohn. Ned arrived in Bellows Falls the morning of the funeral but Hetty had been there all week. She had come, she told her brokers, "to take care of poor Ed." However, by the time she reached the Tucker House her husband was too far gone to be helped in either direction by Mrs. Green's ministrations.

As soon as earth was sprinkled over Mr. Green's remains and Mr. Sanford intoned the last words of the burial service, the funeral party descended a steep hill that leads from the church to the station. Hetty led the procession, outpacing almost everyone except a pair of strangers who kept close by her heels, and a number of children curious to see what their famous neighbor looked like at close range.

Miss Webb had one further recollection of the bereaved widow.

"My father was one of the bearers and he went along from the church to the depot," Miss Webb said. It was a cold March day and steam was hissing from a big circular radiator, with a marble top on it, in the middle of the waiting room.

"Mrs. Green and the two men, who, my father told me later, were her brokers, were standing around getting warm. Nobody was saying anything; everybody was just staring and thinking. All my father could hear was the heavy breathing, the steam, and the ticking of a large clock on the wall.

"This last sound, my father recalled, must have distracted Hetty. Suddenly she looked up at the clock, slapped her dirty, ungloved hand on the marble radiator top, and said, 'Well, gentlemen, don't you think we've wasted enough time? Let's get down to business!'"

Chapter Twenty-one

Purity" was the issue of the 1903 Dallas mayoralty campaign. This was the only threat to Ned's rise in the Republican Party. The incumbent, James Taylor, was spokesman for the Dallas segment of the national Bible Belt. His rallying cry was from the Apocrypha—"He that toucheth pitch shall be defiled therewith." If he won Mayor Taylor promised to "run the harlot and the rich bachelor out of Dallas." There was no question in the mind of the electorate that Mabel was the "harlot" and Ned the "rich bachelor."

Ned's life in Texas had so far been serene. He liked Dallas and had decided he would remain there despite the community's unwillingness to accept Mabel. On the site of what later became part of City Hall, he had built a spacious, three-story brick home topped by an attractive penthouse, the first in Texas. To supply flowers and shrubbery Ned bought a large greenhouse about five miles east of the city, installed an experienced horticulturist and a business manager. Not only did the greenhouse provide him with a cool, shady hideaway, protected from the hot Texas sun by tall bushes and miniature trees, but Green made money by selling surplus plants to Dallas florists.

Mabel disliked all flowers (except orchids), plants, shrubs, vines, trees, and the insects that usually accompany them. She had a particularly strong distaste for the sun, a touch of which usually was enough to burn her fair, delicate skin. Mabel was beginning to hate Texas, and a long life in this state often may have caused her to wonder if the deal she had made was worth it.

Evening and weekend callers at the Green-Harlow penthouse usually encountered Mabel almost completely swathed in towels. The only portions of her lovely body exposed to the heat were the tip of her pert nose and her beautifully shaped feet. The latter were constantly immersed in cold flowing water from a simulated brook that ran through smooth pebbles and a tiny sand beach before it dropped, via a miniature waterfall, into a sewer pipe.

Mabel longed for the cooling breezes that swept upper Michigan, where formerly she had spent her summers, working the hotel trade there. But she knew this never would again be possible if she wished to continue her present career and realized she would have to endure life in East Texas, broken periodically by trips on the *Lone Star*, an occasional visit to the Tarpon Club, or a rare and total fling. Ned, however, soon closed his island retreat and Dallas free-loaders, who were starting to swarm over him wherever he went, had to seek gratuitous weekends elsewhere or pay for hotel accommodations themselves. If Ned ever learned of his housekeeper's indiscretions it is not likely he would have done anything more drastic than reducing her allowance, and that only temporarily. She still had enormous

132

physical attractions for him; he was comfortable in her presence, and he had learned to accept her for what she was.

Now, with Mayor Taylor's "purity campaign," Ned was upset, fearful, and angry. The practical Gooseneck was unconcerned.

"All we needed to beat Mr. Taylor, I told Mr. Green," Bill explained, "was money. He had plenty of that.

"I figured the election would be pretty close but if we scattered about ten or fifteen thousand dollars where they counted we'd build up a big edge. I said to Mr. Green not to worry and even if he didn't want to invest the ten or fifteen I still thought we'd win.

" 'Here's twenty-five thousand,' he told me without a whimper. 'If you need more you know where to come for it.' He was pretty mad."

A contemporary noted that in the 1903 election "purity suffered a decisive defeat at the polls," but McDonald made light of this victory.

"It was easy as falling off a log," commented Gooseneck. "I spread that dough all over the colored wards. The Sheriff didn't lose a single precinct there. We swept him into office by a whopping majority. Mr. Green was happy. Election night after Mr. Taylor conceded to Sheriff Cabele, our candidate, the boss took Miss Harlow for supper right in the main dining room of the hotel. He invited the Sheriff for a drink. Everybody in town understood. They all came over and patted Mr. Green and Mr. Cabele on the back."

The following year Ned was re-elected Chairman of the State Republican Executive Committee for his fourth two-year term. It is hard to tell how much of Green's rising political fortunes were due to his own intelligence, Gooseneck's sagacity, or the golden glow of a hundred million dollars. While no practical politician ever admitted that the party of Abraham Lincoln had a chance in Texas, Green himself was respected as an able and popular leader of a minority group, a position not enjoyed by his predecessors.

133

Ned's potential grew higher in 1904. Teddy Roosevelt had just been elected President by the largest plurality ever given to a candidate for that office. "Trust busting" was the phrase of the day. The expedient economic alliance between Northern Republican followers of President McKinley and their Southern Democratic counterparts rested on shifting bases.

Duly elected Southern spokesmen for the Republican Party, its National Committeemen, in the past either made deals with Democrats or were ignored. Their power was restricted to the distribution of state patronage plus a voice at Presidential Conventions. The picture changed when Teddy reached his zenith. His determination to enforce the Sherman Antitrust Act threw economic royalists Baer, Morgan, Harriman, Hill, and other moguls into dithers.

Support for T. R.'s policies came from many unlikely places but none more so than the one occupied by Mrs. Hetty Howland Robinson Green. After a lifetime of contempt for the welfare of her less fortunate fellows, it is a bit difficult to attribute Hetty's defense of Roosevelt's policies to altruism. Yet there is her voice, conveyed to an astonished America via a syndicated article first appearing in the Boston *Herald.*

"The poor have no chance in this country," lamented Mrs. Green, the richest woman in the world. "No wonder Anarchists and Socialists are so numerous. Some blame the rich, but all the rich are not to blame. . . . Who breaks the law? The great railroad magnates!" (And herein lies a clue to Hetty's belated obeisance to democracy.)

"There is Huntington. He and his railroad and the men about him have been grinding wealth out of the poor for years and years and defying the authorities. But the militia are never sent against him. When some poor starving fellows get desperate and cars don't run, how quickly they send the troops."

Ned's voice did not join Hetty's. When T. R.'s election thrust Green into a spot where he could have demanded Federal investigation of Texas corporations undoubtedly in violation of the Antitrust Act the Republican State Chairman was silent. He was no reformer. He merely wanted to be well liked, and that he was. Even the Texas press agreed that the minority party kept a good man in office when it continued to re-elect Mr. E. H. R. Green.

"We congratulate the Republican Party of Texas that during the past . . . years, under the able personal direction of the Honorable E. H. R. Green, the interests of the party have been wisely guarded," declared the San Antonio *Times*.

"Under his management it (the party) has developed and grown throughout the entire state, extending to the frontier counties on a successful and satisfactory basis. He has . . . corrected gross abuses."

The *Times* failed to identify the "abuses" and Gooseneck Bill conducted business as usual during and after Ned's regime. However, McDonald never questioned his protégé's power. On one occasion, when asked under oath to explain whether officers were elected by the Republican Party or were hand-picked by Mr. Green, Gooseneck's answer was short and to the point.

"Mr. Green *was* the Republican Party," he replied.

Then to make sure his interrogators were not under the impression that Mr. E. H. R. Green was a dictator, McDonald added, "There never has been anyone close to Ned Green's popularity in my day and time." It should be noted that Gooseneck's "day and time" stretched (politically) over a fifty-two-year period.

As to his own role in behind-the-scenes power plays, McDonald's answer was becomingly modest.

"I believe some Texas Republicans thought I was a factor," he said.

Far more interested in having a potent voice at National Conventions than in consolidating gains it made within Texas during Ned's chairmanship, the State Republican Convention split in 1906. One faction, an expansion of the old Lily Whites, was headed by Colonel Cecil Lyon, and the other, the "Reorganized Republicans," was led by E. H. R. Green.

When the State's Attorney General refused to recognize the

Reorganized Republicans at the Houston Convention in 1906, this group "took a walk."

"Mr. Green was in Dallas," recalled McDonald. "I kind of figured what was going to happen and I told him to stay away from Houston. Then if the fight got hot, he wouldn't be in any personal controversy and all factions could rally around him as a compromise.

"Actually the purpose of the convention was to nominate a state ticket but nobody was fooled. What we wanted was to have the say in the 1908 National Presidential Convention. I thought if we put Ned Green to head our ticket in 1906 he might make a good showing even though we knew he couldn't win.

"He had friends everywhere, all over Texas, who might jump party lines to vote for him. A good many newspapermen liked Mr. Green. They couldn't help it. And that Mr. Kiest swung a lot of weight and if he threw it behind Mr. Green. . . .

"A lot of us had in mind that maybe—just maybe, in 1908 he might have an outside chance to get the Vice Presidential nomination. This is what we planned. Mr. Green knew the score and he agreed to go along."

The Reorganized Republicans nominated Green for Governor. Normally the selection of a regular or rump Republican candidate in this strictly Democratic state was about as newsworthy as a strawberry festival at Shiloh Baptist Church even in Texas newspapers. Outside the state it was ignored. But when Green received the nomination this was important news everywhere.

The Chicago *Inter-Ocean* carried the Green nomination on page 1 and on September 6, 1906, the Philadelphia *North American* ran a two-column cut of the President of the Texas Midland, with headlines four columns wide and a page of copy in its magazine section.

"HETTY GREEN'S SON RUNNING FOR GOVERNOR OF TEXAS," said this Quaker City newspaper. Beneath the headline is a picture of the candidate himself. His face is pleasant; forehead high, jowls heavy, and hair thinning. He wears a piccadilly collar and

136

a dark bow tie. In the background is a photograph of his mother. Mrs. Green is purported to be saying, "I'm proud of Ed. He's a shrewd one."

"Ed Green is a big man," declared the *North American*. "He's big physically and since he settled in Texas . . . he has proven himself a big man mentally. This is a combination that Texans like, and they are not different from other folk in that respect.

"'There goes Ed Green,' a resident of Terrell may remark to a stranger, pointing out a commanding figure bustling along the street. 'He's off to the Gulf to try the tarpon fishing, or going out to the race track to speed his new high-powered motor . . . or to his railroad office.'

"President Green loves jolly company and is fond of a joke, even when it is aimed at himself. A big framed man is generally fitted by nature with extremities of enormous proportions, but the good dame was unusually liberal in equipping Ed. Not at all sensitive over such personal matters, Mr. Green joins heartily in any laugh aimed at his physical make-up."

(In the light of the *North American*'s further comment, Gooseneck's appraisal of Green as a potentially important national figure makes more sense.)

"When Green was sent to Philadelphia in 1900 as a delegate to the Republican National Convention, his personality attracted instant attention. He entered the national camp with a breezy dash that was unusual, even in a Texan.

"In hotel corridors a crowd was nearly always about the tall, broad-shouldered delegate from the Southwest, who smiled so pleasantly, shook hands so cordially, and conversed so interestingly. Indeed, many of the other delegates were calling him 'Ed' before they had known him two hours."

Then this Philadelphia journal posed a question that must have been uppermost in the minds of many readers.

"Can this genial man of democratic manner and mixing ability be really Hetty's son?" asked the *North American*. "For the

137

mother's reputation throughout the country has been rather for austerity and taciturn devotion to moneymaking. . . ."

As if to confirm its own opinion of Hetty and to emphasize the contrast between mother and son, this same newspaper, exactly two weeks later, ran the following Associated Press dispatch under a Bellows Falls dateline:

"Like an injudicious player in a poker game, the Bellows Falls Board of Listers raised Mrs. Hetty Green, credited with being the richest woman in the United States, $2,000 on her $10,000 tax assessment. Now they are sorry.

"Mrs. Green's daughter, Miss Sylvia, appeared in the village hardware store early this morning and bought locks and bolts to close up their . . . old fashioned cottage (the Tucker House) on the brow of the hill, with its view down the Connecticut Valley.

" 'When I fight, there is usually a funeral and it isn't mine, either,' Mrs. Green said today.

" 'The Board of Listers is mistaken if it thinks that by driving me out it can get possession of my homestead at a low figure for a library. I shall never give it to Bellows Falls. I do not approve of such things. . . .' "

The story concludes with a moving, albeit contradictory, display of sentiment.

" 'Everything I think the most of is here,' said Mrs. Green. 'It is my home and its associations are very dear to me.' "

Hetty soon bludgeoned her son's political aspirations. The game was over. Ned was thirty-eight years old; he had had his fling; it was time to come home.

"My dear son," she wrote on September 27, 1906. "In the compliment your great and adopted state has tendered to you, I know you will *not forget* your *Mother* who *needs* and *demands* your assistance. . . ."

The message was understood. Green declined the signal honor offered to him, and the Reorganized Republicans hastily substituted as their standard bearer Dr. Atchinson, Surgeon General

138

of the M. K. T. Railroad. While there is no assurance Candidate Green would have polled more votes than Candidate Atchinson, he scarcely could have polled fewer. Out of a total of 405,652 votes, Dr. Atchinson received 14,410. Excluding what others contributed to the party coffers, the cost per ballot, based only on Ned's gift of $75,000, was slightly over $5.00. Tammany would have shuddered at this profligacy.

Hetty's bombardment of her son's defenses continued.

"I am very tired since I came home," she wrote on December 10, 1906. "So much care for an old lady. I need you every day...."

Her pathetic reference to fatigue was understandable. She had just returned to Hoboken from trips to (A) Chicago, where she had vigorously prosecuted a clerk accused of forgery; attacked the local police for their failure to apprehend the alleged criminal; threatened her attorney, Charles T. Ogden, of San Antonio, Texas, in open court, and berated His Honor for a display of "weakness," and (B) Cincinnati, where she foreclosed two mortagages; sold a block of business properties at a large profit; bought 800 acres of suburban farmland for real-estate development; posed for a picture, and granted an interview to a newspaper reporter who, in a nationally syndicated article, compared Mrs. Green favorably to her contemporary fellow scavenger, the late Russell Sage.

Ned was not ready to yield to his mother's entreaties. After Sheriff Cabele became Mayor, Green took Mabel wherever he pleased although he was considerate of attitudes apparent in Ed Kiest and other friends and was careful to keep his housekeeper away from them.

Often Ned and Kiest had dinner together in the latter's home, then rode downtown to watch Kiest "put the *Times-Herald* to bed." Frequently Kiest and others were Green's guests at productions of the Dallas Playhouse, where Mary Cammack played bit parts. Ned was evincing more and more interest in this young lady who was developing into an attractive woman, and she, in turn, grew fonder of "Uncle Ned."

On August 27 of that year Ned went to Philadelphia on the *Lone Star*. Mabel stayed home. "Mr. Green is in the Quaker City to attend the national Florists Convention being held there," said the Terrell *Weekly Transcript*. "In an address before a large group President E. H. R. Green praised Texas. . . . He is staying at the Bellevue Stratford Hotel. . . . Mr. Green said he will leave for a visit to his Mother in New York and will return to Texas the following week."

Ned did not return to Texas the following week. He remained in New York with his mother for more than a month, and when he went back to Dallas his first move was to appoint Larry Wells "Assistant to the President," on October 15, 1907. To the initiated it appeared that Hetty's persuasive powers were starting to pay off and Ned was preparing his withdrawal from the Texas Midland.

Ned's circle of close friends sensed a growing unhappiness in him. They were saddened by his frequent references to a final departure from Dallas and his increasingly long absences. Even if Kiest, Allen, Corley, and the others disapproved of Ned's political associates and their wives disliked his mistress, they found him kindly, generous, warm, and intensely loyal.

Ned gave a practical demonstration of this last quality before the year ended.

The failure of New York's Knickerbocker Trust Company sparked the panic of 1907. Within days of its closing, depositors all over the country began to pull out cash and savings from home-town institutions. Banks everywhere either failed, suspended operations temporarily, or restricted withdrawals. The Harris Trust Company of Terrell was badly hurt by a wave of fear that swept the United States.

"Like everybody else, people in Terrell were uneasy," recalled Tom Corley. "We were solvent but not liquid and a run would have smashed us. You just couldn't get your hands on currency.

"I'd go to work every morning scared half to death. When I'd see a line of more than two people I'd be sure it was the beginning of the end. The strain was awful. I hadn't slept for a week. Business men who *knew* we had assets to cover every cent we owed would come to the windows, eye us kind of funny, and maybe put in less than usual or take out more than they required. All it needed was for just one guy to pull out all his capital, and the run would be on.

"Well, one day, I guess it was a week or so after the Knickerbocker hit the skids that I ran into Ned Green. I must have looked bad. Of course he knew what was happening and he asked me how the Harris was weathering the storm.

"'I might as well admit it, Ned,' I told him. 'I'm scared. We haven't enough cash on hand today to last an hour if they start a run.'

"'How much do you need to tide you over?' he asked.

"'About twenty-five thousand dollars would do it,' I answered.

"'O.K.' he said. 'Stop worrying.'"

By the time Corley returned to his bank the lobby was filled and people were crowding through the front doors making it difficult for the cashier to edge his way inside.

"We had three tellers," Corley recollected, "and each one knew what to do. He was working as slowly as he could. You know, counting every bill twice; questioning endorsements, and so forth. Not one cent was being deposited; everything was going the other way. It was not that anybody had much money in the bank, maybe two, three hundred dollars. But if you multiply that by all the depositors you can see what was bound to happen. Friends I'd known for years wouldn't look me in the eye. You could almost smell the fear.

"I'd been back for about ten minutes when Ned Green shoved his bulk through the doors. He had a big cardboard box in one hand and took his place in the line in front of John McWilliams, the first teller.

"Everybody recognized him and for a moment they all figured he was trying to get his money out just like them and if he got there before they did, there wouldn't be any left.

141

"But Ned didn't let them think that for long. In a real loud voice he yelled, 'John, I got a lot of cash I'd like to get rid of. It's pretty heavy.'

"How that line faded to make way for Mr. E. H. R. Green! He stood in front of McWilliams, gave him a big wink, and sang out, 'Lift 'em up, John.'"

McWilliams raised the bars as high as he could and Green dumped the contents of the box onto the counter.

"You should have seen the bills pour out, beautiful green bills and a lot of gold ones, too," Corley said.

"'Here's thirty thousand dollars,' Ned spoke out still loud so that everybody in the place could hear him. 'And more where that came from. My mother and I figure this is about the safest bank in the country.'

"That was the end of the run. Customers started grinning at each other, kind of embarrassed, and in a couple of hours all the money they'd withdrawn the preceding week was back and then some.

"I tell you that if Ned Green had been a candidate for President of the United States and Booker T. Washington his running mate on the Black and Tan ticket, they'd have had my vote!"

Chapter Twenty-two

Hᴇᴛᴛʏ drew her will in 1908. She was then worth about $150,000,000, give or take ten million. The language of the document was comparatively simple, but in the words of her attorney, William Crapo (apparently in Mrs. Green's good graces again), "It was tight." With the exception of one clause there was nothing unusual about Mrs. Green's testament.

First, Hetty disposed of her father's estate. "To my beloved son, Edward Howland Robinson Green, of Terrell, State of Texas, and to his heirs and assigns forever . . . I give, devise, and bequeath all the . . . residue and remainder of the Estate of my deceased father, Edward Mott Robinson," declared Hetty.

This was an outright gift and was worth approximately $7,500,-000.

"All the rest," continued Mrs. Green, "I give, devise, and bequeath to my son . . . and to my daughter, Hetty Sylvia Ann Howland Green, . . . as Trustees, to be had and beholden by them and the survivor of them, for a period of ten years from the date of my death, in trust. . . ."

Most of the assets Hetty listed were the "blue chip" securities of her day, as well as first mortgages, railroad bonds, outright ownership of business properties and other real estate in New York, Buffalo, Boston, New Bedford, Chicago, St. Louis, Cincinnati, and elsewhere. She also held nearly $6,000,000 in New York City's "gold exempt" Assessment Bonds. In addition she kept between $20,000,000 and $30,000,000 in cash, used for short-term loans on which she was frequently able to collect usurious interest.

If one of her two children predeceased the other, moneys which would have accrued for the benefit of the deceased would then become a part of the trust, eventually to be inherited by the survivor. Ned was appointed his sister's trustee to serve without compensation.

Income was to be divided equally between the pair until the expiration of the trust period. In addition Sylvia was to receive an amount to equal the bonus Ned inherited from his maternal grandfather's estate.

The seventh codicil contained restrictions not normally found in last wills and testaments. This one stretched Hetty's hand beyond the grasp of most mothers.

"All (his bequests) . . . shall be for the sole and separate use and benefits of my said son, to the exclusion of any interest therein or control thereof by any wife whom he has or may wed," stated this clause.

On June 12, 1908, Hetty telegraphed her son that he was needed urgently in New York. He replied saying that his presence in Texas was imperative because of contemplated expansion of the railroad. As if to justify his continuing stay, Green increased his activities there.

"This morning," said the Terrell *Weekly Transcript*, "a number of local men left for Tyler to inspect the territory of a proposed railroad extension. The party included W. P. Allen, T. E. Corley and at Willis Point will be joined by Mr. E. H. R. Green and a party from Dallas who will come to the Point on the Cannonball."

The following week the *Transcript* reported that "Mr. E. H. R. Green was considering expansion of his Dallas flower farms. . . ." A month or two later Ned informed Ed Keist he intended to buy a tract of land in suburban Dallas and develop it into a residential community with a brand-new home for himself there.

"I wasn't fooled a bit," recalled Keist. "I knew what pressures were on Ned and that he'd eventually have to succumb.

"I'll say this, though, that year was the first one since he came to Texas that he didn't visit his mother a single time. He went to St. Louis. He went to Chicago, and once he went to the West Coast but never to New York."

This year Ned determined he would not go East. He probably was afraid he would not be able to resist Hetty's pleas made face to face. Mabel was to go to Highland Park to visit her aunt, Mrs. Campbell. Ned planned to take her as far as St. Louis in the *Lone Star*, then return to Texas and spend several weeks with the Kiests, who had a cottage on the Gulf.

The evening prior to Mabel's departure Ned returned home to find Mary Cammack there, in tears. She had just received word that her mother had died suddenly in San Francisco, where Mrs. Cammack and her husband had moved the preceding year. Mabel offered to give up her trip to Highland Park and go home with Mary, but the latter refused.

"The least we can do then, Ned," Mabel suggested, "is for you to take Mary as far as Fort Worth on the *Lone Star*. I'll go to my aunt's by myself and you can meet me in St. Louis whenever you're ready."

Ned agreed. Since Mabel's north-bound train did not leave until a few minutes after the *Lone Star* pulled away, she was able to wave good-by to her Ned and Miss Cammack. Mary did not get off the *Lone Star* at Fort Worth nor did Ned visit the Kiests. He took Mary to the Coast, stayed in San Francisco until after the funeral, and went back to Dallas two weeks later. The only other passenger on the private car of the President of the Texas Midland was the discreet and loyal Lige.

It is probable that Mabel could have predicted the turn of events. She certainly was aware that for the past few years Ned had not been the eager bed companion he once was. She also must have noticed his increasing interest in Mary. Mabel was almost forty, Mary just twenty-four.

While Mabel was still attractive and would have aroused most men, her glamour was fading. Mary was only then developing into an extremely desirable young woman, tall, long-legged, and slender, with narrow hips, high, firm breasts, soft brown hair, and deep-set hazel eyes. Mabel was hardly the type to believe in or practice monogamy, and if Ned wanted a fling she would not stand in his way as long as he came back to her. She would even be willing to act as his procurer in order to keep him contented and away from a woman he might be willing to marry. Mabel realized that her best cards were Ned's loyalty and gratitude. She felt these would be sufficient, if she did not press too hard, to give her the winning hand.

"When we came back from California," Mary said, "I moved in with Ned and Mabel. It was an odd arrangement and I wasn't altogether comfortable. Three months later I told Ned I wanted to leave. He got me a job in a road show and I didn't see either of them again for two years."

Chapter Twenty-three

I⊤ had been Hetty's habit to discourage every potential suitor for her daughter's hand. She was convinced that no man possibly could wish to marry Sylvia for the girl's sake alone and that the only reason a man would wed this plain, dowdy, repressed woman was the money she would inherit.

Most gentlemen brave enough to endure Mrs. Green's biting sarcasm and sharp temper paid only one visit to the Greens' wretched Hoboken flat. Any romance that might have developed despite Sylvia's lack of social graces and physical appeal soon withered beneath Mrs. Green's cold, hard stares. Nobody knew how long the tenacious Hetty would last, and to discourage male callers still further, she used to relate stories of an ancestor who lived to be one hundred and ten. "No Howland ever died before he was ninety," she would add gleefully. Hetty then was a mere seventy-two.

Only one man was undismayed. His name was Matthew Astor Wilks. He had met Sylvia two years before at one of Countess Leary's dinner parties. Miss Green was thirty-eight, and Mr. Wilks, a kindly, aging, sexless bachelor, was at least twenty-five years her senior. He was a grandson of the John Jacob Astor who built his fortune by defrauding Indian fur trappers, bribing high officials, and stealing funds from the Federal Government. Wilks lived on dividends and spent much of his life here and abroad evading predatory mothers with eligible daughters.

Most likely Hetty could have smashed this budding romance easily, but instead she gave it her encouragement. She had no fear that Wilks was a fortune hunter. He was worth several million dollars and his reputation was unimpeachable. He owned a huge tract of land near Galt, Ontario, where a Canadian branch of the Astors had settled a generation before.

While Sylvia never had been a stimulating companion, she was a good, economical cook and a neat, uncomplaining housemaid. It would be a distinct sacrifice for Mrs. Green to let her go. Yet, weighed against these losses was the fact that Mamma would be alone and her demands upon Ned would have more substance. A long, private talk with her son, begun the moment the bride bade a tearful good-by to her weeping mother, might be the proper way to break down Ned's resistance to renewing life with her.

The wedding was set for February 23, 1909. Hetty telegraphed the news to Ned, asking him to give the bride away. Ned sent his sister congratulations, a magnificent sterling silver dinner service, a carload of flowers from his Dallas nursery, an offer to lend the newlyweds his private car for their honeymoon, and his deepest regrets.

Ceremonies were held in St. Peter's Protestant Episcopal Church in Morristown, New Jersey. The event was well covered by the press. Stories of the marriage were carried by nearly every newspaper in the United States and in most major capitals of the

148

world. Typical was the eight-column spread, complete with pictures, appearing on the society pages of the New York *Herald,* February 24, 1909.

"Miss Sylvia Green, daughter of Mrs. Hetty Green, 'America's wealthiest woman,' was married yesterday noon to Mr. Matthew Astor Wilks in a little church in Morristown, N. J., after a journey from her mother's Hoboken flat," reported this journal.

"Every effort had been made by Mrs. Green to forestall the curious and in consequence even stolid Hoboken thirsted for information about the wedding. The neighborhood of her apartment house, at No. 1309 Bloomfield Street, had been picketed all night, and by sunrise there was a brigade of searchers after news . . . in the side streets. . . .

"Soon before nine o'clock, a self-possessed young woman in a blue gown hurried down the stoop and gave a signal. A one horse cab, of unpretentious pattern, was driven to the door and a moment later Mrs. Green, Miss Green and the young woman in blue entered it so quickly that those accustomed to the financier's slow walk were astounded by her activity. The venerable horse responded to the crack of the whip and all the old Dutch city suddenly seemed to move."

Hoboken, never attuned to society, had its big moment.

"Automobiles, hacks, hansoms and delivery wagons joined in pursuit of the cab. . . .

"The party arrived at the Lackawanna Station for the train . . . to which a special parlor car, 'Ivorydale,' had been attached [Ned's substitute for the rejected *Lone Star*], and in it were friends of the family from New York. The three women went quickly from the cab to the train shed, and as they entered the car were warmly greeted by the waiting company."

The *Herald's* rival, Mr. Greeley's New York *Tribune,* displayed a two-column cut of the bride, her mother, and the groom, who stands between Hetty, on his right, and the bride, on his left. You've a feeling all this has been a bit too much for Mr. Wilks. This elegant little gentleman tilts forward, supporting his right

149

hand on the back of Hetty's chair while his left rests heavily on Sylvia's. His head lists to one side so that his long, drooping white moustache almost caresses a glistening collar, the only bright spot in Mr. Wilks' somber attire.

His dark eyebrows are heavy but his head is balding and the hair is brushed to cover as much of his pale and high forehead as possible. There is a sad, bewildered look about him, as though everything moved just a little more quickly than he expected. You can almost hear a prayer issuing from his thin lips, asking the Almighty to banish the whole nightmare and return him to the hushed peace of the Club, there to spend the rest of his days reading the London *Times* or playing whist with other dignified gentlemen, over a bottle of vintage sherry.

Hetty looks perfectly at ease. She is clothed in a long and hideous black coat, trimmed with lace scallops. From beneath a two-level pyramidal hat, topped by more lace, a curl (product of Miss LeClaire?) swoops over her brow. Her jowls sag but her mouth is as defiant as ever and she stares ahead threateningly.

The only member of the trio who appears happy is Sylvia. She is wearing a Queen Mary hat and over her silk dress there is a feather boa that drapes both shoulders. This sweetly smiling woman looks almost pretty, perhaps for the first time in her life. If not radiant, the bride, whose age can no longer be called tender, seems to emit a cheerful, anticipatory glow. Escape is close at hand!

"The ceremony was carried through without incident," reported the *Tribune* as if to infer it fully expected one. "The bride appeared somewhat nervous but her mother, who occupied a front pew, maintained her characteristic impassivity. Miss Green stopped for a moment in the vestibule and then went up the aisle on the arm of Mr. Howard Pell who gave the bride away.

"The bridegroom, accompanied by his best man, Mr. Woodbury G. Langdon, Jr., who is also his nephew, was waiting at the chancel. He is slight in form and his hair is white. . . . Miss Green is many years the junior of the bridegroom, thirty perhaps, and yesterday she appeared still more youthful.

"As the party moved up the aisle the strains of the Lohengrin wedding march were heard. The ceremony was performed by the Rev. Philemon F. Sturgis, rector of the church."

Following the services, the wedding party moved on to the Inn.

"There," continued the *Tribune*, "was a cheery scene and the déjeuner, which had been prepared by the French chef, was served. The wedding breakfast was bright and gay."

We return to the *Herald* for the last scene.

"Mrs. Green was all geniality and sunshine, the reverse of the wet sky overhead," reported this paper. "As she emerged, a detachment of photographers began to take the range.

" 'If they want a picture,' said Mrs. Green, 'let it be a good one.'

"She walked not far from her daughter and smiled."

There was reason for Mrs. Green to smile. Reposing in a large black handbag that never was far from her, was a single sheet of paper, signed the previous evening by Mr. Wilks, in the presence of his bride-to-be and a notary.

"Being about to marry," declared the Party of the First Part, "I hereby desire to waive and relinquish all interest in such properties to which I might otherwise be entitled . . . by reason of my marriage to Miss H. Sylvia Ann Howland R. Green. . . ."

This was the antenuptial agreement without which Mrs. Hetty Sylvia Ann Howland Robinson Green never would have permitted the marriage to take place.

Chapter Twenty-four

Hᴇᴛᴛʏ renewed her siege. Her first few sorties had been beaten back, but soon she brought up the heavy cannonade.

"I am so tired," she wrote to Ned, June 2, 1909.

"I want you to come back soon," she wrote, July 15.

"They are stealing the ground from under me. I kiss you on both cheeks. Keep well, my darling son," she wrote, August 15.

After that one Ned weakened a bit. He attached the *Lone Star* to a north-bound train and spent the last two weeks of August and the first two of September with Hetty and Sylvia. He did not stay in Hoboken with his mother, nor was he a guest of Mrs. Wilks, then living in her husband's town house at 440 Madison Avenue. Instead, he rented a three-room suite at the Waldorf-Astoria. He installed Mabel in one room; he occupied the center one himself; while in the third connecting bedroom was an eager eighteen-year-old Texas blonde, the first of Mr. Green's young protégées. This one was a gesture from Mabel, happy to do almost anything to keep the master contented.

Somehow Ned made his escape from his mother. The southbound *Lone Star* dropped him at Asheville, North Carolina, where he hoped to recover from a month's activities more vigorous than his forty-one-year-old body was accustomed to. The ladies continued their journey home alone, at least as far as the record shows.

With slight variations Hetty's endearing mail continued.

October 10: "I need someone now that Sylvia has gone."

December 10: "I wish I could see you now. Sylvia sick in bed with her troubles. Oh, how I wish you was [*sic*] here."

December 16: "I need you every day. I implore you to be careful of your health. I have a bad cold."

Hetty pulled out all stops in her letter of January 10, 1910.

"My Dear Ned," she wrote. "I have not been out of the house for over a month. Sylvia is ill. We have dreadful weather and the doctor tells me it would be dangerous for me to go on a little journey. . . . This year I am feeling the effects of my age. Kiss on both of your cheeks from your loving Mother who wishes you was here every minute. In haste.

"Hetty H. R. Green

"*Hoboken*"

Ned's resistance was broken but he made one last weak attempt to entrench himself further in Dallas.

"Mr. E. H. R. Green has joined Max Hahn in the Max Hahn Packing Company business," said the Terrell *Transcript*, January 19, 1910. "Plans are being made to extend the already large operation, with Mr. Green taking an active interest."

But Mr. Green realized it was all over and his mother had won. He began to wind up his personal affairs in Terrell and Dallas and early that spring asked Ed Kiest and Walter Allen to be on the lookout for a good male secretary. Qualifications included efficiency, willingness to travel, and, above all, discretion. Allen heard of a young Texan, Walter P. Marshall, who had just returned from Mexico where he had been assistant to the General Manager of the National Rail Lines, and arranged a meeting between Green and Marshall at the American National Bank in Terrell.

Marshall was then about thirty years old. He had an excellent reputation in Dallas, where he was born. He was quiet and Ned was impressed by the fact that he politely refused to answer questions concerning the lives of his former employers, volunteered no information about anyone else, and replied in as few words as possible to direct questions about himself.

"We got along well right from the start," Marshall said. "I knew exactly the kind of relationship Mr. Green wanted to establish between himself and a secretary: a setup that would allow friendship but never intimacy.

"I never addressed him any way except formally and he never called me anything but 'Marshall' without the 'Mister,' and not once was it 'Walter' or 'Walt.' If that's the way he wanted it, that's the way he was going to get it."

Marshall was hired on a trial basis. His first assignment was to rent a suitable New York apartment for Green. Mabel's future was as yet undecided but Ned had no intention of living with Hetty again. He determined that no matter what she said or did, his personal life would be exclusively his own.

At first Hetty found it difficult to comprehend that Ned, who had capitulated to the extent of coming "home," would not share her Hoboken cold-water flat. But Ned soon made clear the extreme limit to which she could push him.

Green's new secretary returned to Dallas after a three-week stay in Manhattan and resigned.

"I'm sorry, Mr. Green," he said. "I'm afraid this job won't work out."

Marshall refused to elaborate. But Allen discovered the reason.

154

Apparently, during the time the manager of the Waldorf-Astoria Hotel was showing Marshall a suite of rooms, Hetty, who somehow had found out her son's newly engaged secretary was in New York and what his purpose there was, stormed in.

"She raised holy hell," Marshall revealed to Allen. "Told me I had no authority to negotiate anything more than the purchase of a two-cent postage stamp. She wanted to know what the rent of the suite we were looking at would be. When the manager informed her she called him a 'high-classed thief.' I thought she was going to clobber him with her umbrella. Then she turned on me and accused me of accepting a bribe to influence 'my boy to pay out that crazy kind of money when he could live with me for nothing.'

"It was horrible. I figured there wasn't enough money in the world to pay me for this abuse. So I quit."

When Ned found out, he was angry and called on the Marshalls at their Dallas home.

"He didn't speak a word against his mother," Marshall remembered, "but he did point out that I ought to be more sympathetic to the 'peculiarities' (he called them) of a sick, elderly lady. He said he'd see to it that similar incidents wouldn't recur.

"Then he gave me a big smile, told my wife she'd love New York, took a beautiful gold necklace out of his pocket and handed it to my six-year-old daughter, and offered me a hundred dollars more a month than he'd agreed to pay me. I reconsidered and went back to work."

It was hard for Ned to part from his friends and give up the life he loved in Texas. However, he sold his house and planned to leave Dallas late in June. But the month passed and he was still there. On July 1, he, Kiest, Allen, Wells, McKay, Corley, and one or two other members of Green's intimate circle boarded the *Lone Star* for Reno to watch the Johnson-Jeffries championship fight there three days later. When they returned to Texas the group gave Ned a farewell dinner at the Harris.

"I will always consider Terrell my home," Ned said in parting,

155

although at the moment his only personal possessions in that community, in addition to what he was wearing, were an old pair of trousers he had left in his furnished but unused room at Jarvis'.

On July 23, Ned checked into his suite at the Waldorf. The New York *Times* took cognizance of his arrival and this paper's headlines, and the lengthy story which followed, signified the importance of that event.

"HETTY'S SON COMES TO HELP HER," said the *Times*. "RETURNS FROM TEXAS TO ASSIST IN DIRECTING HER MANY INTERESTS. WILL MAKE HIS HOME HERE. OUT OF POLITICS HE SAYS.

"Edward Howland Robinson Green, of Dallas, Texas, came to town yesterday and took up permanent residence at the Waldorf-Astoria to look after and direct the vast interests of his mother, Mrs. Hetty Green, who is now in her 75th year.

"Mrs. Green appeared to be in excellent health when she greeted her big son. Although he was not expected until 9:30 she was there an hour ahead of time. Mr. Green said he was delighted to find his mother so well and predicted she would live for years.

"A suite has been specifically fitted up for Mr. Green, a combination of office and living apartments but as the decorators had not completed their work, he took temporary quarters for a few days. He was revelling in the breeze of an electric fan in his shirt sleeves when he talked about his plans.

" 'I just dropped everything in Texas,' he said, 'when Mother wrote for me to come and relieve her of some of her financial cares. . . . I intend to live at the Waldorf. . . .

" 'Mother . . . will go to Bellows Falls, Vermont, for a well-earned rest. I am very proud of my mother. She is one woman in ten thousand, although she will insist on working despite her years I am big enough to do her share and mine, too.' "

Early in August, Mabel, her fate decided upon, appeared at the desk of the Waldorf, completely unheralded. She registered as "Miss Mabel Harlow" of Dallas, Texas, and stated that she was Mr. E. H. R. Green's confidential secretary. Shortly after Labor Day, Miss Cammack, her somewhat less than starring career on

Chicago's stage over, joined the ménage. She listed herself only as Mr. Green's "guest."

Unhampered by the Texas Code of Morals, a new phase in the life of Mr. E. H. R. Green was about to begin. New York's Commissioner of Police, unlike his Terrell and Dallas counterparts, cared little what Mr. Green did in the privacy of his own castle. As for the Waldorf-Astoria, that elegant hostelry cared even less, providing its new tenant paid his rent promptly.

Chapter Twenty-five

After Sylvia's marriage and Ned's refusal to live in Hoboken, Hetty vacated the four-room cold-water flat she and Sylvia had shared and rented two furnished rooms on the fifth floor next door. She could have done with a single room but modesty forbade this. Mrs. Green handled much of her business in the evening when brokers, prospective borrowers, and others called and she needed a place, other than a bedroom, to receive these gentlemen.

Hetty's days were spent on Wall Street and behind a desk that the Seaboard National Bank gave her at 18 Broadway. Frequently, officials of that institution must have wondered if the business they got from Mrs. Green was worth the trouble she caused them.

First of all, Hetty was visible from the main lobby and this brought in more curiosity seekers than depositors. Then, too, she rarely bathed. Since she wore the same inner and outer garments for long periods without a change or wash, the combined bouquet that was wafted to nearby desks must have been less than fragrant.

Hetty also insisted on bringing her own lunch and eating it in the presence of employees and customers. If she had been content with sandwiches her dietary habits would not have caused much of a disturbance. But she was a firm believer in the efficacy of hot oatmeal. A huge bowl of this cereal, which cost a fraction of a cent per serving since Hetty ate it dry, would, in Mrs. Green's own words, "give me the strength I need to fight those Wall Street wolves."

The Seaboard, like most institutions of its day, was heated by a system of ventilators, which provided no place for Mrs. Green to warm the large tin of oatmeal she brought from Hoboken every day. For a while she tried to eat the stuff cold but this was too much even for her insensitive gullet. She solved her problem by using the facilities of a nearby broker, Stephen T. Kelsey, whose son, Stephen T. Kelsey, Jr., recalls Hetty's prompt arrival in the office each morning.

"I was very young when I first worked for my father," Mr. Kelsey said. "Each morning I used to see an old, dowdy-looking woman, dressed in a long black, trailing skirt, come in and deposit a covered pail on our radiator. She'd pat my head, then speak to my father for a few minutes and leave. She'd return at noon, say hello to the clerk, take the package off the radiator, and go out again.

"I used to think she was some unfortunate creature in to ask my father for a handout. Well, one day I asked our clerk who the lady was and what she was warming on our radiators.

"He laughed. 'That's Hetty Green,' he told me, 'and what she's heating on our radiators is oatmeal. I don't know how she eats the stuff when summer comes.'"

But the worst annoyance the Seaboard had to endure was, strangely enough, Hetty's large amounts of surplus cash.

"We were only a medium-sized bank in those days," an official said, "and you'd have thought we'd have welcomed the big deposits Mrs. Green made with us. But it wasn't worth a thing. All it did was take up space. We couldn't invest it; we couldn't lend it even on short-term notes. No! It made us uneasy and Hetty knew it.

"There were times when she'd have as much as thirty million dollars lying around for a month. If we could have loaned it out, or put it into Government bonds at two per cent for only thirty days, we'd have made fifty thousand dollars. But we didn't dare. The money *had* to be on hand at all times. There wasn't a morning or afternoon when Hetty wouldn't walk over to the first teller's cage and say, 'Joe,' or 'John,' or 'Bill, I might need all my money today.'

"Then she'd purse her thin lips and add maliciously, 'Just you be sure to have it for me when I call!' "

Ned, used to freedom, found life with his mother highly distasteful. As long as he was two thousand miles away, Mrs. Green rarely interfered with his business ventures. But in New York, she again regarded him as Mamma's little handicapped boy and continued to make all financial decisions herself. Ned's confidence, slowly built up over nearly two decades, began to fade.

Green spent part of each day on Wall Street, but instead of being able to buy or sell he now could only say, "Wait until I've discussed this with Mother," or "I'll let you know later," probably hoping Hetty would not have the strength to do everything herself. But Mrs. Green was as sharp at the end of her fourteen-hour day as she was at the beginning. There was no further mention of a long, well-deserved rest or retirement at Bellows Falls.

Occasionally Ned spent an evening with his sister, who, if not radiantly happy, was at least content. Her marriage was satisfactory and she lavished what affection she had on her gentle, aging husband. Like Elsie Dinsmore, Sylvia addressed her mate quite

160

formally in public, always prefixing "Mr." to his surname. He, in turn, called Sylvia "Mrs. Wilks" when anyone else was present.

The Wilkses entertained very little and guests were, for the most part, visiting members of the Canadian branch of the Astor family. Countess Leary went there to dinner infrequently, but Hetty scarcely ever appeared at 440 Madison Avenue. It was as though now that Sylvia was no longer Mrs. Green's exclusive possession whatever intrinsic value the "girl" possessed vanished and all accrued dividends belonged to someone else.

"I don't think Hetty ever liked Matthew Wilks," Mary Bolles said, "and the feeling might have been mutual. Mrs. Green once referred to him as 'a gouty old man.' I do believe Mr. Wilks learned about this remark.

"I think Sylvia was content," Mrs. Bolles said. "She had a home of her own and could do what she liked in it without consulting Mamma. I was happy for Sylvia's sake. I wish Ned had been more considerate. I knew Sylvia loved him deeply and I think she was hurt that he rarely came to see her."

In November, after Ned had been in New York little more than three months, he sent Mabel and Mary on a cruise to the Orient, packed his bags, and fled to Texas for a fling.

"Mr. E. H. R. Green has returned from a . . . stay in New York where he has been in direct charge of the management of his mother's property," said the Dallas *News* on November 1, 1910. "Through most of this time his mother, Mrs. Hetty Green, has been ill and the burden of looking after the estate has fallen directly upon the shoulders of her son.

" 'It has not been that I was overworked but that the responsibilities are enormous,' Mr. Green said yesterday. [You wonder if he said this with a straight face.] 'Had I the same problem in Texas it would have been much easier for me because I have so many good friends here. In New York I have to go it alone.' "

The T. M. had not turned over the *Lone Star* to anyone else and President E. H. R. Green was able to use it for living quarters. Lige and his twin brother, Isaiah, returned to the fold and the blonde who had left the Waldorf to make way for Mary Cammack was installed. She brought with her a statuesque Texas brunette. Ned once described this latter girl to Joe Epstein, the New Bedford newspaperman.

"He said she was exactly his own height, six feet four inches," Joe recalled, "and that a couple of years afterward he got her a job with Ringling's circus. He claimed she married a Singer midget but I don't believe it."

Ned exercised his franchise on November 8, and this was duly reported in the Terrell *Transcript*.

"Smiling and jovial as ever," said this paper, "E. H. R. Green, President of the Midland, arrived in Terrell this morning. He was met at the Union Station by Auditor T. E. Corley. . . . Mr. Green came over from Dallas to cast his vote in the general election, still maintaining his legal residence in Terrell."

When Ned and Corley returned to the station an hour or two later, the flag of Texas flew over the *Lone Star*. Green's smile was even wider and his mood more jovial when he dragged himself up the vestibule steps and limped inside. The table was set; the girls were gone, and in their places were Kiest, Allen, McKay, Wells, and a half-dozen other close friends of Green, and Texas' Governor O. B. Colquitt. When the afternoon of eating, drinking, and singing was drawing to a close, the Chief Executive rose to his feet and proposed a toast. This was to be the biggest moment in Ned's life, one he treasured as long as he lived.

"To 'Colonel' E. H. R. Green," said the Governor, "the newest and finest member of my staff."

Two days later the appointment was made official.

"My dear Sir," wrote the Governor. "Confirming my personal interview with you on your return from Terrell Tuesday afternoon, I am writing to tender you the appointment as a member of the Governor's Military Staff . . . with the rank of Lieutenant Colonel.

"Kindly let me have your written acceptance and oblige. . . ."

Ned replied in haste.

"Dear Governor," he wrote on November 12, ". . . I take great pleasure in accepting the honor. . . . I appreciate it most highly, not only on account of the dignity of the office itself, but also by reason of the personal confidence and esteem which the tender implies and which, I may add, is fully reciprocated by me.

"Assuring you that I shall, at all times, endeavor to meet the requirements and duties of the position, to the full measure of my ability, I remain,

"Most cordially yours, E. H. R. Green."

It should be pointed out that chores performed by a member of a Texas Governor's military staff are about as arduous as those endured by Southern gentlemen holding similar better-known but equally humorous Kentucky Colonelcies. As a matter of fact, the duties, obligations, and responsibilities are nonexistent.

Colonel E. H. R. Green took his appointment seriously. For the rest of his life he rarely signed his name without prefixing the honorary title. The magnificent, sword-bedecked uniforms he had Brooks Brothers tailor for him immediately upon his return to New York were the most elegant ever seen in the history of Texas inaugurations, the first of which Colonel Green attended that January.

Before the curtain is drawn over this phase of Ned Green's life, it might be stated that at this inauguration neither Gooseneck Bill nor other members of the Black and Tans, whom Ned Green had led so gallantly, were present except as waiters, bootblacks, and washroom attendants.

Chapter Twenty-six

N ED was back at the Waldorf physically, but his heart, an old pair of trousers, and a discarded cork leg were still in Texas. He sent this last item to his Terrell landlady, Mrs. Jarvis, about January 15, 1911. It was an obvious effort to add proof that the President of the Texas Midland, well trained by his mother to obfuscate tax collectors, was still a resident of the Lone-Star State.

Early in March, Hetty caught pneumonia and became seriously ill for the first time in her seventy-five years. She called Ned to her Hoboken bedside. Her thoughts there, however, were not so much on her health or what for her might well be an irrevocable change of domicile, but on the Fortune. She wanted reassurances that Ned would be considered a bona fide resident of Texas rather than New York, where taxes were considerably higher.

Mr. Ogden, counsel for the T. M. and a tax expert, was summoned from San Antonio. He added a clause or two to her will,

164

strengthening Ned's position, and left Mrs. Green in a contented frame of mind.

"Now I can rest in peace," she sighed.

The world's press at once queried Ned not only about his mother's condition but also what would happen to her vast interests in the event that Mrs. Green were to die. The New York *Evening Telegram* was one of hundreds of daily newspapers that ran the story of Hetty's chances for recovery together with her son's hopeful answers.

"Mrs. Hetty H. R. Green, the richest woman in the world," said the *Telegram*, "is gravely ill in her Hoboken flat and she may never again engage in trading on Wall Street. . . .

"Her son, Colonel E. H. R. Green, was summoned to his mother's bedside. A daughter, Mrs. Matthew Astor Wilks, was out of the city and could not be reached.

" 'My mother is a very sick woman,' Colonel Green said. 'She has turned over her affairs for me to operate. I have already outlined a plan for the management of her interests included in which will be a chain of banks stretching from coast to coast. . . .

" 'Mother will take a well-deserved rest if she should recover and her doctor says there is a fair chance.' "

Hetty recovered slowly. On April 5, while she was still recuperating, it seemed that she really meant what she said when she thought her days were numbered.

"Mrs. Hetty Green . . . ," declared the Dallas *News*, "has found the task of properly caring for her vast fortune . . . too strenuous for her declining strength and has called her son to her aid.

" 'I have not really retired,' she said. 'But my son has come to me from Texas where his successes there have shown him completely competent to assume active administration of our interests.

" 'I feel fine now and I am not a bit tired. I attribute the fact that I am well and happy and useful at my age to having worked hard, lived plainly, kept a clear conscience, and never let my heart get hard.' "

By November 21, Hetty was completely well. Her avowed intention to let Ned take over by then was forgotten.

"Mrs. Hetty Green, the wealthiest and most successful business woman in the United States, today completed the seventy-sixth year of her strenuous life in perfect health and vigor which many a younger man . . . might well envy," reported the Chicago *Inter-Ocean*.

"Mrs. Green is not much given to sentiment and did not in any ostentatious manner observe the anniversary of her birth. She went to her business offices as usual. Notwithstanding her age Mrs. Green continues to look after her interests herself."

With this announcement Colonel Green gave up the battle. He still retained Marshall to handle his personal affairs but no longer went to the "office" or pretended to have a share in the direction of the Green interests. He was present about an hour a week at meetings of the Seaboard and Columbia banks, where he was listed as Director, but his attendance was perfunctory; he took no part in the proceedings.

Ned made his initial appearance in the Social Register that year. His residence was listed as New York and his clubs as the Union and the New York Athletic. He never went to either. His marital status was noted as "single"—a condition, Colonel Green declared, he was ready to change if he could find the "right one." His idea of a large-scale practical joke, which he still enjoyed playing, was to notify the press that he was seeking a bride.

"I promised my mother I would not marry until I was twenty-five years old," Colonel Green declared in an interview given to the New York *Telegram*, "and I have kept my word."

Colonel Green neglected to add that his chronological qualification for wedlock had long been reached, since he was then in his forty-fourth year.

"When I get married," he continued, "it will be to a woman, not a clothes horse. I want someone who can cook and sew and not be a parasite. My wife will be from the West, from my own State of Texas, if possible, a woman who wants a real home and children.

"I have been searching far and wide for this woman and I will not rest until I can find her."

The *Telegram* pointed out that Ned "is one of the most eligible bachelors in the world," that "he is heir to a hundred million dollars," and that "he lives in a luxurious suite at the Waldorf Astoria Hotel."

The bait was irresistible. Within hours of the *Telegram's* appearance on New York's streets, the crowd of females in front of the Waldorf was enormous. Clamoring women of all shapes, sizes, and ages and in various costumes pushed the terrified doorman aside and forced their way into the hotel trying to find the Colonel's suite.

Someone would cry, "It's on the fourth floor," or the "eighth," or the "fifth," and the mob, unable to enter the elevators, closed at once by the frightened management, would run screaming up broad staircases, banging on strange doors, and startling guests in this usually quiet establishment.

Colonel Green, seated in the lobby with a newspaper held in front of his face, was a delighted spectator. He remained there, unrecognized, while a detail of New York police cleared the Waldorf of its unwanted visitors, except for a few of the craftiest ones, who were combed out several hours afterward by house detectives.

The mail began to pour in the following day. It came from New York first. Then, as papers all over the United States and the rest of the world picked up the *Telegram's* story, letters came from everywhere in a dozen languages. Women enclosed photographs of themselves in all manner of alluring poses. They vouched for their beauty or charm, their wit or their sympathy, their virtue or experience. Meanwhile, the Waldorf urged its most lucrative tenant to forgo mentioning the location of his residence the next time he talked matrimony to the press.

For weeks to come Ned was kept busy reading his mail. To be sure, he would have preferred to read and answer the correspondence his mother received daily, but since this was not to be, at least his present activities staved off boredom.

Chapter Twenty-seven

ABOUT a year after her return from the Orient with Miss Harlow, Mary Cammack began to tire of her position in the Green-Harlow household.

"There was no future in it," she said. "I got sick of going to vaudeville shows and ball games with Ned. Even breakfast in bed gets dull after a while and how much pheasant under glass can you eat! By that time chitlins sounded good. There was a doctor in Texas wanted to marry me for a long time and I said yes. So I told Ned."

Mary Cammack became the bride of Dr. William Eckles, of Dallas, Texas, in April, 1912. The marriage lasted less than a year. By that time the Green-Harlow ménage had moved from the Waldorf to 5 West 90th Street, Manhattan. Hetty abandoned her Hoboken flat and moved next door to 7. These were twin, three-story brownstone houses and had been acquired, together with other real estate, by Black Hawk Robinson during his years in New York.

It was a strange move for Hetty. She loathed Mabel and except for rare references to "Miss Harlot," never acknowledged the woman's existence, and according to Sylvia she never entered her son's home. Miss Harlow, however, denied this and claimed that Hetty was more than an infrequent visitor at 5 West 90th Street.

"Almost the first week we moved there," Mabel said, "Ned's mother walked in. I almost collapsed when I saw her. Ned was out. She gave me a nasty glare and grunted out something like 'Humph!' Then she marched through the place from cellar to attic. I didn't budge.

"When she came downstairs she stared at me again.

" 'You got it pretty damned soft, haven't you?' she told me. 'Stand up while I take a good look at you.'

"I didn't say anything. I was half scared to death. I just stood. She looked me up and down from my head to my toes for a couple minutes. She didn't say another word. Then she turned around, walked out, and slammed the door. I thought to myself, That's the last I'll see of *you*, Mamma Green.

"But a month or two after, when Ned went out someplace with a couple of his Texas cronies, damned if the old witch didn't walk in again. She had a comb and brush with her.

" 'You might as well make yourself useful,' she said. 'I'm going out tonight. Comb my hair and fix it up. You ought to know how to do that.'

"We went upstairs to the second floor back sitting room and she let her hair down. The old bitch was damned near eighty then but her hair was long and thick and reached to her waist. I brushed it for an hour, then I put it up how I thought they were wearing it those days. The whole time she hardly spoke a word. When I finished I gave her a hand mirror.

"She took a good look, muttered something that might have been 'Thank you,' and left. That was all. I'd say this happened a dozen times more. Same thing each time, and always when Ned was out."

There is no evidence to support Mabel's story of Hetty's surreptitious visits to the house on 90th Street. "A complete fabrication" was the opinion of Sylvia's counsel; later attempting to determine the exact relationship between Hetty and Mabel. Mary Cammack, when questioned, said she did not believe Hetty's visits likely but added, "With Hetty Green, you never could be sure. Maybe she was only trying to save the price of a LeClaire hairdo."

Whether responsibility for Hetty's hair styling rested with Miss Harlow or Madame LeClaire, it was, nevertheless, the subject of favorable comment in the story of another of Mrs. Green's surprising ventures into high society. The Boston *Herald*, under a New York dateline, May 22, 1912, was one of many newspapers to carry the following dispatch.

"Mrs. Hetty Green, a Protestant," declared the *Herald*, "was a guest of honor yesterday afternoon in the Fifth Avenue home of Miss Annie Leary, a Papal Countess. At the reception which followed tea, in the embowered salon, Mrs. Green was seated on the right hand of Cardinal Farley.

"Mrs. Green appeared in a white satin modish skirt, with tunic effect of black satin entrain, and a cloudy white chiffon around the shoulders. To the amazement of guests she wore a pendant of diamonds, each stone the size of a pea and set in Roman gold.

"Her coiffure was elegant and a rope of precious stones— amethysts, pearls and rubies—were attached to her lorgnette. Her black hat was surmounted by long, waving black plumes. Her whole manner was at variance with the generally adopted view of her personality. She smiled and chatted with guests who came to pay respects to the hostess."

Ned got back to Texas twice that year for two brief visits, the

170

first in May when he attended the annual T. M. Board of Directors' meeting and again in November to cast his ballot. The Terrell *Transcript* faithfully reported this second appearance of its first citizen but failed to state that Ned's right to vote in Texas was challenged by Jerry Rutledge, an Election Judge. Rutledge took his oath of office seriously and denied Colonel Green permission to exercise his franchise.

"I'm sorry, Colonel," Rutledge said quite formally when the latter presented his poll tax receipt. "You are not a citizen of this state and I am going to withhold your ballot."

It was a bad moment for Terrell's most important resident. He was inured to humiliation elsewhere but not in Texas. Ned's friends hastily called a conference, and within an hour Wells, Corley, McKay, and others swore that President E. H. R. Green had never gone away. As proof they produced a number of monthly room rent receipts signed by his landlady. The gentlemen, however, neglected to add that Colonel Green had never been inside the home of Mrs. Bondurant N. Jarvis.

The November visit ended on a more pleasant note. When Ned arrived in Dallas he was forced to use a private Pullman rented from another railroad. But he was able to return to New York in true Presidential style. During his absence the old *Mabel,* later the *Lone Star,* and now simply 999, its original name, had been completely refitted and rebuilt, an unwitting gift of T. M. stockholders. Partly to pay the $60,000 construction and refurbishing bill and operating costs of $2.10 per mile, the Texas Midland passed its dividends for 1912.

Chapter Twenty-eight

A<small>N</small> important and long-enduring addition to the Greens' staff—Hetty's, the Colonel's, and finally Sylvia's—arrived in December, 1913. This was the close of the second year's operation of the Federal Income Tax, which, by comparison to current levies, was laughable. Hetty had run out of lawyers. Her refusal to pay Mr. Ogden's Pullman fare from San Antonio to New York and return eliminated him. If Hetty could ride day coach for three days and nights and carry her own food there was no reason why the considerably younger Ogden couldn't do the same. Mr. Ogden disagreed.

Mrs. Green now needed a tax expert plus someone who would maintain a more accurate record of her widespread activities than she herself had been keeping for six decades. Ogden warned Hetty that her books were in a deplorable state with important details known only to Mrs. Green. Until recently, when revenue agents were ready to pounce on Hetty and demand a complete accounting with the alternative of establishing their own arbitrary figures, this condition had been more asset than liability.

The answer to Hetty's problems was Wilbur K. Potter, neither attorney nor certified public accountant. He had a good working knowledge of tax laws and was an excellent statistician. In addition, he possessed to the nth degree a quality important to most successful accountants, bookkeepers, and chess players: total lack of imagination about everything unconnected with the job. When he made Hetty's acquaintance Potter was chief auditor for the Delaware Lackawanna and Western Railroad.

Their first meeting took place at Hetty's desk in the Seaboard. Mrs. Green was impressed not only by Potter's knowledge of his work, which she probed fully, but also by his refusal to veer from the subject at hand. This was salary—Potter's. Hetty attempted her usual tactics of confusion, cajolery, and vague promises.

"Start small with me, Potter," Mrs. Green pleaded after an hour of preliminary skirmishing. During this time the laconic gentleman seated by her side said little.

"How much do you want to begin with?" queried Hetty.

"Seven hundred and fifty dollars a month."

Mrs. Green gasped.

"That's more than I pay my lawyers," she said truthfully, since she usually paid her lawyers nothing.

"I'm worth more," said Potter softly.

Hetty screamed and launched into a diatribe about mercenary, heartless people. Potter listened patiently. When Mrs. Green had finished he put on his coat and hat; said "Good day," and walked off. He got about ten feet away before Hetty called him back. He removed his hat but did not take off his overcoat and shook his head when Hetty asked him to sit down.

"How much will you take, Potter?" asked Mrs. Green.

"Seven hundred and fifty dollars a month."

Hetty began her customary process of bargaining. Her offers gradually increased from $200 to $350. At no time did the accountant utter a word. At the last sum Hetty slapped her hand down on her desk.

"That's my final offer. Take it or leave it!"

Potter didn't even bother to say "Good day." He turned his back and left. He was almost at the door when Hetty's strident voice reached him.

"All right, you robber!" she shouted loudly enough to startle everyone in the bank. "You win but you're going to *earn* your salary."

For the next thirty-six years Wilbur K. Potter was to hear echoes of Hetty's words ring in his ears.

Potter's job began officially on January 2, 1914. He shared desk space with the Colonel in Hetty's home at 7 West 90th Street, where a room on the first floor had been converted into a temporary office. His salary was paid by the Windham Realization Company, one of the two holding companies Hetty formed to handle her far-flung realm. The other was called the Westminster Company. Both were "captive" corporations, stock of which was owned entirely by Hetty.

Even though Potter never became much more than an exalted bookkeeper; never recommended the sale or purchase of anything; never attempted to influence Hetty or the Colonel, and only rarely gave Sylvia advice, his knowledge of the Green empire became greater than that of any one of his employers, including Mrs. Green.

To the end of her days Hetty was cognizant of most of the details of her affairs. However, since she was concerned not only with keeping her money but adding to it, her activities were divided between these not always parallel functions. Nobody denies that Hetty was a financial success. But since it was physically impossible for her to handle everything herself as she tried to do, she never reached the limit of her money-making potentials.

For example, she might dash to Chicago to collect a momentarily forgotten debt of a few hundred dollars, which any zealous bookkeeper could have handled by mail, instead of staying in

174

New York where an on-the-spot investment would have brought her a million-dollar profit. Her constant worry about the minutiae often damaged the notabilia. Potter was the only man Hetty ever trusted implicitly. You wonder how much money she would have garnered if he had come into her life sooner and so enabled Mrs. Green to devote her entire attention to the accumulation of wealth, while he would be its faithful custodian.

Potter, undistracted by the profit motive, completely mastered all the ramifications of the Windham and Westminster Companies. He couldn't have quoted a stanza of poetry, hummed more than a few bars of song, or remembered a couple of lines from a book or play, but when it came to figures—digits, ciphers, integers, fractions, numerals, their addition, multiplication, subtraction, and division—Potter had total recall. His importance to the Greens, particularly the Colonel and Sylvia, became enormous.

Potter could recite chapter and verse from the Book of Green. He knew, without consulting the excellent auditing system he installed at once, the due date of each of thousands of mortgages held in fifty different cities, the purchase price of every parcel of real estate from Vermont to California, the assessment on properties in scores of rural and urban American counties, and the call date of every one of a hundred loans and the worth of the securities guaranteeing them. He knew the cost, the par value, and the daily selling price of every stock and bond held by the Windham and Westminster Companies.

But Potter would not have been able to tell you why Hetty bought or sold; when to call and when to lend; which pieces of land were ripe for development and which should be disposed of; what railroad's future was bright and what railroad would fall apart. Hetty was a genius. Potter was a bookkeeper.

To those who tried to pry information about the Greens, Potter was a sphinx. Even the Colonel's and Sylvia's own attorneys had difficulty extracting necessary facts from this uncommunicative gentleman. It was not that he was taciturn, it was simply that Potter had nothing to say.

Joseph A. Lynagh, an employee who worked side by side with Potter for more than a score of years, could not remember a single occasion when the Greens' auditor uttered a syllable more than he had to in order to operate the office.

"He asked his questions as briefly as he could," Lynagh recalled, "and I answered them without comment. He never asked me about my family and I never asked him about his. He never gossiped, mentioned baseball, girls, politics, or religion to me or anybody else in the place. I suppose the only really superfluous words he used were 'Good morning' and 'Good night.'

"He was very even-gaited in everything. He never spoke loud. He never got ruffled. He never was excited or he never was enthused. He was just as calm under tragedy as he was over prosperity. In my opinion there is no man alive more honest and conscientious than Mr. Potter."

Potter was a trifle under average height, perhaps five feet six. He was in his late thirties when he began to work for Hetty but his hair was already gray. His complexion was slightly florid. He dressed well though certainly not conspicuously. Anybody passing Potter on Wall Street would have a hard time believing this paunchy, unassuming little man, whose pale blue eyes looked at the world through rimless glasses, was the unbonded custodian of more than $100,000,000, of which sometimes as much as $40,-000,000 was in cash.

For a year and a half Hetty's office remained at 7 despite the fact that she continued to change her sleeping quarters. The Colonel and Miss Harlow were at 5, where a ceaseless flow of ladies, who grew younger as the Colonel grew older, kept Ned occupied. The stream was diverted temporarily late in 1914 when Mary Cammack, granted an annulment from her Dallas doctor, joined Mabel and Ned. This visit was a short one. Miss Cammack soon became the bride of Fred Stafford of Chicago, where the couple moved after their honeymoon. Colonel Green did not approve of the marriage but he was in no position to prevent it.

The Colonel grew restless. He ordered 999 sent to New York, where he attached it to a Texas-bound train and spent a few weeks in Dallas and Terrell. Mabel stayed at 5 but Ned was not alone. He was accompanied by two or perhaps three young ladies whom he deposited in Little Rock on the way south to be picked up again when 999 went north once more. For the enjoyment of his guests and himself President Green had equipped his private car with a motion-picture projector and screen. Here he showed the first few collector's items of what was to become one of the world's most extensive pornographic film libraries.

The Colonel's visit to Texas that March was not as pleasant as he had hoped. All was not well with the Texas Midland, he was told, and the railroad was losing business to a new kind of competition—buses and trucks.

"From 1911 to 1915," McKay declared, "the T. M. dropped forty per cent of its local traffic, passenger and freight. I reported this to Ned. We needed him badly. He was a very creative man, and I truly believe that even at this late date he could have saved us. Back as far as 1910 he saw what was coming from highway competition and suggested we get into the trucking business. We were considering that when his mother made him come home.

"But the Colonel wasn't interested. He didn't seem like his old self. Didn't give a damn what happened to the T. M., which he built up from scratch to the finest short line in the Southwest. I could hardly believe my ears when he told Larry Wells and me to dispose of his pride and joy.

"'Get rid of her fast,' he said. We pleaded with him to let us lease the road to a connecting line, so we'd still be in business. Finally Ned agreed and I started negotiations which took a couple years to complete before we persuaded the Southern Pacific to take us over."

Soon after Ned's return to New York, tax collectors closed in on Hetty. Revenue agents, both Federal and municipal, had determined that Mrs. Green's business was being conducted from her official residence and this, they said, was 7 West 90th Street.

To thwart them Hetty made an unprecedented decision: she decided to pay for office space. Potter was instructed to rent a small room at 111 Broadway. Orders to equip it as cheaply as possible were superfluous. Hetty, herself, recrossed the Hudson. Her flight into New Jersey was reported in the New York *Times,* May 11, 1915.

"Mrs. Hetty Green has moved back to Hoboken," said this newspaper, "thereby leaving to tax assessors and collectors the task of deciding whether she is a resident of New York or New Jersey. . . . Mrs. Green enjoys the reputation of being the world's richest woman . . . and consequently her every movement is a matter of concern to tax officials.

"Whether Mrs. Green intends to live the rest of her days or the rest of the summer in Hoboken, or not, a reporter for the *Times* ascertained that she spent the nights of Friday, Saturday and Sunday at 1211 Washington Street, Hoboken, in the apartment of the family of Jacob Van Twist, caretaker of the apartment house.

"The agent for the house . . . owned by the Hoboken Land Improvement Company, said that Mrs. Green had not leased an apartment. However, it is recalled that three years ago, when Mrs. Green lived in the same block, her apartment was in the name of 'Mrs. Dewey.' Mrs. Green owned a dog named Dewey [by then at least 25 years old]."

Either the meticulous New York *Times* erred or else Hetty was able to create another blind trail for her pursuers by tossing in a hitherto undisclosed dwelling place.

"Mrs. Green did not spend the night at her supposed home at No. 9 [sic] West 90th Street," said the *Times*. "She moved from Hoboken to Manhattan several years ago when her daughter was married. . . . No. 5 West 90th Street is the home of her son, Colonel E. H. R. Green. The caretaker at 9 West 90th Street said last night that Mrs. Green occasionally came to the house but that she neither slept nor ate there. . . . He said he had not seen the Colonel for several months . . . and advanced the information that the house was not furnished. . . .

178

"Just what state can boast of Mrs. Green as a resident was not known by her son-in-law, Matthew Astor Wilks. Asked last night where Mrs. Green lived he replied:

" 'I don't know. She visits my wife occasionally. She might be in New Jersey and she might not; she might be in Manhattan and she might not. Good night!'

"Mrs. Green never made any secret of the fact that she just detests interviews with tax assessors. . . . Wherever Mrs. Green's home is—her office is at 111 Broadway. . . . It is to be a game of tag with the N. Y. tax men, and after they find her they may not have her after all, for she's living now in Jersey."

To counteract the *Times*' unkind remarks, Hetty, apparently grown sensitive to public opinion, talked at length to a reporter from the New York *Sun*. The heart of this interview is a single, short sentence.

"The Bible is my guide," declared Mrs. Green.

Hetty was loath to admit it but she was growing old, it was becoming difficult for her to ride in public conveyances, and walking was getting increasingly painful. She was persuaded to allow Ned's chauffeur, Patrick Harlan, to drive her around occasionally in the Colonel's Pierce-Arrow limousine.

Ned's acquisition of that symbol of wealth the preceding year and his employment of a chauffeur were accepted without comment by Hetty. She no longer questioned Ned's personal expenses. His trips, girls, and other entertainment were charged against the Texas Midland. Compared to Mrs. Green's yearly expenditures, the Colonel lived in regal splendor. Actually, considering the amount of money he had at his disposal, his living costs were modest.

Ned and Hetty had joint control of several bank accounts with deposits frequently reaching $50,000,000. Yet, since he had come back to New York, except for his fling at the Waldorf, the Colonel lived at 5, which was rent-free. This home was furnished modestly, and before Pat was hired the staff there consisted only of Ernestina Holcinger, a chambermaid, and the Colonel's Japanese valet-butler. Mabel did the cooking herself. Her allowance

179

had been raised to $500 a month. However, out of this she paid all household operating costs. At the most, Ned dipped into the family till for no more than $20,000 a year while the Greens' annual income then could have been no less than $5,000,000. In addition, he had the $7,500,000 from his father's estate.

Harlan, who was a sympathetic Irishman, noticed Mrs. Green wince with pain every time he assisted her up the Pierce-Arrow's high running board. One day when Hetty seemed to suffer more than usual, he asked her if he might help.

"Madame," he said, "I've a good doctor who lives near here."

"What does he charge?" Hetty asked.

"Fifty cents a visit."

"All right. Let's see him."

Harlan's physician was Dr. Henry S. Pascal, a staff member of St. Elizabeth's Hospital, at 415 West 51st Street. His office was nearby. He had graduated from New York University in 1896 and by 1915 was one of Manhattan's most brilliant surgeons. Except for those who saw him at St. Elizabeth's free clinic, most of his patients were wealthy New Yorkers and occasionally their chauffeurs, butlers, and other domestic servants. The surgeon's fees varied accordingly.

Dr. Pascal recalled Hetty's visit to his office.

"Harlan introduced me to Mrs. Green. Of course I knew who she was. I'd never met her but she looked exactly like her pictures. She was wearing a long, old dress which swept the ground. When I shut the door of my examination room she got right to the point.

" 'I've a hernia,' she said. 'What will you charge to operate?' Obviously I wasn't the first doctor she'd been to.

"I told her I'd have to examine her first. She removed her clothing. Her underwear was in rags and none too clean, either. I thought I'd seen everything but here was something new. She had a hernia, all right, a big one. She was supporting it with a stick, jammed against the swelling and held there by pressure from her leg and undergarments.

"I made no comment about the stick, which fell to the floor.

I asked her how long she'd had the hernia and she told me for about twenty years.

" 'It's from carrying heavy books from my desk to the vault.'

"It must have been very painful and I told her it ought to be operated on at once.

" 'What'll it cost?' she asked.

" 'My fee will be a hundred and fifty dollars. The hospital charges are extra.'

"She glared at me, picked up the stick, put it back in place, and got dressed.

" 'You're all alike,' she said. 'A bunch of robbers!'

"I could have been angry but I wasn't. It was too funny. I asked her where she was going and she said, 'None of your business.'

"I told her it *was* my business until she paid me my fifteen-dollar examination fee. I thought she was going to have apoplexy. She reached into her handbag which was tied about her waist and jammed with bills and papers, and selected fifteen of the oldest singles, threw them on my table, and stalked out."

This was not the last time Dr. Pascal saw Hetty. About a month later the surgeon and his wife received an invitation to dine at Countess Leary's.

"The first person I saw there was Mrs. Green," Dr. Pascal recalled. "She was dressed considerably better than when I'd met her; in fact she looked quite elegant. She had just come out of the powder room when she spied me.

" 'Don't use any of the clean towels in there,' she warned in a loud voice. 'My friend Annie hasn't got a rich doctor to support her!' "

Hetty reached an important milestone that November, and the New York *Times* admitted the lady had again outsmarted the city's working press. That paper thought it worthy of mention that no interview was granted on her eightieth birthday. Indeed, the reporter sent to interview her could not discover her whereabouts.

Chapter Twenty-nine

Hᴇᴛᴛʏ granted an interview to an International News Service reporter the following March. "I'll live to be a hundred," she predicted. "You can bet on that!" If this member of Mr. Hearst's staff had taken Mrs. H. H. R. Green's advice he would have lost his money. Early that summer Hetty became seriously ill.

"Hetty Green . . . ," said the New York *Times* on June 26, "who was 80 years old last Fall, was reported yesterday to have suffered a stroke of paralysis after a drive in an automobile last Thursday and to be confined to bed. It was admitted at her home, 7 West 90th Street, that Mrs. Green had been . . . ill but it was declared she was resting comfortably.

"Mrs. Green's physician, Dr. Henry McM. Painter, of 62 West 55th Street, when asked about his patient's condition last night, said:

" 'Mrs. Green is not as well as she was ten or fifteen years ago, but that is to be expected.' "

After this pontifical remark Dr. Painter added, "It is not true that Mrs. Green had a paralytic stroke. In fact, after I saw her yesterday I gave Mrs. Green permission to sit up. . . . I feel sure she will be quite well again."

Dr. Henry McM. Painter's patient succumbed a week later, the result of a paralytic stroke suffered on June 24.

"Mrs. Hetty Green, believed to be the world's richest woman, died yesterday . . ." reported the New York *Times*. "The woman whose great business acumen had built up a fortune estimated at $100,000,000, and had made her name known in the market places of the world faced death as she had life, militantly and unafraid.

"She did not want to die, but ten days ago she believed that death was near and called her son, Colonel E. H. R. Green, and daughter, Mrs. Matthew Astor Wilks, to her bedside and placed her house in order."

This newspaper revealed that this was not the only seizure Hetty had suffered.

"Mrs. Green," continued the *Times*, "was first stricken April 17 while she was visiting the Countess Leary at her home, 1032 Fifth Avenue. Her left side was paralyzed and as this incapacitated her from moving about she went to live with her son at 5 West 90th Street. . . .

"A week ago . . . Mrs. Green seemed sufficiently improved to go for an auto ride. She returned greatly weakened and another severe stroke followed. It was then she became convinced that the end was near. . . ."

Colonel Green disclosed the fact that Hetty did not die as a Quaker.

"Once, ten years ago, Mother . . . had us take her to Jersey City where she was baptized in the Episcopal faith. She did this because my father was an Episcopalian and it was necessary so that she could be buried in the family plot at Bellows Falls, Vermont."

To former neighbors at Bellows Falls there was an easy explanation for Mrs. Green's conversion from the Friends' unadorned tenets.

"The Greens' family plot at Immanuel was all paid for. There was free space for Hetty there," declared one Vermonter.

Hetty was buried at Bellows Falls, where services were conducted by Father Arthur O. Wilson, Rector of Immanuel. Mamie Nims Bolles was at the funeral and saw her childhood friend Sylvia for the first time in many years.

"My husband was one of the bearers," Mrs. Bolles recalled. "I spoke with Sylvia after and she said, 'Go down to my private car at the station in half an hour and I will be there. I am going to take Mr. Wilks for a drive about town and I hope he will like it so well he will come to live here.'

"In the car I met Mr. Wilks, a small, quiet gentleman for whose comfort Sylvia had a maternal solicitude. A secretary produced a lunch and we were very busy talking when the car started. It was backed over the long bridge into New Hampshire and down the east side of the river into the Boston and Maine Railroad yard.

"I began to wonder if I was being carried off to New York by a devious route and, having no money with me, I didn't like the prospect of asking Sylvia for the price of a return ticket. However, after visiting a water tank the engine returned us by way of another bridge to the place from which we started."

Apparently Mr. Wilks did not care for Bellows Falls well enough to move there from Madison Avenue.

"After her mother's death," concluded Mamie, "Sylvia seldom came back to Bellows Falls."

Few mourned Mrs. Green's passing. Most of the nation's press had something unkind to say about her. Some newspapers deplored Hetty's refusal to share the country's tax load; some decried her business methods, while others were bitter because she neither gave anything to charity while she lived nor left a cent of her fortune to a philanthropic organization or to needy individuals when she died.

The Colonel rushed to his mother's defense but was hard put to find a concrete example of his mother's munificence. He tried to brush off prying reporters with generalities.

"My mother never told me about her charities although they were many," the Colonel declared. "She gave amounts up to ten thousand dollars. There were dozens of families she supported regularly in New Bedford, in Bellows Falls, and here in New York."

But when not one of Hetty's "beneficiaries" declared himself and the press refused to take Green's word for it, the Colonel tried to furnish evidence of Hetty's generosity. After considerable thought he came up with one potential.

"Six months ago Benjamin Lawton, a man ten years my mother's senior, died," Ned told a reporter from the New York *Times*. "He had been her father's bookkeeper in New Bedford and from him she had received her first money, an allowance of $1.50 a week. So when she became a woman of affairs Lawton continued as her bookkeeper. Until his death, he was a bent, helpless old man . . . and came daily to the office and sat at his desk . . . asleep most of the time. I wanted to let him go but he told Mother it would kill him so he stayed and drew his salary."

That there actually was a Benjamin Lawton who did work at 7 was confirmed by Mr. Potter. This usually uncommunicative gentleman, touched by the plight of a brother accountant, recalled that "a poor old ragged-looking fellow named Lawton used to come in to the office the first week or so I was there. He didn't show up one day and I asked Mrs. Green what happened to him. She told me she had to drop him. I never saw Lawton again and to the best of my knowledge I do not recall writing a check for him."

The New York *Times* was able to find something good to say about the late Mrs. Green, fiscally at any rate.

"There is no person of great wealth whose passing could cause less shifting of investments than will follow the death of Mrs. H. H. R. Green," said this newspaper. "Her financial advisors said yesterday that the death of the wealthiest woman in the United States would have no effect on any corporation in which her funds were invested . . . her inheritors, whether individuals or charities would have no reason to disturb the investments. . . ."

But the press of New England was particularly hostile, possibly because it had known Hetty longer. Under a slug line, SHE, TOO, LEFT HERS BEHIND, the Boston *Transcript* tersely described the way most Americans felt about the departed.

"Hetty Green, who lived as a poor woman lives, and moved from one place to another in order to dodge those who pestered her with appeals for aid, was unable to take her immense fortune with her when she quit this world for the next. She may have thought, when she was earnestly and painfully accumulating her millions, that she could do what no male or female miser before her had been able to do, but she went, and her fortune remained.

"And now various states are claiming her as a daughter. Not that they wish to honor her memory by the claim; not that, when the final claim is established, any one of them will erect a memorial to her, but in order that they may tax what she left behind, as they were unable to tax it when she was on earth as its guardian.

"How much good Hetty Green might have done with her wealth if she had cared to use it. How much good others of great fortunes might do if they could receive the inspiration for doing. And how many of them will continue to hoard and accumulate until they are recalled hence and their fortune will remain here —to be fought over in the courts and to be clamored for by rival tax gatherers."

The States of New York, New Jersey, and Vermont immediately staked claims against Hetty's estate, but it took more than three years before Vermont was able to prove to the United States Supreme Court that Mrs. H. H. R. Green was a resident of Bellows Falls. At that, officials and taxpayers of the Granite State may not have felt the award of slightly over $50,000 was worth the effort and cost.

Since the majority of Americans were as yet untouched by the Internal Revenue Service, there was little public furor over the picayune taxes collected from Hetty's estate. One man, however, hardly waited until the body was cold before he used the departed as an example to prove the need of personal income taxes. A few hours after news of Mrs. Green's death was flashed to the world, William Jennings Bryan, then a Congressman, declared, "Hetty Green enjoyed an income which could scarcely be less than three million dollars a year yet lived at a cheap boarding-house and spent only a few hundred dollars. This woman, under our indirect method of taxation, did not pay as much toward the support of the Federal Government as a laboring man whose income of five hundred dollars is spent on his family."

Nobody ever knew the exact amount of Hetty's estate because neither her son nor daughter, as joint trustees, was required to file an inventory or post bonds. But Wall Street appraised the fortune from a low of $100,000,000 to a high of $200,000,000. Whether the bottom or top figure is accepted, annual income was at least twice as high as the "Great Commoner's" estimate.

Hetty had made only a few minor alterations in her will since the addition of the 1911 codicil. Consequently, the ten-year trust fund she often told her son she would dissolve was unchanged. Her two siblings were to share only the income of the estate for the next decade. At the expiration of this time Ned would be fifty-eight and Sylvia fifty-five, surely ages of discretion even in Hetty's measured opinion.

The acquisition of an additional two or three million dollars a year meant little to Sylvia, whose modest way of life with Matthew Astor Wilks continued its even pace. Mr. Wilks, an old-fashioned gentleman, was a firm believer in the principle that a husband's duty was to support his wife. Except for comparatively small gifts, Mrs. Wilks spent little of her legacy.

Her brother, however, set a pace unapproached by other profligates of his day. Before the year 1916 ended the Colonel closed 5 and 7 West 90th Street and took a sixteen-room corner suite in the Waldorf-Astoria at an annual rental of $28,000 and spent $150,000 on its *décor;* bought Mabel a diamond-studded chastity belt for $50,000; hired a personal staff of fourteen young ladies including two "masseuses" and a half-dozen typists although his office contained a single L. C. Smith; had plans drawn for a sixty-room mansion, and placed an order for the largest yacht in the world.

One expenditure, minute but significant, was the cost of a telegram the Colonel sent to Dallas from Bellows Falls the day Hetty was buried. It was addressed to Walter Marshall and read simply:

"YOUR JOB IS OPEN STOP RETURN TO WORK AS SOON AS POSSIBLE STOP REPLY COLLECT WESTERN UNION.   COLONEL E. H. R. GREEN."

Chapter Thirty

To the surprise of everyone, including Mabel, and perhaps the Colonel himself, Ned proposed marriage to Mabel in August of 1916. By then, the couple had been living together for twenty-four years. Hetty had been at rest less than a month. To the surprise of no one, Mabel said yes. It would have been interesting to watch Hetty's reaction to the announcement that soon followed.

Ned had always wanted a ship of his own and believed a yacht would be the appropriate place for a Howland to spend his honeymoon. Since there was hardly any necessity for a speedy wedding, the Colonel decided that formal ceremonies could wait until he was able to buy a suitable vessel.

Marshall was instructed to look over the market carefully but found nothing available. Neither J. P. Morgan's *Corsair* nor Vincent Astor's *Nourmahal* was for sale and nothing else was big enough. At the time, most European shipyards were having trouble supplying sufficient bottoms to keep even slightly ahead of the tonnage that German U-boats were sinking. English and French builders, who had constructed many an American millionaire's pleasure craft, would not consider building a private steam yacht and United States naval architects could not promise delivery for at least two years.

Ned was frustrated, but only temporarily. The Brooklyn ship brokerage firm of Gielow and Orr had a suggestion. Several months before it had been commissioned to sell a comparatively new Great Lakes steamship, the *United States*, which carried passengers and light freight between Grand Haven and Milwaukee. If the Colonel had $1,000,000 or so to spare and was willing to wait until the following August, these Brooklyn brokers and naval architects would guarantee to rebuild and deliver a seagoing boat worthy of Hetty Green's son.

Ned was willing to wait and had the $1,000,000 to spare. As a matter of fact he was satisfied to put even more into the *United States* after seeing the graceful, single-stacked ship cutting through Lake Michigan's waters. The Colonel had one trifling complaint: the *United States* was just a bit too short despite her over-all length of 215 feet. To Colonel Green's question, "Can you saw the *United States* in half and add forty feet to the middle?" Gielow and Orr replied, "Why not—for another $100,000?"

The *United States* wound up her commercial career and steamed through the St. Lawrence, into the Atlantic Ocean and south to Brooklyn, where major surgery was performed. According to the August, 1917, issue of *The Rudder*, "work on transforming the U.S. into the largest, finest and costliest privately owned yacht in the world was begun . . . Dec. 6, 1916. . . .

"The lengthening has made the yacht measure 255 feet over all; her breadth is 40 feet and her loaded draught is 15 feet. Her

190

engines of 2,500 i.h.p. will give her a speed of about 17 miles per hour. Her gross tonnage is 2,054."

There was a considerable amount of additional construction necessary to meet the Colonel's demands for luxury.

"A new upper deck was built," continued *The Rudder*, "and a new promenade deck of Oregon pine on steel beams . . . with nine inches more headroom between these decks than on the original boat. The yacht now has five decks. . . . The flying wings of the bridge are 32 feet above the water line.

"The bridge deck also has a sun deck 24 feet by 15 feet, and from it a commanding view can be obtained because of its height above the water. On the promenade deck forward is the pilot-house, fitted with every thing up-to-date for the use of the captain and his officers in navigating the vessel."

Each of the ten lifeboats cost $1,100, putting it well beyond the reach of the average fisherman, content if he could call a twelve-foot rowboat his own. The *United States* also carried four launches.

"All launches," said *The Rudder*, "are made of mahogany. Colonel Green has named them Alaska, Hawaii, Antilles and Philippines, so that the yacht may be termed the United States and her possessions. The Alaska is the largest, measuring 35 feet by 6 feet 6 inches and is driven by a Speedway engine of 130 h.p.

"The chart room is finished in silvery gray ash, with leather upholstery. . . . The tea room . . . decor is in red and black lacquer . . . upholstery and hangings are of Chinese design . . . and the rug especially woven for the yacht. The library is 12 feet by 15 feet and hangings and upholstery are of maroon leather. The drawing room . . . is Louis Quatorze . . . and the breakfast room Louis Seize."

The Colonel's sleeping quarters were the largest aboard ship.

"The owner's stateroom," continued *The Rudder*, "is 15x20. The tone is Georgian and distinctly mannish. . . . The adjoining stateroom [Mabel's] is Marie Antoinette in design and is a dainty

191

and queenly room. . . . Altogether there are nine master chambers, each having a bathroom. . . . Every room is perfectly appointed and represents some distinct period. . . . All the magnificent interior decorating and furnishing were done by John Wanamaker. . . .

"The living room . . . is 28 feet long and 32 feet wide and . . . decorated in the Jacobean period. . . . At one end is a large stone fireplace for an open fire. . . . Above the mantel is a painting showing the U. S. Frigate United States of 44 guns.

"Nothing that could be done to make the United States the most perfectly fitted vessel afloat has been neglected. . . . The chief inspector throughout the period of alteration was Colonel Green who derived much pleasure from his almost daily visits to the work. . . ."

The shipyard bettered its schedule and, after a satisfactory trial run, notified Colonel Green that the *United States* would be turned over to him early in July, 1917. Ned hired Captain DeWitt C. Moore and a crew of seventy-one, and told them to stand by for orders.

On June 26, Miss Harlow fulfilled the one consideration without which she would never have become Mrs. E. H. R. Green. In the presence of three officers of the Columbia Trust Company and Charles W. Pierson, Ned's attorney, Mabel signed an antenuptial agreement. In consideration of waiving all rights to her fiancé's fortune, the future Mrs. Green was guaranteed a life income of $1,500 per month. This was to be paid out of a $600,000 trust fund that Ned established. As a patriotic gesture to his country, which was then at war, the Colonel included $125,000 of that amount in Liberty Bonds.

The following morning Miss Harlow, who had come a long way since she first met Ned in Chicago twenty-eight years before, returned to that city. She registered at the Blackstone Hotel. Ned joined her the night of July 9, not many hours before the ceremony. This was scheduled to take place the next morning at ten o'clock in the home of Mabel's aunt, Mrs. George Campbell, in suburban Highland Park.

Chapter Thirty-one

THE wedding between Colonel Edward Howland Robinson Green and Miss Mabel E. Harlow was a small one. There were no more than twenty guests, including Walter P. Marshall, the only Texan there. Among those present were Mr. and Mrs. Fred Stafford. The latter was matron of honor. Services were performed by the Reverend P. C. Wolcott, Rector of the Highland Park Trinity Protestant Episcopal Church.

"Although the marriage license placed Mrs. Green's age at 47, she does not look it," the Associated Press declared gallantly. "She could say she was 32 and no one would doubt it. She is very pretty, has an abundance of fine auburn hair, a winning smile and large, sympathetic blue eyes. . . . She wore . . . an ivory crepe gown of ankle length, with a slightly panniered skirt. Her only ornament was a pearl necklace."

The United Press captured the Colonel and his lady in a scene dripping with sentiment.

" 'Look up into my eyes, darling, I want to show the world what a fine wife I have,' said Colonel Green to the hordes of cameramen who surrounded him immediately after the ceremonies.

"But the blushing bride refused and buried her face in a bouquet of lilies of the valley."

Ned and Mabel left at once for New York, where, according to the New York *Times,* "The steam yacht, United States, . . . is moored on the Hudson River at Fortieth Street, to wait the arrival of the owner and his bride. Members of the crew stated that they expected to make a cruise down to the West Indies and the Panama Canal."

With bride, groom, and matron of honor aboard (Mr. Stafford conveniently stayed behind) the honeymoon trip was begun. The *United States,* her flags flying gaily, slipped out of her pier, steamed slowly down the Hudson, then sped out into the open Atlantic. The first port of call was Galveston. By the time this Texas city was reached "Commodore" Green, as he was called by Captain and crew, had made an unpleasant discovery, particularly distasteful to one with so much Howland blood in his veins. The Colonel hated the sea.

His reasons were sound. For a man with a cork leg, walking about a ship in motion, even one as stable as the *United States,* was both difficult and painful. The yacht remained in Galveston long enough for Kiest, Allen, Corley, McKay, and Wells to board her. Their wives, unable to resist the lure of the world's largest yacht and apparently willing to forget their dislike for Mabel, joined husbands in a tour of the ship. Mary Stafford thoughtfully spent the evening on shore.

The *United States* then cruised south through smooth Gulf waters to Mustang Island, where she remained for a week. Heading north, the sea was not rough but Ned was uncomfortable much of the time. His ship docked overnight on Long Island

Sound near Greenwich, where the Wilkses had a summer home. The "Alaska" picked up Sylvia, her husband, and their fifteen-year-old guest, Ruth Lawrence, of New Bedford, and brought them to the yacht for dinner.

This was the first formal meeting between the Wilkses and Mabel. Mrs. Green tried hard, but Sylvia's displeasure was obvious and the meal was not a success. Ruth, however, impressed the Colonel and was invited to visit him later.

The following morning the *United States* sailed for New England. Here, much to the regret of Captain and crew, Commodore Green announced that in the future his seagoing yacht would be used only as a houseboat. To assuage their disappointment Ned agreed to maintain a full crew all year round. This could be done for a bit over $100,000 annually, including wages, and was well within the Colonel's budget. His net income for 1917 was $2,150,972.53.

The Colonel planned to live aboard the yacht during the summer months and wanted to be within sight of Round Hills. At a cost of $150,000 he cleared a wide beach at the foot of the Howland farm; built two conservatories to supply the yacht with daily cut flowers, several bathhouses, a six-car garage and machine shop, a 50,000-gallon tank to furnish the ship with water, and an 850-foot pier, long enough, he hoped, to dock the *United States*. The pier was long enough, but unfortunately the water was not deep enough.

"The ship could come in only at high or mid-tide," admitted Zebina B. Davis, a New Bedford contractor responsible for all construction at Round Hills. "We found that out the first time we tried, and if Captain Moore had brought her all the way in he'd never have gotten her out again.

"So the Colonel abandoned the whole project, left the pier to rot, and bought South Wharf in Padanarum Harbor at South Dartmouth, four and a half miles away from the farm. He built a floating scow at the end of this to moor the launches."

The initial attempt to dock the yacht at Round Hills must have

195

been quite an experience for New Bedforders, including scores of Howlands reared in the tradition of the sea. Having sailed the waters of Buzzards Bay for a dozen generations, they certainly were aware, from the moment construction was started, that the Colonel's yacht would never make it. However, nobody asked their opinion and, with characteristic restraint, nobody gave it.

A frequent guest aboard the *United States* that summer was Miss Ruth Lawrence, who became the first and odds-on favorite of a procession of young ladies the Colonel "adopted." Ruth was the granddaughter of a New York judge whose wife knew Hetty, and namesake of an aunt who was a friend of Sylvia Wilks. She was pretty, intelligent, and well mannered. Both Greens liked her at once.

"The Colonel told me to call him 'Uncle Ned,'" Ruth said. "I called Mrs. Green 'Aunt Mabel.' I remember my initial visit to Round Hills. The yacht was anchored nearby and we took a launch and went to Padanarum and then drove from there in a little red Ford and went to the estate which was then mostly woods. Uncle Ned was waiting for us because it wasn't physically possible for him to have gotten into that little car.

"He showed us around the grounds and told us he hoped soon to build a large home there where his ancestors lived. Then we returned to the *United States*, where I spent the rest of the month. I had to go back to high school in September but I was invited to come to New York to visit Uncle Ned at the Waldorf that winter."

A number of "better" families from New Bedford and some summer residents of exclusive, nearby South Nonquitt visited the yacht once or twice but did not ask Mr. and Mrs. Green to their homes. This may have been the reason Ned temporarily abandoned his idea of building a mansion at Round Hills and even refused to spend more than a few dollars to repair the two-hundred-year-old Howland farmhouse, which was in a state of near collapse.

Bride, matron of honor, and groom returned to the Waldorf early in October. It was a boring stay for all three. Mabel whiled away part of her time shopping and making sure her husband's supply of young ladies was adequate. The latter task was becoming more and more difficult, with quality and imagination, rather than mere quantity, the criteria. Mary Stafford had even less to occupy her. She returned to Chicago, presumably to join the waiting Mr. Stafford.

The Colonel spent a few hours a week behind the desk in the Trinity Building at 111 Broadway with little to do there except to read Potter's reports of a monotonously steady income, which never varied more than a few hundred thousand dollars a year. Rarely was anything bought or sold by the Windham Realization Company or the Westminster Company. The late Mrs. Green had invested wisely. For the caretaker of her estate and her beneficiaries it was merely a matter of clipping coupons, and seeing that rents were collected promptly and interest was paid on time.

The Colonel did order Potter to buy a million dollars' worth of Liberty Bonds. That reduced Sylvia's and Ned's annual income slightly, but since Mrs. Wilks spent practically none of her inheritance, and Ned was hard put to spend all of his, this patriotic move did little except help make the world safe for democracy.

Records of the Seaboard National Bank and the Columbia Trust Company reveal that Ned was present at some of the weekly Board of Directors' meetings but his associates say the only motion they recall the Colonel making was to adjourn.

After a few weeks in New York, Ned was so weary of his existence that against his better judgment he ordered Captain Moore to pick him up for a Texas cruise. With the Colonel, Mrs. Green, and guests aboard, the ship sailed down the Hudson on the evening of October 28, skirting hundreds of gray warships, flying the colors of the United States Navy and the flags of her allies.

The Colonel's yacht arrived at Galveston in time for Ned to

vote as usual. For her owner, this cruise of the *United States* was even worse than her maiden voyage. In addition to experiencing severe pains in the stump of his leg, Ned was violently seasick. The Greens stayed in Fort Worth and Dallas until December, then the Colonel reluctantly boarded his yacht for the return trip. The ship steamed into New York Harbor December 15 and from there proceeded to Padanarum without her Commodore.

Christmas holidays were enlivened by the presence of Ruth Lawrence and the fourteen-year-old daughter of Walter Marshall, Dorothy, and Tom Corley's two daughters, Eugenia, fifteen, and Prudence, fourteen. All three young ladies, it should be pointed out, were chaperoned by their parents. Marshall was particularly careful, since he was aware of his employer's susceptibility to the charms of the adolescent. The precautions were not necessary. The Colonel had already made definite distinctions between his "protégées" and other girls, only slightly older, whom he took to his bed.

Some of the few friends who knew Green well were convinced that the Colonel's preoccupation with youthful females was an expression of a desire for his own family. Others attributed his wish to dominate the lives of his young ladies to his own frustrations at Mamma's hands. By being a substitute "father" Ned placed himself in a position where he could choose his protégées' clothes, select their schools, direct their social lives, and even select their husbands.

Several long-time acquaintances of the Colonel dismissed all these theories as arrant nonsense. They claimed that Ned simply reasoned, "Age has little to do with it. It's size that counts!"

Chapter Thirty-two

Just like Hetty, Ned did his best to evade paying taxes. He suffered acutely from the heat but endured Manhattan's early summer dog-days rather than reach the cool waters of Buzzards Bay before July 1 because he believed it was the only way to avoid paying the Massachusetts income tax. This conclusion was tenable only as long as Ned could prove he was legally domiciled elsewhere. The theory was supported by several members of the bar, including the Colonel's New York counsel, Charles W. Pierson. Evidence of Mr. Pierson's reasoning processes is to be found in the following letter this attorney wrote to his client, January 3, 1918.

"Dear Sir:

"The Massachusetts Income Tax Law provides (Section 12):

" 'Every person who is an inhabitant of the commonwealth at

any time between the first day of January and the thirtieth day of June, both inclusive, in any year, shall be subject to the taxes imposed by this act.'

" 'The word inhabitant as used in Chapter 269 of the General Acts of 1916 shall denote a legal resident in this commonwealth, a person whose legal domicile is herein.'

"As your domicile . . . is Texas it would seem, therefore, that you are not taxable under the present Massachusetts Income Tax Law although you spend part of your time . . . in Massachusetts."

Thus reassured, the Colonel ordered the *United States*, which was lying at Tebo's Basin, on Twenty-third Street, Brooklyn, to proceed to Buzzards Bay. The yacht arrived a few hours before Ned, Mabel, and Mary, who traveled by train. The Colonel's party was soon joined by the Misses Lawrence, Marshall, Corley (both Prudence and Eugenia), and North, and two Texas teenagers, Helen and Ellen Cammack, nieces of Mary Stafford, determined that young ladies of the Lone-Star State get their rightful share of holiday fun.

There was still one more young lady whom the rest recall dimly only as "Popsie." This one did not mix with the others and spent most of her time below deck with the Colonel. She was also the only female minor privileged to enjoy the motion pictures Uncle Ned showed daily in his projection room.

Before the summer ended the Colonel earned his right to be called "Commodore." He surrounded the *United States* with seven recent acquisitions, including a genuine Venetian gondola. The "Green mosquito fleet" (so called by New Bedfordites) was described by Harry R. Bennett, a second steward.

"The Colonel had a Crosley catboat, the *Mabel*," said Bennett. "Then there was a potbellied motorboat he named the *Ruth Dana;* a large powerboat Crosley called the *Moonhanas,* the *Virginia,* the gondola which of course had no power, a supply boat, and a garbage scow.

"The Colonel would have his 'navy' grouped around the *United*

States and assign a 'captain' to each boat. The instructions were that they were to go aboard their boats in the morning and if he raised the flag they would have to come alongside and take him off in one of them."

Meanwhile the regular United States Navy was fighting elsewhere. This unpleasant fact was brought home to Colonel Green shortly after his return to New York. The Federal Government notified him that, owing to the national coal shortage, the supply of fuel allotted to the *United States*—600 tons per year—was to be cut sharply. In fairness to Ned it should be pointed out that inspectors from the First, Second, and Third Naval Districts had previously rejected the Colonel's offer to turn over the yacht for war use.

The Colonel left New York for a visit to Texas, but the trip was not the most comfortable ever taken by the President of the T. M., by Marshall, who accompanied his employer all the way, or by Mrs. Stafford, who was dropped at Chicago. Marshall recalled this particular trip vividly.

"The Government, you know," he said, "had taken over all the railroads and we couldn't get 999 or any other private car. We weren't in the war effort and the best accommodations we could manage were one lower and one upper. Of course you know who got the upper.

"I don't know how they did it but the boss and Mrs. Stafford shared the lower. I can't imagine anybody had much fun. I know I didn't."

While the Colonel was accustomed to seeing his name in print and grew rather fond of publicity, he was shocked to find Sylvia on the pages of some of the nation's newspapers on April 19. This was her first appearance in the press since the wedding ten years before. The story was not only unkind, it was a distortion of the truth.

"HETTY GREEN'S MILLIONS IN A SPITE FENCE SQUABBLE," declared the I.N.S.

"To keep her dog Jack, a collie, in the grounds of Alta Crest,

201

the Greenwich, Connecticut, home of Mrs. Matthew Astor Wilks, daughter of the late Hetty Green, . . . a three foot 'spite' fence has been erected surrounding the magnificent estate.

"Mrs. Wilks said the barricade was not done in spite, but because of the recent poisoning of dogs in the area and was constructed to protect her own pet. She further added that the barrier was inside her own grounds by three feet.

"Mrs. Wilks' neighbor, Mr. L. P. Price, has now obtained an injunction to stop the fence from getting higher and is suing to have it taken down. Sheriff George Jones served the injunction on Mrs. Wilks and contractors already working there."

The suit was never brought to court. Mr. Price later admitted that he had misunderstood Mrs. Wilks' motives, apologized for his actions, and an amicable adjustment was made. When last seen there was no fence, spite or otherwise, surrounding Alta Crest.

Following the Colonel's return from Texas he occupied some of his time with a new hobby, stamp collecting, and some of his time with old ones. Marshall found that his own duties were increasing. He was now beginning to handle the heavy correspondence between his employer and the latter's twenty-four young wards, whom Green was determined to give only the best of educations.

Since he was footing all bills, supplying clothing, spending money, tuition fees, room, board, and round-trip fares to the Waldorf at Christmas holidays and New Bedford in the summer, the Colonel felt he had the right to insist on degrees from Wellesley College, which to him meant "the best possible education."

To prepare for her entrance to the college of the Colonel's choice, Ruth Lawrence was off to St. Mary's School in Peekskill, New York, where she spent a semester before transferring to Wilkes Barre Institute (now Wyoming Seminary).

"I wanted very much to go to Smith," Miss Lawrence said wistfully, "but Uncle Ned wanted me to go to Wellesley. He seemed to want *everyone* to go to Wellesley.

"Before I left he took me to De Pinna's on Fifth Avenue and bought all my clothes. He told me I'd have two thousand dollars a year spending money as soon as I entered college providing I agreed to spend one-third of each year with him and Aunt Mabel.

"Eugenia and Prudence Corley were at some seminary back in Texas, Dorothy Marshall was in Chevy Chase, and the rest were elsewhere getting ready for Wellesley. I think Uncle Ned made the same arrangements with all the others and bought their clothing too. We had to promise to write every week and be sure our marks were better than just passing."

The task of handling the mail that flowed back and forth between Uncle Ned and his wards occupied much of the Colonel's and Marshall's time.

"The correspondence became voluminous," Marshall complained. "There were weekly letters from the wards to the Colonel, then his answers to them. He'd write to each of the girls' teachers and *they'd* reply. When report cards came in (they were all mailed to the Colonel) we'd have to make the necessary comments. When the girls' marks were good he'd praise them, and when they were doing poorly, he'd jack them up.

"Then he'd send letters of invitation to them to visit him and there'd be correspondence about travel arrangements and bills for clothing and letters about tuition and once in a while the Colonel would feel he was being overcharged, then he'd be upset."

An example of Ned's circumspection is to be found in a letter he sent to Mrs. Frances Gill Morgan, of Dallas, complaining about the high cost of acquiring culture in Texas. Mrs. Morgan was the mother of a Green protégée.

"My dear Madam," wrote Colonel Green. "In regard to Margaret's piano lessons: Is there not some mistake about the prices quoted—three dollars for thirty minutes and four dollars for forty-five minutes? In New York the charge ranges from one dollar to a dollar and a half for forty-five minutes for beginners."

At the time the Colonel was spending approximately $150,000

203

annually to prepare his many wards for Wellesley's exacting standards. It must be reported reluctantly that of all the young ladies in whom he placed such high hopes, only Miss Lawrence graduated. Even more lamentably, as far as the record shows, not one of the rest got beyond her first collegiate semester.

This all became too much for Walter Marshall, who again tendered his resignation. He left for Texas in June of 1919. In July the Greens, plus their perennial house guest, Mary Stafford, returned to the *United States* and a summer of fun on Buzzards Bay. All the young ladies who had been there the previous year came back. The jolly group was augmented by Miss Laura Lopez, who had been hired to assist the Colonel in his growing stamp collection, Miss Jennie Turpaud, a French war orphan whom Uncle Ned sponsored, Miss Marguerite Stone, an attractive young chambermaid employed by the Waldorf until she met Colonel Green, and several other Texas and New York teen-agers whose names no one now recalls.

Commodore Green's flagship sank early in the morning of August 21, 1919. Everybody aboard had ten hours to reach the shore, fifty yards away, and there were no casualties. The most the owner, his wife, guests, and crew suffered were slight inconveniences, plus undoubted embarrassment to the Captain. The night was calm with hardly a ripple disturbing the placid waters of Buzzards Bay.

"Keeled on an angle of nearly fifty degrees with her upper plate submerged on its starboard side," reported the New Bedford *Standard*, "Colonel Green's palatial yacht, the U. S., lies locked on a ledge inside the Padanarum breakwater.

"The prize yacht started its tilt after midnight. Peacefully lying at anchor inside the breakwater, the yacht swung around striking a rock. Immediately a hole was stove in the bottom and she began filling. . . . At noon she was lying in 16 feet of water."

Captain David Bosworth, who had replaced Captain Moore, had a difficult time explaining how the mishap, which resulted in total loss of the yacht, could have occurred. With admirable restraint the *Standard* made no comparison between the careers of the 2,000-ton steamship and the 351-ton bark *Morgan*, most famous of Howland whalers. The former traveled less than 10,000 miles in the two years Colonel Green was her master. The latter sailed more than a million miles in every sea during her eighty-four years of active service without a single serious misadventure.

For the balance of the summer all passengers were Uncle Ned's guests at nearby Tibitha Inn. On Labor Day, Colonel Green, to the joy of Mrs. Green, Mrs. Stafford, and those protégées who had not yet been dispatched to ivy halls, arrived in Buzzards Bay aboard the tug-transported *Day Dream*. This was a magnificent houseboat that cost $90,000 and had sleeping accommodations for seventy.

Soon after, the Colonel changed his mind again about building a house at Buzzards Bay and decided to go ahead with plans submitted the preceding year by Alfred Bossom, an English architect. Ground for the Round Hills mansion was broken on September 25. There were no ceremonies. Before he left for New York in October, Ned spent hours every day watching Zabina Davis' men tear up the old Howland farm on the site where the new Green home would arise at a cost of more than $1,000,000.

Mabel also was an interested spectator. She told Mary Stafford that as soon as the house (her first real home) was completed she intended to entertain the neighbors and assume her rightful place in Massachusetts society. Mrs. Green's neighbors at adjacent South Nonquitt included a few Cabots, Lowells, Lodges, Houghtons, Aldriches, and Winthrops of Boston, a Philadelphia Biddle or two, and the Chestnut Hill Decherts, Rosses, and Whartons.

Chapter Thirty-three

NEW Year's Eve of 1921 would have been a lonely one for the Colonel but for the arrival of an old friend. All the young ladies who spent the Christmas holidays with Uncle Ned at the Waldorf had returned to their own homes; Mabel and Mary were on their way to Chicago to see Fred Stafford, who was seriously ill, and Green's numerous teen-age secretaries who assisted him with his stamp and newly begun coin collections had engagements.

Ned was getting ready for bed when the room clerk announced that the Colonel had a visitor. It was Gooseneck Bill McDonald on his first visit to New York. The Colonel welcomed his political mentor with open arms.

"Boy, he sure was glad to see me," Bill said. "Called room

service and had them send up a fine meal with champagne. We talked half the night, and when I was ready to go back to my hotel the Colonel claimed he wouldn't think of it. Had a bellboy pick up my bags and put me up in the Waldorf.

"I stayed for three days. The Colonel had his chauffeur drive us all over New York. I saw all the sights. We even went down to see his office near Wall Street. Went to a midnight show at the Palace, too, and had supper at Lüchow's. First time they ever served a colored man, there, I bet. Well, I had the best time I ever had in my life. Last time I saw the Colonel, too."

Midnight shows became a habit with the Colonel, and he and Mary went to them frequently.

"Ned was getting restless," Mrs. Stafford recalled. "He'd work over his stamp or coin collections all evening. Then he'd try to go to sleep about ten o'clock. Maybe after an hour of tossing around he'd say, 'Let's go to a show.' He'd call Ito, that was the Japanese valet, to dress him and out we'd go.

"He was starting to worry about his sex and thought he was losing his manhood, but so far I'd heard no complaints."

Aging Lotharios of the day, who could afford high medical fees, were being led to believe they could preserve, prolong, or recapture their virility by the use of "monkey glands." The first American to achieve notoriety by allegedly submitting to this operation was Harold F. McCormick, the Chicago millionaire and husband of Polish-born opera singer Ganna Walska.

Inspired by McCormick's example, Colonel Green sought Dr. Pascal's advice. This surgeon, however, struck down Ned's hopes.

"In the first place," the physician said, "no monkey glands were involved. What McCormick had is called a 'Steinach rejuvenation' and I don't think much of it. It won't harm you but I don't believe it'll do you a damned bit of good."

His patient persisted. Under a New York dateline, the Boston *Herald* declared, on March 29, 1921:

"Colonel Edward Green, son of the late Hetty Green . . . underwent the so-called Steinach operation. It was performed by

Dr. Henry S. Pascal, a well-known surgeon, in St. Elizabeth's Hospital.

"After a week's stay in the hospital and brief seclusion in his apartment at the Waldorf, Colonel and Mrs. Green went south. . . . Colonel Green wrote to a friend in New York that he felt better than he had in fifteen years.

"The operation consists of an incision and the ligature of a duct leading from one of his glands which, within modest limits, influences the processes of senility and . . . retards them. . . . Glandular secretion of the patient is thus revived and strengthened."

It is possible that Dr. Pascal's evaluation of the Steinach rejuvenation operation was incorrect. Neither this surgeon, the Colonel, nor anyone else would discuss results. On the positive side, it may be reported that the flow of young ladies continued as usual.

Before President Green left for Terrell to attend the annual Board of Directors' meeting of the Texas Midland, he went to Round Hills to note the progress made on the construction of his new house, and to bury a pet dog in the Howland family cemetery adjacent to the farmhouse. There is little in the record about this nameless canine's funeral except casual mention in Marshall's diary. One thing appears reasonably certain: the animal could hardly have been Dewey.

The incident shows the Colonel's utter contempt for his Howland forebears. Yet less than a month later, when the *Encyclopedia Americana* asked the Colonel to submit a brief autobiography, he appeared proud of his lineage.

"On my mother's side," boasted Colonel Green, "I am a direct descendant of Henry Howland, who came to America in 1621 and settled in Dartmouth, Mass., where he shortly became a leading citizen of the new world."

In his modest self-appraisal, the Colonel also awarded himself a law degree and professed that he was "a lover of art, music, literature, science and the drama." The Colonel did not confine his generosity to himself. Mabel became "the debutante daughter of the late Captain George Harlow, of Gloucester, Mass., who owned a fleet of boats . . . which sailed between Gloucester and Newfoundland."

That spring, Ned, Kiest, Allen, and several other Texans spent a week in Mexico City as guests of President Obregón. The party included Edward Harper, President of the Security National Bank of Dallas. Soon after the group returned the panic of 1921 reached Texas and there was a run on Harper's bank. The Colonel repeated an action he had made some years before in Terrell.

"I was eating breakfast with Ned in the Adolphus," recalled Ed Kiest. "It was May 21. Ed Harper came in all excited looking for us. Harper was a good friend of both the Colonel and me.

" 'There's a run on our bank,' he said. 'It's awful. I need help bad.'

"The Colonel looked up. 'Are you solid?' he asked.

" 'I swear to God we are,' Harper answered. 'It's just that no bank could stand a run like we got without more cash.'

" 'All right, Ed, I believe you,' said the Colonel. He opened up his wallet and took out twenty ten-thousand-dollar bills. (He always had at least that much on him.) 'Put this in. When I finish my grapefruit I'll be down with more.'

"While we were eating, the Colonel sent a boy to his room to bring down an old black Gladstone. The bag wasn't even locked. Ned opened it up, pulled out a thick manila envelope which was stuffed with ten-thousand-dollar bills. He counted out thirty of these and I thought the boy's eyes would pop. I know mine nearly did. He told the boy to take the bag back to his room. Ned stuck the envelope in his coat pocket and said, 'Let's go.'

"I don't recall how much the Colonel had to put in to stop the run, but whatever it was, it was enough. I know the bank stayed in business. Nobody lost a cent and Ned got his own money back the following week."

A month later, Peter J. A. Van der Putten, a decorator with showrooms at 501 Fifth Avenue, added his last touch to "Round Hills." On July 1, the Colonel and his lady moved into their magnificent home, which stood on a slight promontory overlooking Buzzards Bay.

The first sight to greet Mabel's eyes the moment she entered the door and glanced to the balcony above the sweeping circular stairway was a life-size portrait of her late mother-in-law, thoughtfully placed there by Mr. Van der Putten, who had carefully removed the picture from 7 West 90th Street.

"Take the goddamned thing down!" screamed the new mistress of Round Hills, in one of her rare fits of temper. "And if there's an attic in this joint, that's one of the places you can shove it."

Chapter Thirty-four

Iɴᴄʟᴜᴅɪɴɢ furnishings, Round Hills cost about $1,500,000. It was one of New England's show places. The house was a three-story granite structure, roughly rectangular, with wings across each end. The east face of the building was separated from the nearest beach by about five hundred feet of lawn. The main driveway, on the inland side, led to a large portico of Doric design with four columns, two stories high, surmounted by a heavy pediment. The house had a hip roof, heavily tiled and broken by numerous dormer windows.

Along the waterfront side was a wide tile terrace that extended around the south wing and terminated in an open loggia overlooking the south beach. The floor of the loggia was of glazed tile to permit dancing.

The main entrance, under the portico, led into the central hall, which also opened onto a terrace on the other side. The hallway contained a double mahogany staircase to the second floor and an electric passenger elevator. This was deep enough to accommodate an oversize bed, so that if the Colonel was not feeling well he could be taken from floor to floor with little inconvenience.

To the right of the first-floor entrance were Green's study, the library, and a hall leading to the living room, which occupied the entire south wing and measured sixty by thirty feet. Secluded from the main hall to the left of the entrance was an office where the accounts and payrolls were kept.

There were a hundred and seven men and women on the payroll. This included a steward, butler, first and second footmen, chauffeur and his helpers, a cook, cook's helpers, utility men, gardeners, an engineer, night watchman, bus drivers, laundry men, ladies' maids, chambermaids, a baker, pastry chef, parlor and pantry maids, a carpenter, painter, and building superintendent. It did not include the Colonel's valet, a half-dozen "private secretaries," and a masseuse, nor Mabel's personal maid.

Further along to the left the hallway opened into the dining room, which measured approximately forty by thirty feet. At the end of the building were a butler's pantry, the main kitchen, servants' kitchen and dining hall, pastry room, and laundry.

On the second floor the Greens' bedrooms occupied the entire south wing, and opening off the central hallway were six guest bedrooms. The bedroom adjoining Mabel's was called the "Ruth Lawrence Room." It was done in pink, a color chosen by the Colonel's favorite protégée, and reserved for her exclusive use. Each of the rooms had its own fireplace and bath.

In addition to heating and cold-storage equipment the basement contained a heavily constructed vault for the Colonel's valuables and cash. There was also a liquor cellar, the contents of which Mr. Bullard, the New Bedford lawyer, who is somewhat of a connoisseur, described as "simply dreadful."

Mabel was totally unequipped to be mistress of an establishment as large and complicated as Round Hills. Before the summer passed, servants were insubordinate; silver, linens, and other valuables were stolen; chambermaids were sleeping with footmen; liquor was missing from the cellar, and occasionally even a goat from a herd the Colonel was raising inside the old Howland farmhouse would wander into the mansion, there to remain until someone took the trouble to chase it out.

The Colonel spent most of his time on the *Day Dream*. Early that October he fled to the comfort, cleanliness, and efficiency of his Waldorf-Astoria apartment, where he stayed until November 1. Then he boarded the *Independence*, a private Pullman, for Terrell, Texas.

After casting his ballot, Ned left for Dallas, where he registered at the Adolphus. He was not feeling well and went out little that visit. He spent the evening of November 13 with Kiest.

"Ned seemed awfully low down," the publisher recalled. "I tried to cheer him up. I knew he'd started to collect coins because that trip we took to Mexico in the spring, he showed me a 'Star' dollar and I couldn't identify it. In my pocket I had a fifty-peso gold piece given to me by President Obregón when his delegation stopped into my office. It was a special minting but I don't guess it was worth more than twenty-five dollars.

"I pulled the coin out of my pocket, tossed it to Ned, and asked him what it was. He looked at it, turned it over, and I can see him yet, taking his finger and feeling it. He said, 'I don't know.'

"I said to him then, 'Well, you haven't this one in your collection, have you?' and he answered, 'No, I haven't.' Then I said, 'Let me present it to you.' I told him how I got it. He said, 'You mean you want to give it to me?' and I said, 'Sure. It's something you haven't got and I'm tickled to death to give it to you.'

"He took the gold piece and tore off a piece of newspaper and folded it up, put it in his pocket, and said, 'Thank you.' I honestly thought he was going to cry. Well, the next time I saw it, he had a chamois bag for it and carried that Mexican coin in his pocket all the rest of his life."

The following morning, while his valet was out, Ned tried to

213

hop to the bathroom by himself. He tripped on the rug and fell, throwing all three hundred pounds on his good leg. Allen, who had a breakfast appointment with the Colonel, found him stretched out on the floor, in excruciating pain. Allen called a doctor, who ordered Green to remain in bed for several weeks. The Colonel returned to New York November 16. He was examined by Dr. Pascal, who advised a blood transfusion and suggested that the patient remain in bed for at least a month.

The physician thought that natural baths would help the Colonel recuperate and suggested Hot Springs, Arkansas. But Ned, who had been there before and did not care for its ostentation, preferred the Buie Clinic at Marlin Springs, Texas. He arrived there without Mabel on January 24, 1922. He was in a wheel chair.

Before leaving New York, Uncle Ned set up twenty-four trust funds of $100,000 each, to insure the future of his wards. Marshall pointed out that the Colonel's 1921 contributions to charity were approximately $3,500.

"Nobody ever taught Colonel Green how to give," Marshall said once.

Chapter Thirty-five

THE Colonel, still in some pain but able to walk after three months at the springs, spent a week or two in Dallas before returning to New York. Dr. N. B. Buie, Chief of Staff at the Marlin clinic, advised Ned to rest as much as possible and cut down on his weight, which had gone over the three-hundred mark.

The winter passed as usual with the normal complement of young female guests but without the presence of Mabel and Mary, who were at French Lick, Indiana, where they stayed until May. Sylvia visited Ned several times and once brought him a Boston terrier he named "Stella." The Colonel rarely discussed Mabel with anyone and seldom mentioned his personal problems. But he must have told his sister about the mismanagement at Round Hills because the first visitor there that July was Mrs. Wilks.

Mabel, apparently aware of her own inadequacies, temporarily surrendered her position as mistress of Round Hills to her sister-in-law. Sylvia stayed there only a week. But in that short time she had one dishonest chambermaid arrested, fired a dozen more she suspected of stealing, put a stop to the custom of 20 per cent commissions some New Bedford merchants were paying the cook, inspected servants' uniforms and coldly berated those whose attire was not immaculate, hired an honest majordomo and gave him complete authority, chased a stray goat off the terrace and made the carpenter build a fence around the herd of forty. Although Sylvia, who loathed Mabel, came back to Round Hills only once, the remaining staff remembered Mrs. Wilks' icy anger every time one of them was tempted to do something wrong.

The Colonel bought a new car for himself which the young ladies promptly named the *Cream Puff*. It was delicate-looking with a high body painted light orange. The car was operated by storage batteries. When Ned felt well enough and was helped into the seat he could drive it himself and often took one of his wards for a ride around the estate. At the same time Ned gave each of his protégées except Ruth Lawrence a Model T. For his favorite, he ordered a more expensive car from Warren Bartlett, a New Bedford automobile salesman.

"Dear Sir," wrote the Colonel. "If you can furnish one Buick, Model 22-6-54 Sport Roadster, f.o.b. New Bedford including freight, war tax, and all extras, as per catalogue, $1,940, you may consider this an order.

"Upon the door the party to receive same would like to have the initials 'R.L.L.' in monogram, to occupy no more space than a ten-cent piece."

The Colonel's fun was short-lived. His "good" leg began to pain him and he was confined to a wheel chair for the rest of the summer, unable to drive the *Cream Puff* or spend time aboard the *Day Dream*. He grew depressed, wrote to Dr. Buie about his worsening condition, and asked for Dr. Pascal.

Dr. Buie's prescription was Ed Kiest.

"I got a telephone call one day from Dr. Buie," the publisher said, "telling me Ned was sick and discouraged and that I ought to go up to see him.

"When I got to New York I wired the Colonel and he wired me immediately to come at once. I took the New Bedford boat and got there at five o'clock in the morning. It was raining like everything. Ned's chauffeur came to my stateroom and woke me.

" 'The Colonel's outside waiting,' he told me. I got dressed, walked down the gangplank, and there was Ned sitting in the car.

"Boy was he glad to see me! We went right back to the house and I said, 'Ned, let me fix breakfast' and he said, 'All right, but I'm not very hungry.' Well, I knew what Ned liked. He was crazy about grits and some kind of sweet rolls called 'snails' that Mrs. Kiest used to make. My wife had put a pokeful of them in my suitcase and some special grits she'd added bacon fat to.

"I went into the kitchen. It was a hell of a big one with nobody there but a cook who was getting breakfast ready for the help. I took my coat off and went to work. The cook grinned and said, 'I don't know what you're going to prepare, Mister, but I hope you can get the boss to eat something. He's been way off his feed.'

"I fixed the stuff just right and served it myself. The Colonel was sitting in his wheel chair by the table. I put the grits and hot snails in front of him and the cook brought in a pot of coffee.

" 'It smells pretty damned good, you know, Ed,' he told me. He ate the whole thing and then he settled back in his chair and said, 'Best breakfast I ever had.' It was worth the trip up from Texas just to hear him say that.

"I could see he was feeling better. We sat around talking and drinking coffee till around nine o'clock, when Mrs. Green and Mary Stafford came down and said they were going to Fall River to take the boat to New York. I don't sleep too well except on

217

solid earth and I hadn't gotten a lot of rest for four days. I suppose I looked tired and Ned said I should go to my room and rest for a couple of hours.

" 'There's three young girls from Dallas here as guests of Mrs. Green,' he said, 'and I'll amuse myself with them while you take a long nap.' On my way upstairs Mary came over to me and whispered, 'I'm glad you came, Mr. Kiest. It's the first time in a long while the Colonel wanted to do anything like that.' "

Envious of the good times Ned's several dozen young ladies were having at Round Hills, swimming in the terrace pool, spending days and nights aboard the *Day Dream,* or enjoying the luxurious service inside the mansion, a number of local teen-agers tried to become part of the Colonel's circle. Only one succeeded, a plump but pretty fifteen-year-old. This enterprising miss, by sharp attention to details, learned that Uncle Ned stopped at a New Bedford drugstore every week to replenish his supply of the Bromo Seltzer he was beginning to take in unhealthful quantities.

Dressed in as little as possible, she planted herself on a soda fountain stool waiting for a Hollywood-style "discovery." Her perspicacity was rewarded. Scarcely a week after the Colonel saw her, she was invited to enjoy all rights and privileges of a full-fledged protégée. It would be an inspiring success story to report that the percipient young woman graduated *summa cum laude* from Wellesley, but such would not be the truth. She flunked out of this Massachusetts institution before her first semester was half over and had to be content with Uncle Ned's $100,000 consolation prize.

The Colonel became interested in radio and told John Bullard he would like to build a station at Round Hills. The attorney formed a nonprofit corporation with the announced purpose of "broadcasting by radio telephone or telegraph news, music, concerts, weather reports, lectures, sermons, speeches and other matters of general or special interest. . . ."

Call letters were WMAF and Ned named his station "The Voice from Way Down East." In August, Western Electric installed an experimental 100-watt transmitter. Several trial broadcasts were made and heard as far off as Terrell, Texas. Ned, who was taught to handle the controls, which he could do easily from his wheel chair, became so enthusiastic that he immediately ordered WMAF's power increased to 500 watts. On July 1, 1923, WMAF broadcast its first official program, which included an organ recital and a number of classical violin and piano solos. There were no commercials.

In an illustrated brochure bearing a picture of the Colonel, Ned's own part in the development of this new field was depicted with characteristic modesty. Following a brief history of the Howland family, the pamphlet declared that "Colonel Green's interest in radio began in 1896."

"Learning of Marconi's transatlantic experiments, Colonel Green attempted to adapt this new art to railroad use. Two baggage cars of the Texas Midland Railroad . . . were equipped with receiving sets and a sending set was installed at Terrell, Texas. It was not satisfactory on a moving train but messages were handled for some months between two fixed stations eleven miles apart.

"It is fitting that Round Hills should be the home of a great radio station. In olden days the Master of Round Hills watched his own ships bearing cargoes of all lands to and from the port of New Bedford. . . . Cargoes now arrive at Round Hills—cargoes of good-will from radio listeners . . . letters from lonely farms and frontier camps, from ships at sea, from those isolated by sickness. . . ."

South Nonquitt residents had no objection to their neighbor's desire to share his radio station with the outside world. But when they became captive audiences and involuntary hosts to the thousands of visitors "The Voice from Way Down East" attracted, the aloof residents of this summer colony were furious. In the words of John Bullard, "Ned Green became a public benefactor and a private nuisance."

"To make his excellent programmes available to all," the brochure concluded, "Colonel Green . . . installed on the top of a water tower (80 feet high) a group of loud speaking sound projectors connected to another amplifyer . . . known as a public address system. . . . Near the water tower is ample parking space for automobiles and Colonel Green has invited his neighbors to drive in and listen to the programmes which will be audible for a half mile or more." (Bullard says the range was more likely five miles.)

According to Thomas Andrew Clarence Tulloch, ground superintendent, the farm resembled Coney Island.

"It was really something," Tulloch recalled. "The noise was awful between blasts of music from WMAF, klaxons honking, kids screaming, and hawkers selling hot dogs, balloons, and Bon Ami. They used the Bon Ami to sprinkle on car windows so they couldn't be seen when they got undressed to get into their bathing suits.

"On a hot summer Sunday there'd be maybe eight, ten thousand cars parked on the grounds in front of the mansion, jammed in any way they could get space. And they'd all try to get out at the same time. There'd be cars backing into other cars, drivers swearing at each other, and women fainting from the heat and excitement. There were probably twenty-five thousand people."

Many of New Bedford's ethnic groups were represented and formed homogeneous nuclei in beach areas of their own choice.

"There was a Little Italy, a Little Greece, a Little Portugal, a Little England, a Little France, a Little Africa, and even a Little Jerusalem," Tulloch said.

"Meantime the Colonel would be watching everything. He might be sitting up in his bedroom with binoculars, but most of the time he'd be in the *Cream Puff* parked where he'd be in the center of the crowd. He didn't mind a bit when they recognized him and shook his hand. In fact, he seemed to enjoy it and he didn't care a bit what they did to his beautiful estate.

"But *I* did. The next morning the place would be a goddamned mess. The beach and lawn was littered with orange and banana peels, newspapers, stale bread, and broken bottles. I ought to add there were no toilet facilities."

Chapter Thirty-six

Mᴀʙᴇʟ bore the brunt of her neighbors' displeasure with the Colonel. A housewarming she hoped would launch her into South Nonquitt society was a failure. The Cabots, Lowells, Lodges, Biddles, Pattersons, etc., all sent regrets. The only "acceptable" guests to appear were the Bullards. The attorney and his wife felt sorry for Mabel and liked Ned despite the fact, the lawyer said, that "the Colonel used to annoy me every time he saw me by purposely mispronouncing my name, which he knew damned well was 'Bullard.' He insisted on calling me 'Ballard.' "

Mrs. Green began to drink again and to entice any available man into her bed—gardener, farmer, cook, butler, valet—it didn't matter. For a while the Colonel, who was aware of his wife's infidelities but in no position to complain, ignored them. But when rivalry between the mistress of Round Hills and a housekeeper over the affections of a New Bedford delivery boy became common knowledge, he admonished Mabel so severely that she told Mary Stafford she intended to sue for divorce.

"She thought better of it after a while," Mary said, "even though Mabel was pretty well fixed by then.

"Mabel kept all her valuables in the vault of the Knickerbocker Safe Deposit Company. I remember the box number was three sixty-three. I was deputized to open it when she wasn't around and needed something. The password was 'Terrell.' "

Mary herself didn't fare too badly at Colonel Green's hands. Before she left to attend her husband's funeral in August, Ned set up a $100,000 trust fund for Mrs. Stafford, who, unlike other recipients of his generosity, was not required to matriculate at Wellesley.

The Colonel did not respond quite so generously to an appeal from his old Texas sodality.

"Dear Brother Kerr," Colonel Green wrote on October 14, 1924, to the Keeper of Records and Seal, Terrell Lodge No. 5, Knights of Pythias. "I am in receipt of your favor of the 6th instant, in regard to the erection of a Girls' Dormitory to the Orphans' Home at Weatherford, Texas, and in response it gives pleasure to enclose herewith my donation of one dollar toward this very worthy cause."

Attrition at Wellesley was particularly high that semester. At least five and possibly six of Uncle Ned's protégées, including both Corley girls, were dropped from the rolls. Only Ruth Lawrence, then a sophomore and doing well, remained. She continued to spend all holidays with the Greens, either at Round Hills or at the Waldorf, where she also had her own room. One visit to New York was marred by a telegram.

"I had written to ask permission to visit at the Waldorf on Washington's Birthday. This was to be an extra trip. My housemother came to my room with a telegram which said, 'Uncle Ned dead, you may come home.'

"I was horrified and hurried to get packed and permission

from the Dean. All the way to New York I got newspapers at New Haven, New London, etc., but couldn't find anything about Uncle Ned's death. My father met me at Grand Central and was glad to see me. I wondered how he could be so jolly.

"I told him and he couldn't believe it. When I got to my room at the Waldorf I heard the radio playing loudly and I wondered why they would be listening to the radio at such a time. Mrs. Green heard me coming. I burst into tears and she thought my father had died. I finally told her and she said, 'Oh no, he's fine. He's in his room.'

"I could see him sitting in his wheel chair about to have his dinner. I had to take a few steps to him and it was the longest walk I ever took. I finally got to him and cried and laughed until he calmed me down. The nurse gave me a sedative and then Uncle Ned teased me, saying I was so disappointed not finding him dead that I cried. This was a standing joke with him and he used to embarrass me before his Texas friends by telling it.

"Incidentally the telegram should have read, 'Uncle Ned *said* you may come home.'"

The Colonel got his first taste of Florida in 1923 and liked it so well he returned the following year. Because E. H. R. Green didn't travel like the ordinary rich, preparations for the trip kept Marshall busy for weeks in advance.

"It took two private railroad cars to handle the Colonel, his masseuse, valet, chauffeur, stamp and coin secretaries, Mrs. Green, Mrs. Stafford and their personal maids, and a half-dozen of the Colonel's protégées," the secretary said. "Then we needed a baggage car to handle all the luggage.

"The Colonel never traveled with less than forty trunks. In addition to his clothing and medicine (and this took one trunk) he carried his collections with him. Then all the others had luggage. It was like getting an army on the march.

"That second year we stopped off at Jacksonville and picked up a houseboat the Colonel ordered. He named this one the *Colonel*. It was the biggest one I ever saw, bigger even than the

223

Day Dream. We couldn't get her through the canal after we left Jacksonville and had to come back there and go down to Miami Beach on the ocean."

Ned took possession of another of his acquisitions when he arrived at Miami Beach.

"When we checked into the Royal Palms," Marshall said, "the Colonel was notified that a new car he bought had just arrived. It was a special job, all hand-tooled by Nicholas Rommelfanger, a Boston automotive designer. I don't remember the cost exactly but I think it was twenty thousand dollars. It was powered by a twelve-cylinder Packard special motor. There was a glass roof and an inside toilet.

"The car got to be the most familiar in Miami and Miami Beach. Every cop knew it. They gave the Colonel extra privileges; he could park double, and had the right of way over everything except a fire engine. They gave him a title too, 'Deputy Commissioner.' As soon as he'd reach Florida he'd stop the car at every corner and shake hands with the traffic cop. Then he'd present him with a twenty-dollar gold piece. When he'd be ready to go north again, he'd come around again and give them another twenty dollars."

Hotel life palled and the Colonel bought two adjacent lots on Star Island, one of which contained the abandoned Yacht Club. Star Island was one of a number of artificial islands built in the early '20s by pumping earth from the bottom of Biscayne Bay. It was a kind of feudal principality and access could be gained only via a carefully guarded causeway and bridge.

Would-be buyers were carefully screened and limited to white Protestants wealthy enough to build a small palace and maintain a yacht at least 100 feet in length. The Colonel passed all tests. His land, at the end of the island, commanded the best view on the Bay. On a clear day, Ned Green and his neighbors could see Al Capone, only a short distance away.

Before he left Florida for the North, Ned approved plans to convert the Yacht Club into a fitting residence for himself and his entourage. Construction was begun at once. Mabel, Uncle Ned, and his protégées spent their usual summer at Round Hills. Mary, her period of mourning for the late Fred Stafford ended, was engaged to marry young Billy Moore, son of Dinty Moore, the famous New York restaurateur.

Ned grew bored with radio. He learned that attempts were being made to transform the old Howland whaler, the *Charles W. Morgan,* into a museum and present it to the City of New Bedford.

"I owned her, or at least twenty-nine thirty-seconds of her," recalled Harry A. Neyland, a South Dartmouth artist, "and I agreed to give the ship to New Bedford if they would guarantee a fund for maintenance. Also if I could get enough people to pay out all of my shares except one. The first man I called on was Colonel Green.

"After all, I felt he'd have a stronger interest in the vessel than anybody, inasmuch as the *Morgan* was owned by Isaac Howland, Jr., and Edward Mott Robinson.

"He got real excited and wanted to go right over to see the whaler, which was lying in a wharf at Fairhaven across the river. The ship was in pretty bad condition but the Colonel insisted on seeing as much of her as he could even with his bad leg. We rolled him up the gangplank in his wheel chair and he stayed aboard all that day.

"Next morning he was waiting at my studio at half past eight and said he had not slept a wink all night, thinking this thing over.

" 'I want to buy her,' he said. I told him the *Morgan* was not for sale but that he could purchase up to ten shares. He told me he wasn't interested in that. Well, he fooled around for a couple of weeks and in the meantime I got rid of all the shares except one, which I kept for myself.

"Finally the Colonel decided to come in. If the City of New Bedford refused to pay for maintenance, he said he'd pay all expenses for refitting the ship, salaries of a captain and a crew of six, and set up the *Morgan*. It had to be at Round Hills, though.

"Of course the City of New Bedford refused to pay for anything so we took the Colonel up on his offer and John Bullard drew up the papers. We called the project 'Whaling Enshrined' and moved the *Morgan* to Round Hills. There the Colonel set up the whole works, ship, countinghouse, oil refinery, cooper shop, and everything else pertaining to whaling. While the Colonel didn't own a single share of the ship he paid for everything else and before the first year of 'Whaling Enshrined' ended we drew about thirty thousand visitors."

Uncle Ned spent the summer in a wheel chair near the *Morgan*. On September 17 he attended the wedding of Mrs. Stafford and Mr. Moore in New York. Following a brief honeymoon, the bride and groom moved into the Greens' Waldorf suite. There they remained until Bill and Mabel quarreled and the gentleman struck his hostess on the jaw. The blow resulted in Moore's immediate banishment from the Waldorf and separation from his bride. Mary, her devotion to Mrs. Green stronger than her loyalty to her husband, stayed on. A divorce followed soon after and Mary was free once more.

Chapter Thirty-seven

ARCHITECTS and builders worked for almost two years before Ned was satisfied with the design and construction of his new Star Island house. Meanwhile, during the Colonel's annual Florida visits, he and his entourage lived aboard the *Pioneer*, another of his palatial houseboats, which had been used by President Harding when the Chief Executive was in Southern waters with his Teapot Dome cronies.

Ned was feeling better than he had for a while and attributed his improved health to Florida's sun. He heard that Sylvia was not well and invited her to come south.

"Dear Sylvia B.," he wrote on February 2, 1925. "I've just learned you had a very bad attack of laryngitis. Since leaving New York, January 2, we have not seen a day down here when the temperature was below 72. . . . The roses and all the flowers are in bloom. The motto here is: 'It is always June in Miami.'

"You will remember that in New York your bad brother told you that you would have to quit suffering from throat trouble in the future. We have room to take care of you here and you can take a train and in two days be where your throat will not trouble you. As I am writing this letter the thermometer stands at 76.

"Hereafter your brother is going to insist on your coming down to Florida during February and March. . . . If you come once, you will come every year. Drop me a line and tell me how you are getting along. You are always welcome here and I will see that you are properly cared for.

"Your loving brother,

"Ned."

Apparently Sylvia preferred laryngitis to Mabel and never accepted her brother's invitation to visit him either on the *Pioneer* or at Star Island.

Unlike the Round Hills house, which servants nicknamed "Alcatraz" because of its forbidding exterior and its proximity to the gray Atlantic, 46 Star Island was a cheerful, sunlit mansion, only a few yards from the bright blue waters of Biscayne Bay. The architecture was glistening white Spanish mission, and the house was surrounded by a magnificent garden dotted with hundreds of royal palms. Wide windows and French doors on every side looked out on myriads of perpetually flowering tropical plants.

There was a large central living room, two stories in height. To the east was a wing that contained a room used for showing moving pictures. To the rear of the projector was a vault containing the Colonel's library of pornographic films, which experts considered the world's choicest.

Four balconies opened off the second-floor rooms in the east wing. Every bedroom had its own sitting room and bath. Several of the baths were especially designed by the Colonel himself, according to James A. Dixon, one of Florida's most distinguished lawyers, who represented the Green interests in that state.

"Each 'throne,'" explained Dixon, "was mounted on a pedestal about eight inches over the floor. Thus, unless the user was well over six feet tall, he would be extremely uncomfortable, with his legs dangling in midair. To make matters worse Ned had a full-length mirror installed directly in front of the water closet.

"If there was any way to make a man feel humble all he had to do was to use this toilet. That was Ned's general idea of knocking piety into the stuffed shirts who annoyed him. He made sure they were assigned rooms with these peculiar baths."

To the distress of his neighbors, Colonel Green opened the grounds of 46 Star Island to the children of Miami and Miami Beach every Easter.

"They flocked in by the thousands," recalled F. Lowry Wall, President of the Miami Beach National Bank and one of Ned's friends. "He would hide hundreds of eggs all over the estate and he himself would hand each kid a basket. Then on a given signal he'd turn them loose.

"It was some sight! The children would be scrambling all over the lot; digging up plants, knocking down flowers, climbing the palms, and generally raising hell. But Ned didn't give a damn. He loved to see the kids having fun and after all he had about twenty gardeners to take care of the havoc the next morning.

"But the neighbors! They were wild. They used to barricade their homes that day and put guards at the gates. They called on the Colonel and argued with him but he told them off. Said it was his place and if they didn't like it they could move over to Al Capone's.

"Ned was so goddamned inconsistent. Those Easter lawn parties must have cost him ten thousand dollars to replace trees and flowers damaged or destroyed every year. But try and collect more than a hundred dollars from him for some charity like the Red Cross or Salvation Army!"

The Colonel enjoyed the fanfare he caused every July by his return to Massachusetts. A preliminary step was to telegraph his hour of arrival to Joe Epstein, a New Bedford *Times* reporter (now the *Standard-Times*). With John Bullard and former

Mayor Charles S. Ashley, Joe formed the Colonel's tiny circle of Round Hills intimates.

"The guy really made news," Epstein recalled. "It was almost all I could do to keep up with him the minute I got that wire. You know, New Bedford's a pretty conservative town and the sight of two loaded private Pullmans and a baggage car coming into the station was something to watch. The depot'd be filled with people.

"First the Colonel would emerge and wave to me. He knew I'd be there. If he was well enough he'd limp down from the vestibule with a cane. Or if he wasn't up to that his valet and chauffeur would put a ramp against the car and wheel him down. Then came Mabel, dressed to kill. There'd be a couple nurses in uniform and the Colonel's masseuse, 'private secretaries,' his regular one, Walter Marshall, Mabel's personal maid, and anywhere from six to a dozen 'wards.'

"The servants traveled in the second car and they'd pile out from that. He always took thirty from Round Hills to Star Island every year. The town would really hum the moment Colonel Green got here. He did most of his buying in New Bedford for Round Hills and the boats. Food, gasoline, equipment, etc., and they were no small items. With his household staff, outside workers and crew I'd say he employed well over two hundred people. All these would do their own buying here, too."

In addition to the large quantities of supplies needed for Round Hills and the "Green mosquito fleet," Ned made many personal purchases, including diamonds and other precious stones.

"He had a favorite jeweler," Joe continued. "This guy would pay ten per cent to anyone who'd steer the Colonel into his store. One of Green's trusted employees made himself a small fortune just on commissions. But don't think the Colonel didn't know what was going on. It was just that he didn't give a damn. Money didn't mean to him what it did to ordinary people. For the Colonel it was a kind of commodity, like he had a huge bin full of cash and regarded it as so much sand. No matter how much he shoveled out there was always more left than when he started.

"He couldn't spend it all and he wouldn't give it away. Even if he lost a million dollars it wouldn't have mattered. I'll tell you a joke he played with his money and jewels once. When he'd send his stuff from Florida to Massachusetts he had somebody get him a couple of cardboard cartons, the kind they have in grocery stores. He stuffed these full of jewels and cash, maybe a half a million dollars in large bills and that much in diamonds. Then he tied up the cartons with twine and sent them by ordinary express.

"A couple of days after, when they were on their way, the Colonel called the main office of the express company and got to the executives. He said he was a friend of Colonel Green and told them what that crazy fellow had done. Well, the express company went nuts trying to trace the packages before anybody else found out what was inside of them.

"Can you imagine what would have happened if word leaked out that there were a couple of packages with a million bucks' worth of cash and diamonds in them? The express company's whole system would have been shot to hell. Trouble shooters followed the route of the cardboard boxes all the way from Star Island to New Bedford. Do you know where they were finally found? In a delivery truck on its way out to Round Hills. It was parked outside of a diner. The driver was inside having a hamburger."

In August of 1925 the Colonel grew alarmed at his deteriorating health. He asked Dr. Pascal to come to Round Hills and, if the physician wished, bring his wife with him.

"It was the first time I'd met Colonel Green," Mrs. Pascal recalled. "He was seated in a wheel chair on the terrace and he greeted us quite cordially. At least I think he did. You could hardly hear what he was saying because of the noise of a blimp which was flying right over our heads.

"At the same time there was some kind of mad scramble on the other side of the porch. I looked around and saw a dozen young girls dash down the steps, hop into little runabouts, and take off. I didn't know what this was all about until later although Henry had prepared me to expect anything.

"It was an extremely hot day and it had taken us about eight hours to get to Round Hills. I wanted to go to my room for a shower and a change of clothing before dinner but our host would have none of that. The first thing we did was take a ride in the blimp. This was his hobby that summer. We didn't go very high up but I was scared to death looking down from the gondola. It seemed like we were miles above the ground.

"We had a wonderful view of Round Hills. It was a magnificent place but terribly depressing. I suppose what made it still more depressing was to have to spend an evening with Mrs. Green."

While the doctor was giving his patient a checkup, the duties of hostess fell upon Mabel.

"For me, it was an evening of utter boredom," Mrs. Pascal said. "We sat there for three hours. I didn't know what to talk about. I tried books, music, theatre, politics, cooking, and I got no response at all. When I stopped talking there was complete silence. She just sat there, totally emotionless, and I was so bored I could hardly keep awake.

"Finally, later that evening, Mrs. Green suddenly perked up at the sound of some distant whistle. She leaped out of her chair and ran to the window. 'Look!' she said. 'It's the New Bedford boat. I watch for it every night before I go to bed.' It was quite sad. This was Mrs. Green's big moment. 'Now we can go to bed,' she said."

Ned remained at Round Hills longer than usual the summer of 1925 and was still there on October 30, when he wrote to Dr. Pascal.

"My pulse has remained at 80 and I am continuing to take one drop of digitalis every night. . . . I am eating with fairly good appetite and not restricting my diet to any particular line. . . .

"If you have any suggestions to make, I will try to carry them out. Yours very truly, E. H. R. Green."

Dr. Pascal said he had one important suggestion.

"I told him to quit using Bromo Seltzer. He was taking about fourteen a day and fast developing acetanilic poisoning. This was causing all manner of complications and affecting his system generally. I couldn't make him stop. Everybody around him tried—nurses, masseuses, Marshall, and the young ladies—but somehow he'd sneak them in. It was a shame, too. He was a very intelligent man otherwise with a wide range of conversation and some damned sensible opinions."

Ned grew weary of his Goodyear blimp and "Whaling Enshrined" and took a fling at aviation. He built an airport at Round Hills and set up a training school operated by Bert and Priscilla Hill, both of whom were skilled pilots. The Colonel paid all expenses, which, according to Bert, were far in excess of what was necessary.

"He had some wild ideas of economy," Hill recalled. "For example, I might tell him we needed a tractor for the field. He'd look at me over the top of his glasses, the way he did, and ask me if I *really* needed one, and I'd say, 'Sure, I wouldn't say so otherwise,' and he'd say, 'All right. I'll take care of it.'

"A couple weeks later I'd hear a hell of a roar, look out of the classroom window, and see a dozen tractors jogging up the road. I'd be sure there was a mistake and I 'd hunt up the Colonel. I'd say, 'For God's sake, what's all this about?' This would be his answer:

"'I was checking tractor prices in town. One Caterpillar cost thirty-eight hundred dollars but the dealer told me if I bought a dozen the price would be twenty-seven hundred dollars apiece. Do you realize that's a saving of eleven hundred dollars a tractor?'

"There was no use trying to explain that one Caterpillar would last us a lifetime. He did the same thing with everything else. I'd need maybe fifty gallons of flat paint, which cost two dollars a gallon. I'd tell the Colonel and before I knew what happened a truck would be up unloading a carload of paint from a New Bedford railroad siding. Sure, he bought the paint for a dollar a can. But he never figured what the hell we'd do with two or three thousand gallons left over."

Chapter Thirty-eight

Sʏʟᴠɪᴀ became a widow on August 4, 1926. Matty's passing was accomplished modestly and his obituaries were correspondingly brief.

"Matthew Astor Wilks died . . . at his home, 7 West 81st Street," said the New York *Herald Tribune.* "He formerly lived in Galt, Ontario. He was a member of the University, Metropolitan, Badminton, Turf and Field, Fencers, Knickerbocker, New York Yacht Clubs and the A.A.A. He is survived by his widow, Mrs. H. Sylvia Ann Howland Robinson Green Wilks. . . ."

Mrs. Wilks was richer by $1,500,000. Less than three weeks before, she and Ned each had come into about $60,000,000, their share of the trust fund that ended on the tenth anniversary of Hetty's death.

Sylvia, who had depended on her gentle husband to make all decisions for the past eighteen years, at once turned to Ned for advice.

"Dear Princess," he answered on August 24. "I do not think it a good plan for a lady to live by herself. I think you should move into an apartment but do not take a long lease. Be careful of your neighbors. . . . I don't see anything to prevent your living in New York since you pay your personal taxes there anyway.

"Why don't you come up and visit Uncle Ned and his goats? You want to remember that you are always welcome at Round hills. . . .

"With lots of love,

"Your affectionate brother, 'Prince' Ned."

Sylvia took her brother's suggestion, closed her house on West 81st Street, and moved into a twenty-room duplex at 988 Fifth Avenue. She did not accept the invitation to visit Round Hills, although she could have had the "Ruth Lawrence Room," which had become permanently vacant.

"Miss Ruth Lavinia Lawrence, daughter of William M. Lawrence, Jackson Heights, Long Island, and Stuart M. Briggs, of New Bedford, will be married at 6:30 this evening in Old Trinity Episcopal Church," declared the New York *Times* on October 23. "Miss Lawrence graduated from Wellesley last Spring. She is a ward of Colonel E. H. R. Green. . . ."

Only Mabel represented the family; Ned stayed home. "He was angry with me," Mrs. Briggs admitted, "and did not approve of Stuart."

Ned grew despondent about his health and depressed over the sale of the Texas Midland, which lost its identity on May 10 when it became part of the Southern Pacific. The Colonel, no longer a railroad president, left Star Island earlier than usual, spent a month at Marlin Springs and two weeks at the Waldorf, and arrived at Round Hills on July 1, as usual.

By then he had recovered his health and spirits sufficiently to resign from the swank Wamsutta Club because it expelled a friend of Mayor Ashley's, to entertain his new protégée, a sixteen-year-old Fort Worth redhead, and to activate another hobby, "fog dispersement," and with it the promotion of air safety.

Ned's neighbors were alarmed by justifiable fears of something else being added to the prevailing turmoil of Round Hills and spilling over to their own snug summer retreats. They also were disturbed by one of the Colonel's practical jokes, which they took seriously. Green told Joe Epstein to spread the word that WMAF would construct a 1,000-foot tower and increase its wattage to 50,000.

"If this were done," Joe explained, "we'd be able to hear music merely by turning on our water faucets. You can hardly blame Ned's neighbors for heeding the most preposterous rumors about him because so many of his remote contingencies became facts."

On advice of counsel, Ned made the effort to explain his interest in aviation and to allay some of his neighbors' fears. His letter to Mrs. Texas (her real name) Brooks, chairwoman of a committee of troubled South Dartmouth summer residents, is indicative of the Colonel's vision.

"My dear Madam," Ned wrote. "I think I should endeavor to prove that I am not such a menace as unconfirmed reports would make me appear. Only the other day I read in the paper the following headline: 'Salter's Point and Nonquitt Declare War on Colonel Green.' Not true! My thought has always been to do things which would tend to elevate mankind.

"With some others I decided that research in fighting fog should be started. . . . I do not believe much can be done in aviation until flying through fog has been made safe. I sincerely think that in long flights across the country, and especially across the Atlantic, there is a great field for the airplane and now is the time to make it as popular as the automobile.

"In the event of war I think the welfare of our country lies in the air, and to be successful we should be able to control man in the air by radio communication."

236

Ned turned over wmaf, his airfield, several buildings adjacent to Round Hills, and some cash to Massachusetts Institute of Technology. Professor Henry G. Houghton, an eminent meteorologist and Director of M.I.T.'s Department of Meteorology, was placed in charge of fog experiments; Howard A. Chinn, an M.I.T. aeronautics engineer (now Chief Engineer for C. B. S.), was appointed Resident Manager, and assigned to short-wave study; and the Hills did the test flying.

"It was a fair setup," Professor Houghton recalled, "and I think we accomplished something of lasting value. Results of our studies in 'cloud physics,' the technical name for what we were doing, are still quoted in scientific magazines. But we didn't accomplish enough although Professor Edward L. Bowles, of the School's Department of Electrical Engineering, who was largely responsible for arousing Green's interest, did his best to get us sufficient funds.

"What we really lacked was operating money. M.I.T. paid all our salaries and the Colonel gave us a place to work and to live but he didn't give us the funds he led us to expect. He'd hand us amounts up to ten thousand dollars, which you might call a 'good-sized drop in the bucket.' And it came in irregularly. We needed ten times as much and we needed to know when it was coming in so that we could plan accordingly.

"I'm afraid that basically the Colonel was a scientific dilettante with little knowledge or curiosity. It seemed to me he evinced a great deal more interest in his collection of coins, jewels, stamps, and 'protégées' than in what we were doing.

"What he enjoyed more than anything else was a sense of movement about him. He liked to see things being built. He liked to be surrounded by people. He enjoyed more than anything else the idea of construction and would watch for hours while something was being torn down and something else erected in its place.

"Every afternoon, when the Colonel was at Round Hills, he would 'hold court' in his little electric car. None of us was able to

237

have sustained conversations with him—too many interruptions from people trying to get something from the Colonel. My relations with Green were pleasant but aloof and the only times I went into the mansion were to discuss finances. We had no social contacts whatsoever."

Chinn shares some but not all of Professor Houghton's opinions about the Colonel and was closer to Ned than his colleague.

"The Colonel was a pretty bright guy," Chinn said, "despite the fact that he had little scientific knowledge. We had many conversations and he'd ask really intelligent questions, based on good lay scientific reading. For example, he'd say to me, 'Why can't I hear New York radio programs directly here, and why can't something be done about it?'

"Then I'd try to frame uncomplicated answers so that a layman such as the Colonel would understand. But he couldn't maintain his interest in one idea for long and he'd veer from project to project. I remember once, we'd concluded a long talk on short wave and I thought he was absorbing what I said.

"Suddenly he looked up at me and said, 'Howard, do you know how to build a tennis court?' This was scarcely my 'discipline' and I said, 'No, but if you want I'll find out.' He said, 'O.K. Go ahead; build me a couple.' I did.

"But for what Professor Houghton and the rest of us were trying to accomplish we were terribly short of money. What we got just dribbled in. And it was hard to get through to the Colonel. He was surrounded by scoundrels, some of whom had to be bribed merely to reach him. I think he knew it but at this stage of the game I don't think he gave a damn.

"I used to go up to Round Hills frequently for lunch. It wasn't very pleasant. There seemed to be little communication between Ned and his wife, and practically no social life except when Mrs. Green would entertain an occasional guest. The Colonel was extremely lonely."

The Colonel grew lonelier that September when Mary Stafford made her final departure from the Green houshold.

"I'd had it," she said. "Poor Ned was sick and losing interest. Mabel was drinking a lot, and Round Hills was going to pot. The hired help was divided into teams, one for Mabel and one for the Colonel. The squawking was terrible. I'd known Ned for a long time and I hated to walk out on him again, but what could I do?

"We said good-by on September 15 and two days later I sailed for Europe. I stayed there a good many years. I never saw Ned again."

The colonel made efforts to assuage his loneliness.

"My dear Elizabeth," he wrote to a protégée on October 21, 1929. "Delay in replying to your letter has been due to waiting for the picture you requested. I have at last received some and am sending you one under separate cover. . . .

"As you know I am now at the Sherry-Netherlands since they tore down the old Waldorf. I was the last tenant there.

"Your Uncle Ned is always very glad to have his girls call on him, any time, and bring their little girl friends with them. Just let him know and he will have a car meet them at the station."

Chapter Thirty-nine

A new life began for Mabel in 1930. She became the darling of Miami society and was listed in the Blue Book. Her parties in the Star Island house or in a Mississippi showboat the Colonel bought and rebuilt at a cost of $300,000 were the most popular on "the Beach." Mabel limited her drinking to an occasional highball; discharged all servants not on her team, thereby establishing household order; became a patron of an excellent modiste; and in general played the part of the charming, well-behaved wife of Florida's wealthiest resident. No one knew her background.

"Even if we had," admitted a contemporary who regards Miami's *haut monde* with considerable cynicism, "I think we still would have accepted her. Wealth is our common denominator.

That was particularly true in the twenties and thirties. We were 'first generation,' without the few hundred years of breeding you find in Boston or Philadelphia. We'd accept anybody with money: Presbyterians, Methodists, or even Baptists. It didn't matter if a man's wife had been a stenographer, choir singer, or waitress, just so long as we didn't actually *know*. Naturally, you had to be a Protestant.

"Mostly everybody was a transplanted Midwesterner. The hill-billies went to Los Angeles. We got the 'better class' Okies in Miami and Miami Beach. We had all the inhibitions and self-terrifying insecurities developed in our native states. As soon as our rolls were filled we ruthlessly mowed down all others left at the gate. Sinclair Lewis would have loved us."

A perusal of Miss Jefferson Bell's well-read society column, which appeared daily in the Miami *Herald,* reveals the extent of Mabel's acceptance by the community's elite. Scores of items appear in which Mrs. E. H. R. Green is either a hostess or guest of honor during the season. A condensation of a few of these stories follows:

March 10, 1930: "Colonel and Mrs. E. H. R. Green entertained a number of Central and South American diplomats at their Island home on 'Cuban Goodwill Day.'"

April 4, 1930: "Colonel and Mrs. E. H. R. Green gave a luncheon for 80 guests at their Star Island home. The guest of honor was Mrs. William Bartlett."

March 27, 1931: "Mr. and Mrs. Richard Massey gave a large garden party. The guest of honor was Mrs. E. H. R. Green."

April 16, 1931: "Mrs. Harrison Brentley gave a tea party in honor of Mrs. E. H. R. Green."

As if documentary evidence of Mabel's stratospheric social position were not enough by itself, the Miami *Herald's* society editor added a clincher.

"At teas, other than her own," Miss Bell declared, "Mrs. Green usually poured."

While it is likely that neither Mrs. Vincent Astor nor Mr. Ward

McAllister would have considered the distance between a Chicago bordello and the heights of Miami society much of a climb, others more tolerant surely would have regarded Mabel's self-developed eminence as quite an accomplishment.

The world that took Mabel to its bosom was patriarchal, and that may have helped. Its leaders were and are Lino L. Sertel, who determines *Blue Book* eligibility, and Alfred I. Barton, Vice President and operating head of the swank Miami Beach Surf Club. Barton is a sophisticate who views his fellow man's struggle for social recognition with amusement. His opinion of Mabel comes as something of a shock to those who followed her career.

"Mabel," he recalled, "reminded me of a retired schoolteacher, rather severe-looking and quite prim, almost the New England type. Mother and I met her a few years after the Greens came to Florida. Mother liked Mabel at once and in a sense was her sponsor. I think she felt sorry for Mrs. Green. The Colonel, on the other hand, didn't appeal to us at all. His relations with his wife weren't particularly pleasant. The few times we saw them together he either spoke roughly to her or ignored her.

"We knew nothing of Mrs. Green's background. As a matter of fact, it's a surprise to find she wasn't reared quite properly, with a limited education, of course, but considerable surface polish. She didn't say much, but she was an excellent listener. She rarely swore, only an infrequent polite 'damn.' We often wondered about her romance with the Colonel. We were curious as to why she remained with him in the light of his attitude toward her and the tales we heard about his fascination with young ladies."

According to the story Mabel spread among her new Miami friends, Hetty was anxious to see Ned married to a "nice" girl because she had heard her son was running around with fast Chicago women.

"I suppose I was the first 'nice' girl Ned ever met," Mabel told Mrs. Barton. "When my future mother-in-law was introduced to me she said she'd give her son two hundred and fifty thousand dollars if I'd marry him. I accepted. Then they tricked me into signing away all my rights."

Mabel's version of the marriage was believed.

"We all went out of our way to be kind to her," Barton said, "and accepted invitations to her parties, which were huge but rather fun. In Philadelphia and Boston they long ago abandoned these vast, expensive affairs, but you have to realize Miami Beach is a 'pioneer' town. Then, too, those were Prohibition days and we were wild and young. Mrs. Green, herself, drank sparingly but didn't put a damper on others."

A well-remembered affair was Mabel's St. Patrick's Day Ball, held March 18, 1930.

"It was the biggest job we ever had for a party," recalled Eugene Franklin Holland, a Miami electrical contractor. "We strung seven thousand five hundred lights all over the grounds, in the palms and around the driveway and so on, along the boats and dock. The bulbs were all green and they went on to the showboat and the others.

"Then we built a huge electric shamrock in front of the house. I guess it was higher than the house itself. You never saw anything like it: designers worked on that shamrock for a couple of months ahead. Our bill for lighting alone ran close to ten thousand dollars for that one night."

Another Miami business to profit by this event was the catering firm of Mrs. Margaret H. Allen.

"That St. Paddy's Day party was the most elaborate affair ever held in Miami, before or after," Mrs. Allen said. "There were at least three hundred couples present. We furnished nothing but the best. Our flower bill alone came to over two thousand two hundred dollars. We brought in a staff of ninety-five in extra help. This was not counting Mrs. Green's own servants.

"Vintage champagne was served in almost every room in the house. There was dancing on the terrace and on the boats and on the lawn. About eleven o'clock a troupe of Irish players performed from the stage of the showboat."

The cast placed no strain on the intellect of Mrs. Green or her six hundred guests.

"It seemed to me," Mrs. Allen continued, "all they played was 'The Harp That Once Through Tara's Hall,' and 'Killarney,' and the acting was nothing more than Irish jigs, clogs, and reels."

The Colonel was present at most of his wife's parties but was rarely visible.

"When we did the plantings on Green's Star Island grounds and floral treatments inside the mansion," recalled James Donn, a Miami landscape gardener, "the Colonel asked us to fix him up a place where he could watch what was going on and no one would know. We built a concealed niche on the balcony. Here, I understand, he would sit for hours and watch all his guests dancing and having fun and never show himself."

Mrs. Allen, too, remembered Ned's sanctuary.

"The night of the St. Paddy's party, Mrs. Green asked me if I'd mind bringing the Colonel's dinner up to him," Mrs. Allen said. "I told her I'd be glad to. I'd wondered where he was. She took me to one side and pointed out the spot where to find him. It was behind a permanent floral decoration on the balcony.

"He was seated in a big armchair all by himself. He smiled and thanked me for serving him. I stayed up there for a while and he complimented me on everything and told me I deserved a wreath. There's no reason for me to remember but Lanin's orchestra was playing 'The Girl I Can't Forget,' and the Colonel said it was one of his favorites.

"After a while I thought I'd better go down and check on everything so I excused myself and said good night. It was sort of sad. I couldn't understand why he wasn't with his guests instead of hiding. It didn't make sense."

The same year that Mabel renewed her zest for living, the Colonel began to take less and less interest in outside activities. He no longer went to Terrell to vote nor did he visit Dallas, where he used to enjoy reminiscing with his old cronies. He stopped building ships and houses and spent more hours in sedentary hobbies—the further acquisition of jewels, coins, and stamps. By this time expert philatelists declared that the Green collection was one of the world's greatest, exceeded in size and value only by King George's.

Ned's most valuable stamps were the famous "inverted air mails." He acquired these in 1918 when he first began his collection and their value constantly increased. Wealthy philatelists— kings, maharajas, princes, and multimillionaires—from all over the world besieged him with offers to buy. But the Colonel, having no need for money, refused to sell. However, in 1930 he indicated his willingness to dispose of this set, which is to philatelists as the Hope Diamond is to gemmologists.

Many stories have been told about the inverted air mails and Ned's acquisition of them, but the one accepted by most philatelists was related by Willard Snyder, a well-known Philadelphia dealer who made a study of the Colonel's stamps and coins.

"On May 13, 1918, a young man named W. T. Robey came into the New York Avenue branch of the Washington, D. C., post office to buy some air-mail stamps," Snyder said. "A clerk pulled out a sheet of stamps and handed it to Robey, who in turn gave the clerk twenty-four dollars, the cost of a hundred stamps.

"Almost simultaneously the clerk, who knew a great deal about stamps, and Robey, who knew enough, noticed something amiss with these. The clerk made a grab for them, but the customer was quicker and jerked them away. He said he'd paid for them, refused to give them up, and walked out of the building.

"As soon as Robey got around the corner he looked at his buy and discovered that the plane in the center was upside down. He must have felt like the guy who discovered the Comstock Lode. At the time nobody knew how many of these irregular stamps were in circulation but dealers believed there couldn't have been many because the error was obvious; it was a first run, and they had just been put on sale.

"As it turned out there were only four hundred and they never should have left the Government Printing Office. We don't know what happened to the other three sheets but we do know the history of Robey's buy. Robey, acting on the advice of Percy McGraw Mann, then an Eastern philatelist and publisher, sold the set to Eugene Klein, a Philadelphia dealer, for fifteen thousand dollars. That was a neat profit for Robey and must have started a million kids collecting stamps.

"Colonel Green heard about the stamps and offered Klein a fast two-thousand-dollar profit. Klein held out for three thousand dollars more and sold the stamps to Green, on May 21, 1918, for twenty thousand dollars. The Colonel took out the choice 'positions' from the sheet and hung on to them for years. He made a smart move when he decided to sell his stamps individually. By doing this he created a market where none existed.

"He kept the prime positions, including the center line block. These were the most valuable. He numbered every one of the stamps lightly in pencil on the back so that a buyer would know the exact position his stamp held on the set. This is important to philatelists. The Colonel now had for disposal nineteen straight-edge stamps and the rest with perforations. Perforations make a stamp worth more. He put them on the market and they were grabbed up so fast it would take your breath away."

He would like to have a couple himself, Snyder admitted. "What price would they bring in today's market? Oh, at least twelve thousand dollars apiece," he said.

Many philatelists claimed that Ned bore the ignominy of being a hoarder rather than collector. Norris Barratt, a Philadelphia attorney and philatelist who owns some of the Green collection, believes the Colonel squandered much of his money buying stamps he didn't need or want.

"The Colonel would come in to a dealer here in Philadelphia or on Nassau Street in New York," said Barratt. "He'd look over the stock for a few hours, then ask the owner, 'How much do you want for everything you've got?' If Green thought the price was right and if he was in the mood he'd say, 'All right. Wrap it up.' Then he'd unpeel cash from his pocket and go out with the dealer's entire stock in his possession.

246

"That's no way to collect. I'd call that hoarding."

Snyder had a further criticism.

"The trouble," Snyder said, "was that Green was purchasing more rapidly than he could absorb. What used to make collectors furious and jealous was that the Colonel could and did buy almost anything he really wanted. But he knew his values and I'd put him in the category of 'greats,' both in philately and numismatics. You'll find in their pedigree that many famous stamps bear the notation, 'From the Colonel E. H. R. Green Collection.'

"What also bothered collectors was that he hung on to almost everything even when he had a complete monopoly. Take the 1913 'Liberty head' nickels. If you were a coin collector when you were a kid you must have seen ads in magazines which read: 'Will pay up to ten thousand dollars for a 1913 Liberty head nickel.'

"Naturally, kids went nuts examining five-cent pieces wherever they saw them. That ad probably was placed by Colonel Green as a practical joke. The truth is that 1913 was the year the 'Buffalo' nickel was minted and there weren't supposed to be any more Liberty heads. But five and *only* five were minted and these were illegal. The Colonel owned them all. I don't think he meant to be cruel and I don't believe he was when he placed that ad. He was simply having fun, providing excitement and creating lots of new collectors.

"Nobody knows what the Colonel paid for the nickels but the 1962 catalogues list them at forty thousand dollars each."

By 1930 Ned was spending most of his time in a wheel chair. His use of patent medicines made frequent blood transfusions necessary. He became friendly with his donors and paid them well. To one, Thomas J. McCann, a New Bedford fireman, the Colonel spoke longingly of his early days in Texas.

"After I gave the Colonel a little more than a quart up in his bedroom at Round Hills, he asked me to sit around and talk to him. He seemed kind of lonesome and I thought this was crazy. Me with a twelve-hundred-dollar-a-year job and him with about fifty million bucks. But he was a very nice fellow and democratic too.

"He asked me about the state of my health and I asked him how he got to be a Colonel. He told me he used to be on the staff of a Texas Governor and I said kiddingly, 'I don't understand how a rock-ribbed Republican like you could get himself in such a position.'

"Well, he smiled and said, 'I guess that's pretty hard to understand but I *belong* in Texas. I used to make them and break them down in the Lone-Star State. That's where my friends are. I wish I was there right now.'"

Each time the Colonel's health failed, Mabel became concerned over her own position if Ned were to die without either dissolving the antenuptial agreement or changing the will in which he left everything to Sylvia. Ned refused to discuss the subject. Mrs. Green grew desperate in the late summer of 1930 and approached Walter Allen, who came up from Terrell to visit his ailing old friend.

"No sooner did I walk in the house," Allen recalled, "when Mabel nabbed me. She was all agitated and she must have been watching for me from the window. She told me Ned was upstairs asleep and would I talk to her about a personal matter.

"I said, 'Sure, go ahead.'

"'Well,' she said, 'I guess the Colonel discussed our antenuptial agreement with you.' I said, 'No, but I'd heard about it.'

"'I guess you know where that leaves me if Ned dies, only eighteen thousand dollars a year.'

"I was thinking to myself, It sure leaves you a damned sight better off than when you started out, but I just nodded my head. She asked me as a special favor would I plead with the Colonel to double the limit and make it thirty-six thousand dollars a year so she could maintain the status she was accustomed to.

"I thought, Lady, you got one hell of a nerve, but I didn't tell her that. I didn't say I would or I didn't say I wouldn't, but believe me I had no intention of butting in on the Colonel's private affairs. I figured he knew exactly what he was doing and if that's what he wanted that was his business, not mine."

In October of that year Dr. Pascal was summoned again. He spent a few days at Round Hills and gave Ned several blood transfusions. Ned's improvement was remarkable and on October 30, Mabel sent Dr. Pascal the following telegram:

"The day before yesterday the Colonel walked into a barber shop. Today he walked from about eight feet inside the front entrance all the way to his car and got in without any assistance whatever. We all say hurrah for Doctor Pascal. Mrs. E. H. R. Green."

The following summer Ned felt well enough to enroll two more protégées and install several slot machines at Round Hills. As evidence of the Colonel's lack of intent to corrupt the morals of minors by introducing them to gambling, the testimony of one of his artless young ladies is offered.

"See, it was like this," recalled a ward, remembered now only as "Snookums," "there was no risk at all. Uncle Ned set up three 'one-armed bandits' in the library but the machines were rigged to pay off at better odds than you could get at any other place in the world. The house take was only thirty per cent with seventy per cent for the 'sucker,' instead of the other way around.

"You couldn't have lost even if you'd put in your own dough. But we didn't have to do that. The Colonel handed each of us a couple of stacks of quarters. We were to keep feeding the bandits until we hit a jackpot. Then we had to go in the other room and 'thank' Uncle Ned. It got tiresome after a while."

While Ned maintained his Sherry-Netherland apartment, he and Mabel were beginning to spend less than a month in Manhattan each year and went there only to buy stamps, coins, precious stones, and to enroll an occasional protégée. He still claimed that he was a citizen of Terrell, Texas, but also was calling himself a "Florida cracker" and stretching his Star Island visits to six months out of every twelve.

Miamians were happy to consider the Colonel one of their

own. They sought his financial help whenever it was needed. He responded and gave fifteen hundred dollars to the Greater Miami 1932 Community Fund and five dollars to the Boy Scouts. For this second ennobling gift Colonel Green became a sustaining member of the Dade County Council, Boy Scouts of America, and was permitted to take the Scout oath in a public ceremony.

The Colonel was even more generous if a request for funds had a particular appeal. When Ann Booker, a twenty-year-old Miami aquatic star, broke her back during a diving exhibition in Vienna in July, 1931, and died in a Miami hospital the following March, Colonel Green paid most of the girl's hospital bills and all of her funeral expenses. The total was over three thousand dollars.

Although the depression of the '30s had increased the purchasing power of the Colonel's dollar enormously, his bounty did not extend to New Bedford. Those who recall that era are not likely to forget the bitterness of 1932, when prosperity, despite promises to the contrary, was not just around the corner and a fair-sized portion of our citizenry was in imminent danger of genteel or indecorous starvation. Those were the days when apples made their appearance along Main Street, when thousands of Negro women milled about Harlem's dollar-a-day "slave markets," and hundreds of American cities issued "scrip" to pay their bills and to feed, clothe, and shelter their desperately poor.

New Bedford was in sad financial straits. Schoolteachers, police, and other public servants had not been paid for months and relief funds were exhausted. The city in which the Howland fortune was built appealed to its wealthiest son for help. Ned's answer was reported without comment in the Boston *Herald*, March 18, 1932.

"Colonel Green telegraphed from his winter home at Star Island today that he would be unable to aid New Bedford as he had been asked to," said the *Herald*. " 'Very sorry but at present time impossible for me to assist New Bedford in sale of temporary loan notes.' "

Ned's refusal to help New Bedford was received indignantly by many of that community's citizens.

"This was the kind of action that caused the people of New Bedford to believe that Colonel E. H. R. Green had no interest in the city or in its future. He was never a popular personality in his home town, and he did not share in its problems," commented Charles J. Lewin, Editor and General Manager of the New Bedford *Standard-Times* and a civic leader.

"The number of persons who benefited by generosity at the hands of Colonel Green were few, indeed. He permitted folks to park their automobiles at Round Hill and to listen to broadcasts of outstanding sports and other events; he allowed visitors to swim at his beach and a select few to dip in the pool on his estate.

"But, he did not participate in community, charitable, educational, or cultural events. And, he failed to make any provision to maintain the famous whaleship, Charles W. Morgan, which was enshrined at his estate. The result was that New Bedford lost the Morgan to The Marine Historical Association, Mystic, Connecticut.

"Colonel Green was disinterested in the general welfare of New Bedford."

Chapter Forty

Iɴ September of 1932, the Colonel collapsed while he was riding from South Dartmouth to New Bedford. A local physician
diagnosed the illness as a "mild coronary" and Dr. Pascal confirmed this opinion. Ned was put to bed at Round Hills, where he
remained until October 22. Then he went to Lake Placid at Dr.
Pascal's suggestion. He stayed at the Lake Placid Club until mid-
December when he had recovered sufficiently to spend a few
weeks in New York and make his annual trip to Florida. This
time he traveled without protégées.

At Star Island he did little more than rest, stretched out on a
reclining wheel chair near the water's edge, his Boston terrier,
Stella, by his side. Two or three times a week he had long talks
with Lowry Wall, the Miami banker, and once that year Allen,
McKay, and Ed Kiest went to see him.

Ned did not go to his Sherry-Netherland apartment at all and, instead of stopping off in New York City on the way to Round Hills, he went to Lake Placid, where he stayed for six weeks, arriving at South Dartmouth on July 1, as usual. By October he had recovered sufficiently to worry about dodging process servers.

A United States Senate investigation into the operation of several Manhattan banks uncovered evidence that Albert H. Wiggin, Chairman of the Board of Chase National, had received excessive remuneration and "was not faithful to the trust and confidence reposed in him; and that breaches of trust committed by him during his regime cost the stockholders . . . many millions of dollars."

A number of suits were filed against bank officers and process servers were subpoenaing every Chase Manhattan Director they could locate. Because the Colonel was the richest of all Directors, service on him would have been particularly desirable. But he had to be caught within the borders of New York State. He wrote to his attorney for advice on November 14, 1933.

"Mr. Charles W. Pierson
Alexander and Green
120 Broadway
New York City

"My Dear Mr. Pierson:
"I am in Massachusetts and can remain here for a reasonable length of time, but the weather is getting very cold. I know of no way of getting to Florida without going through the State of New York and going down on the train in our car we will have to go over Hell Gate Bridge and come into the Pennsylvania Station where we would remain for about an hour and a half during the midnight hours. I am open to any suggestions you care to make. . . ."

Pierson's answer the following day enabled the Colonel to proceed south without undue alarm.

"Dear Colonel," wrote the attorney, "I do not suppose anybody is picketing the ports and terminals and as a practical matter I feel reasonably confident that one could pass through the city on a night train without being molested by process servers, providing he did not burn red fire or advertise his plans in the newspapers.

Sincerely yours, Charles W. Pierson."

By 1933 the Colonel's interest in girls was academic. Only precious stones seemed to be able to arouse the Colonel from a state of ennui. Jewelers from all over the East flocked to Florida and tossed their gems on his lap. Between 1930 and 1936 Ned purchased more than $10,000,000 worth of jewelry, most of which was bought while he was sitting in his limousine, double parked on Miami's Flagler Street.

Ned's favorite dealer was H. S. Fischer, of Philadelphia, who followed Green wherever he went and who sold the Colonel about two-thirds of the total. Gemmologists who appraised the Green collection said that while the Colonel was rarely "stuck," few stones were outstanding. Green seemed to enjoy fondling the gems in public, much to the alarm of Miami's Department of Public Safety, aware of the community's rising gangster population. Police were fearful that the sight of the several million dollars' worth of sparkling jewels covering the rear seat of the Colonel's automobile might tempt technically vacationing mobsters to return to work forthwith.

Two brief communications from Ned to his Philadelphia dealer reveal the frequency, quantity and cost of the Colonel's purchases.

June 9, 1934

H. S. Fischer, Inc.,
1242 Widener Building,
Philadelphia, Pa.

Gentlemen:

     I enclose herewith my check No. 3092 on The Chase National Bank for $128,000.00, in payment for the following purchases of jewelry:

February 14, 1934

2 - Loose emerald cut diamonds
    weighing over 200 carats-------$55,000.00
    Less ----------------------------- 5,000.00 $50,000.00

February 22, 1934

Lot 1 Antique Jeweled Elephant
    Six lots of emerald, ruby and
    diamond jeweled necklaces,
    brooches, rings & earrings.

    7 lots ruby necklaces----------$40,000.00
    Less--------------------------- 3,500.00 $36,500.00

February 27, 1934

3 - Lots consisting of 15 emerald,
    ruby and diamond bracelets;
    diamond necklace; genuine em-
    erald & diamond aviator's clip;
    brooches; diamond necklace--- $45,000.00
    Less------------------------- 3,500.00 $41,500.00
                                            $128,000.00

    Please acknowledge receipt.

              Very truly yours,

255

H. S. Fischer, Inc.,
1242 Widener Building,
Philadelphia, Pa.

Gentlemen:

    Enclosed herewith please find my check No. 3117 on The Chase National Bank for $55,000.00, to cover purchase of jewelry as follows:

        March 5, 1934
        Seven lots of jewels, consisting of necklaces, brooches, rings and earrings.
           Rubies, Emeralds and Diamonds.

        Very truly yours,

Another hobby, jigsaw puzzles, tickled the Colonel's fancy in 1933. Men and women old enough to recall the problem of finding inexpensive entertainment during the depression are likely to remember the jigsaw rage that swept the country. Tired of anagrams or poker for matches, a family might get hours of surcease from worry, if not actual pleasure, by attempting to assemble a five-cent puzzle. After the puzzle was finally solved, it was disassembled and exchanged for another from a neighbor.

Ned, however, could afford variety without troubling the folks next door. Just as he acquired stamps, coins, jewels, tractors, ships, and protégées, he bought puzzles. One order he placed with Milton H. Bradley, of Springfield, Massachusetts, called for delivery of 149 pounds of jigsaw puzzles at a cost of $456.00.

But by the following February, it did not look as though Ned would be around long enough to get through many pounds of puzzles. He was examined by Dr. Charles Frederick Roche, a Miami Beach physician, who declared that his patient was suffering from "heart trouble, pernicious anemia, with the condition growing steadily worse."

Green was able to get to Lake Placid in May and to South Dartmouth on July 1. He felt a little better by then and while he added no stamps, coins, or protégées to his collections, he bought a million dollars' worth of precious stones from New Bedford jewelers. He was also able to pick up, at the reduced price of only $1,700, a real bargain which might be of interest to psychologists. This was a whale's penis, fourteen feet in length. Ned had it mounted and placed on the top of the balcony facing the Round Hills doorway. Only a chosen few knew what this trophy really was.

Ned, who must have realized how seriously ill he was, talked to Mr. Bullard about turning Round Hills into (1) an orphanage, (2) a hospital, (3) a home for aged couples, (4), a sailors' retreat, (5) a new M.I.T. project for the development of television. But actually the Colonel did nothing about any of these ideas.

After an absence of almost eight years, the Colonel returned to Texas and tried to recapture his health at Marlin Springs. He arrived there May 13, 1935, and was greeted by most of his surviving Terrell and Dallas cronies—Kiest, McKay, Wells, Allen, and Corley. By this time neither they nor the stimulus of hot Texas air helped.

"The Colonel was in poor shape," Dr. Buie reported. "He slept badly; his blood pressure was very high; he had profound anemia; he was taking liver extract intravenously, and had no appetite. His weight was down to one hundred and twenty-four pounds."

Ned was too ill to accept a dinner invitation he would have enjoyed.

"Dear Colonel," wrote Mr. W. H. Wright, President of the

Terrell Chamber of Commerce, November 19, 1935. "On Tuesday, November 26, County Agents and agricultural leaders will gather from the corners of Texas to pay tribute to you, Walter C. Porter and Dr. S. A. Knapp, commemorating the thirty-second anniversary of the first demonstration farm in the United States.

". . . A monument will be raised paying a lasting tribute to you . . . for the rich heritage you have left in the history of agriculture. . . . It will be a great honor to have you as our guest on that memorable occasion. . . ."

Ned returned to Florida in 1935. He was asked to contribute to the Miami Beach Community Fund by Henry Mangles, an official.

"We talked about what makes a good community," Mangles recollected. "He started to reminisce. He said, 'You know, when I was a young man my mother sent me to Texas to take over one of her railroads. I'd go to a town and ask the citizens what they wanted. Invariably they needed a new depot, or something of the sort.

"'I'd ask them, What have you got in the city that will warrant it? These citizens would say we have fine schools, we have fine churches, fine people, etc. And I'd say, Is that all? Haven't you got any saloons? Haven't you got any gambling houses? Haven't you got any sporting houses? I'd tell them it takes all kinds of people to make a good town and that I'd think it over.

"'Well, Mr. Mangles, I don't have to think over Miami Beach. You qualify. Here's my check for one thousand dollars!'"

Ned paid his last visit to Star Island in 1936. He spent almost all of his time in the wheel chair facing Biscayne Bay, looking at the ships or talking to his few friends.

"I remember one evening very well. I sat with the Colonel," recalled Mark L. Watson, of Miami. "I'd known him only a short while. We'd met in front of the old Post Office Building at the corner of First Street and First Avenue. I was passing by and he was all by himself in his car except for his little dog, Stella. I had one just like this so naturally I stopped to talk.

"Well, the Colonel invited me to see him at Star Island and I did. Late one April day he and I were sitting on the lawn watching two little sailing canoes. He had his dog cuddled up in his arms. The Colonel was very quiet for a while. Then he got a look on his face that was very sad. He seemed like he was tired. The sun was just about setting. He had to go up to the house and I had to go home.

"Maybe what he said was pretty corny, but I never forgot it.

" 'This is really beautiful country, isn't it?' he asked me. 'I just wish I could stick around a little longer. You know, some of it's been fun.' "

Chapter Forty-one

Ned Green never saw Round Hills or Terrell again. He went directly from Star Island to the Lake Placid Club, arriving there on April 28. He was so slight that a single attendant was able to carry him to his room. Ed Kiest came up from Dallas to see his friend, but he was a day too late. Only Mabel was with the Colonel when he breathed his last, June 8, 1936. He was sixty-seven years old.

"His body," said the New York *Times*, "was sent to his eastern home, Round Hills, South Dartmouth, Mass., where a funeral service will be held. Burial will be in Bellows Falls, Vt.

"As one whose life covered a wide range of interests, Colonel Edward Howland Robinson Green became almost as picturesque a figure in the United States as his mother, Mrs. Hetty Green, eccentric financier. His name was associated with railroads, radios, television . . . aviation, politics, athletics and the arts and sciences. His pastimes and hobbies were innumerable. . . ."

Almost every newspaper in the country noted the Colonel's passing. The New Bedford *Standard-Times* carried a full page of pictures of Ned, his homes, and some of his hobbies. Joe Epstein wrote the obituary.

"New Bedford, which knew Colonel Green personally through the years," wrote Epstein, "remembers him as a friendly and extraordinarily interesting neighbor whose sharing of his hobbies was as notable as the hobbies themselves.

"His great shoulders and kindly, sallow face, his straw colored mustache and spectacled blue eyes, his sunburned sailor and invariably loose fitting wing collar, identified the Colonel to hundreds as he drove through New Bedford in his high-slung limousine. . . .

"His estate, save for a few hundred yards of driveway immediately adjoining the house, was as well known to the motoring public as any public park, a fact in which the Colonel took personal satisfaction."

Private funeral services were held at the South Dartmouth mansion. These were preceded by a viewing during which thousands of men and women filed past the coffin. No doubt many of these came out of curiosity, but certainly there must have been a few who were grateful for individual kindnesses and others who were delighted to have been summer inhabitants of Little Italy, Little Portugal, Little Africa, or Little Jerusalem. How else would these "little" people have had the chance to scatter orange peels all over the estate of a millionaire?

Ned's last journey was to Vermont. He made the trip in his usual style via private railroad car.

"Colonel Edward Howland Robinson Green came back to his boyhood home," said the Bellows Falls *Times*. "He was laid at final rest in the beautiful cemetery of the Immanuel Episcopal Church in the same burial lot in which are interred his mother, father, grandfather and grandmother.

"The widow, Mrs. Edward Green, was the only immediate

relative present. A sister, Mrs. Matthew Astor Wilks, was unable to attend as she is recuperating from a serious illness."

Sylvia, now expecting to be richer by untold millions, which she didn't need, didn't want, and wouldn't know what to do with, believed herself the sole heir and executrix of her brother's estate. After recovering her health, her first official duty was to evict Mabel from Round Hills. Joe Epstein recalled the occasion.

"I was working at the office one evening doing an 'overnight' when the phone rang. It was Mabel and could I come out to Round Hills? I said 'sure,' finished the story, hopped into my car, and drove to South Dartmouth. The mansion was almost completely dark and Mabel was standing on the front patio waiting for me. We went upstairs to the Colonel's study, where he and I used to talk. Except for us and Ned's dog Stella, who followed at Mabel's heels, there wasn't another soul in the place.

"'Well,' she said, 'Sylvia got me. Everybody's deserted and Bullard told me I had to be out of Round Hills by tomorrow morning at nine. If I stay longer I'll be a trespasser.'

"I felt pretty sorry for Mabel even though I knew she wouldn't have to worry where her next buck was coming from. But anyways, it was a little sad. She'd been mistress, maybe not a good one, but still mistress of a damned big place with a hundred or more servants and now she was nothing. Just a beat-up old woman all by herself except for a reporter and a dog.

"We talked for hours and she did most of it. She didn't tell me much about herself. It was mostly about the Colonel, the funny things he did and the strange way they lived all the years they were together, over forty. She never said a mean thing about him.

"Finally, when dawn came, I said good-by and she said, 'So long, Joe, I'll see you around.' But she never did. She cleared out right away. Later that morning when I went out with a couple of lawyers who took possession of Round Hills, she was gone."

Bullard, whose firm had represented Hetty and occasionally the Colonel, now had Mabel for a client. One of the attorney's tasks was to make sure everything at Round Hills was accounted for.

"We weren't worried about what might happen to the furniture and other household effects once we got a padlock on Round Hills," Bullard said. "We were concerned over small 'portable' objects, like coins, cash, stamps, and jewels, and there must have been at least twenty million dollars' worth of these in the house. Most of them were in the basement vault or in the wall safe in the Colonel's bedroom, but there was still plenty lying around loose.

"An appraisal was not necessary yet but we had to have an inventory and it took us days to conclude that. We needed several armored trucks to haul the stuff off to Boston, where we stored everything in a huge bank vault.

"This was an incredible experience, checking those stamps and coins from all over the world; counting out ten-thousand-dollar bills and small binfulls of loose diamonds, emeralds, sapphires, rubies, pearls, amethysts, etc. And the necklaces, rings, watches, pendants, earrings, bracelets, and other ornaments. It was like a scene from the *Arabian Nights* or the *Count of Monte Cristo*; didn't seem to belong to real life.

"But it's strange, you know, how dull it all became after a few days. We welcomed a break like trying to identify an odd ornament—a diamond-studded chastity belt, for example."

Later, expert appraisers at the Boston bank shared Mr. Bullard's experience. As one of them, who had been on the job steadily for nearly a week, told Joe Epstein afterward, "I suppose we'd become a bit punch-drunk. One item fooled us. We came upon what we assumed was a magnificent jeweled crown.

"There were four of us on the appraisal and each of us tried it on and looked at ourselves in a mirror. We were about to label it when one of the men picked up the ornament and after examining it more closely turned and said,

" 'This is no royal headgear. I hate to tell you but it's the Colonel's own chamberpot. Furthermore, gentlemen, it's been used!' "

Chapter Forty-two

Mabel did not choose to sit back on her annuity, lick the wounds her sister-in-law had inflicted, and spend her remaining days in some modest retreat. As a matter of fact the retreat would not have had to be modest. In addition to lifetime take-home pay of $1,500 a month, all tax-free and guaranteed by Ned's premarital trust fund, the Colonel's lady had an additional income of approximately $75,000 a year, derived from her private fortune of $1,750,000. Since Mrs. Green had no other visible means of support during her years as the Colonel's housekeeper and wife, and was not likely to have scraped together quite so much by stinting on the kitchen budget, it is reasonable to assume that her busy little hands did more than pour at society teas.

Mabel proposed to fight. The stakes were high. If Terrell were truly the Colonel's domicile, as he had always maintained, then, in accordance with Texas community-property laws, his widow would be entitled to so much of his estate representing retained income of their married life. Mabel claimed that this was a substantial part of the estate.

Less than two months after the Colonel breathed his last, Mrs. Green struck the first blow. Reinforced by a battery of Philadelphia lawyers, Mabel sought action in the Texas courts. The Widow Green's counsel was headed by no less a personage than the late U. S. Senator George Wharton Pepper, one of the nation's most highly respected gentlemen of the law, who occupied a Texas command post himself. He was supported by one senior partner, Isaac Pennypacker, scion of an old Quaker City family, and several juniors. Included in the last category was the Senator's nephew, Ernest Scott, a sharp young man fresh from a recent victory in which he represented the President of the United States in a conflict between the White House and the Senate.

Mrs. Green's counsel requested that their client be placed in sole charge of her late husband's earthly possessions. This action was noted with keen interest by millions of Americans.

In far-off Massachusetts, which for generations had been oriented to lawsuits involving the Howland fortune, those remote sounds of battle in Texas were heard with more than academic interest. The antenna of the Bay State's politically ambitious Attorney General Paul A. Dever caught the vibrations clearly. Should Terrell, rather than Round Hills, be declared the Colonel's domicile, then Dever's constituents would loose approximately $5,000,000 in estate taxes. On the other hand, if the Attorney General could prove the Colonel's actual home was South Dartmouth, there was no telling where grateful voters would send him. For the moment Dever's policy had to be one of "watchful waiting."

Mabel won the first round. Her victory was reported in the

265

New Bedford *Standard-Times*, August 10, 1936, under a Kaufman, Texas, dateline.

"Mrs. Mabel H. Green, widow of the late Colonel Edward H. Green . . . of Round Hills, was named permanent administratrix of his vast estate, estimated at $80,000,000, in a brief hearing here today . . . ," said this newspaper.

An aroused Mrs. Wilks sprang into action. Unlike her mother, who dearly loved the panoply of the courtroom, Sylvia's only previously recorded appearance in the halls of justice was as a character witness more than a quarter-century before. Sylvia, however, had a big advantage over Hetty. Mrs. Wilks' integrity was spotless and any attorney she might engage would be sure of his legitimate fee. She was thus in a position to seek counsel of the caliber retained by her sister-in-law.

The Widow Wilks selected the Wall Street firm of Milbank, Tweed, Hope and Hadley. Three senior partners, countless juniors, clerks, and investigators took upon themselves the assignment of protecting the Fortune and preventing it from falling into the hands of the Philistines. Included in the category of "seniors" were Harrison Tweed, one of the best-known corporation lawyers in the United States; Timothy N. Pfeiffer, a brilliant trial lawyer whose defense of Mrs. Hall in the Hall-Mills case was regarded as "classic"; and George W. Jaques, who knew as much about the intricacies of estate law as any member of the New York bar.

Until a will could be produced—and Sylvia had every reason to believe her brother had made one—initial strategy for the Widow Wilks was to restrict Mabel's newly granted rights to the disposition of only that portion of Ned's earthly possessions which lay within Texas' borders. Then, even if Mabel could resurrect the aged, and by now certainly moth-eaten, pair of trousers left in Mrs. Bondurant (Rezia) Jarvis' Terrell home, her victory would be hollow. The Colonel's total assets in the Lone-Star State were $2,220. Mrs. Green was welcome to that, and good riddance!

Potter came to Sylvia's rescue and blocked Mabel's opening

move. The faithful bookkeeper, from the depths of 111 Broadway, produced not only the Colonel's will but also the antenuptial agreement which Mabel had somehow neglected to mention at the Kaufman County hearing. Ned's last will and testament, drawn in 1908, was succinct. He left everything he had to Hetty. If Hetty predeceased her son, the estate then went to Sylvia without any restrictions. Ned never added a single codicil or changed so much as a comma in this document, which, it should be remembered, was written long before he came into any sizable inheritance.

Now that the matter of the will could be disposed of satisfactorily (for Sylvia) by removing claims of intestacy, thus depriving Mrs. Green of Texas community property rights, counsel for Mrs. Wilks would have the more difficult task of proving the validity of the antenuptial agreement. They had every reason to believe Mabel would cry "fraud." Which would be more inclined to believe her, judge or jury? Mrs. Wilks' counselors at first were not impressed by their client's appearance and were afraid her dour, unattractive face and sharp, embittered tongue would repel a panel. Consequently, should the occasion arise, her counsel leaned toward a one-man rather than a twelve-man decision.

Another and far more serious question faced the Manhattan firm. This was the matter of the Colonel's domicile. Only recently two sovereign states, New Jersey and Pennsylvania, had concluded a long and costly war to determine the real residence of John T. Dorrance, founder of Campbell's soups. To the horror of the Dorrance heirs, both states proved their points and were permitted to divide much of the late soup king's $150,000,000 fortune between them.

Because of the Colonel's lifetime pattern of tax obfuscation, there was a better than even chance that at least four states, and possibly five, would claim the late E. H. R. Green as having been a resident. Should this legal nightmare occur, then there would be literally less than nothing remaining for either of the widows,

267

and not quite enough to pay each state's own tax bill. The Internal Revenue Service had no problem. It was ready, willing, and able to skim off the top layer and let Texas, Florida, New York, Massachusetts, and possibly Vermont squabble over the remainder.

Ned rightfully could have blamed Hetty for the large Federal tax bite because her practically tax-free estate so incensed the Congress of the United States that this body passed laws to increase inheritance taxes enormously. Actually it was the minus quality of the Colonel's inheritance that saved the day for the final victor.

Sylvia's counsel were forced to make the next move. They had to put the Colonel's testament on record. No place was ideal but Mrs. Wilks' lawyers decided to probate the will in the New York county of his death, Essex. Here they hoped to prove that both the will and the antenuptial agreement were valid. Hearings, which were to last for twenty-nine months and move into the four claimant states (Vermont after a fast look decided its chances were too remote even to make the try), were begun September 14, 1936, at Elizabethtown. Surrogate Harry E. Owen presided.

As Ernest Scott (former Chancellor of the Philadelphia Bar Association), who was at the first and the last of the Surrogate hearings, phrased it, "The Green circus followed the sun—Florida in the winter, Texas in the spring, Massachusetts in the summer, and New York in the fall."

Chapter Forty-three

O<small>N</small> the eve of the morning Surrogate Owen was to open court, only a score of attorneys were present at Elizabethtown. There were a half-dozen of Mrs. Wilks' Philadelphia lawyers, including a new arrival, Joseph J. Fischer, whose brother Harry sold the Colonel $10,000,000 worth of jewels. Senator Pepper's firm was augmented by several Essex County members of the bar, while the Widow Wilks' counsel was joined by a rising young Texas barrister, Dillon Anderson, of Houston. Present also was a sufficient number of reporters to provide counsel with not only an unseen national audience but also the courtroom laughter and applause so necessary to the beatitude of performing lawyers.

By morning, counsels' ranks were swollen with so many new arrivals that hotel accommodations in the village burst. Traveling members of the bar, accustomed to only the finest of hotel suites, were forced to occupy humble rooms and share baths in Elizabethtown's private houses.

Messrs. Chrystie and Chrystie came to represent the Commonwealth of Massachusetts. Attorney General Dever was not quite ready to make his own appearance. However, the Attorney General for the sovereign state of New York, the Honorable Seth T. Cole, was on hand. He was supported by a goodly staff of assistants, plus Mortimer M. Kassell, counsel for the Empire State's Tax Commission, and *his* staff of assistants. To make sure any fruit likely to fall in neighborhood backyards would be gleaned by local tax collectors, the Honorable Shelden F. Wickes was there to protect Essex County interests.

Then there were the witnesses! Dozens and dozens of witnesses. Since strategy of counsel for Mrs. Wilks was to show the Colonel's true relationship with Mabel and his actual domicile, they intended to re-enact Ned's life. It was the hope of Sylvia's attorneys that before the hearings ended, the Colonel, off stage forever, would be as familiar to Surrogate Owen as he was to anyone during his peripatetic lifetime.

To accomplish this, the defenders of the Fortune subpoenaed every friendly witness who knew the Colonel from his birth to his death. Those who were unfriendly were summoned to Elizabethtown by Mrs. Green. It should be added that there were a great many in the second category, including, to the surprise of Mrs. Wilks, Walter H. Marshall. Secretary Marshall, however, was more than balanced by Mary Stafford, who developed a strange (and helpful) fondness for Sylvia, whom she had never before met.

Moving within a wide aura of French perfume she herself had purchased at its source, Mary, gowned as though she were part of a Fifth Avenue fashion parade, swept into the village. Without even asking, Mrs. Stafford was given the best accommodations at the inn by a goggle-eyed clerk who unhesitatingly transferred the assigned guest, Senator George Wharton Pepper, of Rittenhouse Square, to a hall bedroom.

Witnesses came from almost every state in the Union and several from outside continental limits. Since all expenses were, so to speak, "on the house," many brought husbands or wives and frequently children. On the morning of September 14, 1936, Elizabethtown took on the air of almost any rural American county seat on the opening day of the annual fair.

The man in charge, Surrogate Owen, was an experienced, perspicacious country judge, learned in the law, and delighted with the novelty of presiding over a courtroom filled with brilliant, even-tempered, jousting men of Harvard, Princeton, Columbia, and Penn, including a law school dean and a few quondam Fellows.

From counsels' point of view the case was ideal, involving two rich widows, fascinating and undetermined points of law, heterogeneous congeries of witnesses, and well-fed, brilliant courtroom antagonists who, when the day's battles were over, became charming dinner companions.

Within hours after the hearings began the first witness produced by Mrs. Wilks' counsel effectively destroyed any hope Mabel had of proving intestacy. Three old friends of the Colonel, all Vice Presidents of the First National Bank of Dallas, were signatories to Ned's 1908 will. One of these officers, Alvin Valentine Lane, survived.

Placed on the stand by Pfeiffer, Lane, a tall, distinguished-looking gentleman of seventy-six, vividly recalled details of that day, thirty-nine years before, when Colonel Green walked into the bank and requested the trio of Texans to affix their signatures to his will. Opposing counsel was unable to shake or change Lane's testimony in any way.

The next step was to determine whether the antenuptial agreement was valid or had been obtained, as Mabel claimed, by "fraud." If the former were true then the Widow Green had no interest, legally speaking, in the estate and therefore neither she nor her counsel any standing in Surrogate's Court. On the other hand, Senator Pepper's team averred that its client's signature to her waiver of the Colonel's fortune was obtained by "subterfuge,

271

chicanery, and deception." The relationship between Mabel and her late husband had to be clarified and Ned's character determined.

As the months rolled by the Colonel's life was revealed in all its intimate details on stages at Elizabethtown, at Port Henry, Surrogate Owen's home town a few miles away; in Manhattan, where the New York Bar Association was host; at Miami Beach, in Dallas, and in Marlin.

Mabel, dressed appropriately in widow's black, her hair no longer rich auburn but coiffured in a style becoming to gray, with only the most ladylike traces of make-up on her still attractive face, took the stand. In well-modulated tones, the Widow Green, gently prodded by Senator Pepper, told her side of the story.

"On the morning of June 26, 1917," Mrs. Green declared under oath, "while we were living in New York, the Colonel asked me if I'd go downtown with him.

"'I want to show you Diamond Jim Brady's jewels,' he said. 'They are on display at the Columbia Trust Company.'

"On our way Ned said, 'When we're married I don't want you to run up any bills on me. I can't stand charge accounts. I'm going to give you pin money and you'll have to care for yourself out of that.'

"When we got to the bank we went to a side door which was opened by a man who said, 'Right this way, Colonel.' We were taken to a side room and he (the Colonel) said, 'I am now arranging for your pin money.' Ned gave me something to sign and I signed it without looking, in the presence of a gentleman named Pierson, who I understand was the Colonel's lawyer, and one other man whose name I don't recall.

"When we finished the Colonel said, 'Now, come out and look at Jim's collection.' I remember the jewels very well. There was one in particular which appealed to me a great deal. It was a diamond-studded automobile."

After several hours on the stand, during which she was subjected to Pfeiffer's not-so-gentle cross-examination, the Widow

Green concluded her testimony by declaring she didn't know what she had signed; she had no legal counsel and furthermore, she neither mentioned it again to anyone nor saw it until after her husband's death. Mabel's testimony was supported by Walter Marshall, by several Miami friends, and by one former colleague of Miss Harlow's early Chicago days. This last was an excellent witness. Subsequent to her association with Mabel she had become the wife of a respectable Milwaukee wholesale grocer, an active local clubwoman, and a leader in the Eastern Star.

Mrs. Stafford was chosen to be Pfeiffer's star for the rebuttal. She seemed eager to take the stand and appeared quite happy to be able to testify against her old friend, with no thought of Judas Iscariot entering her mind. After tracing the witness' early friendship with Mabel and Ned, counsel asked Mrs. Stafford if Mrs. Green had ever discussed the antenuptial agreement.

"Often," was her answer.

"Do you recall the first time it was mentioned?"

"Oh, yes, very shortly after Mabel signed it. I don't remember the exact date but it was around July 1, 1917. The Greens were married on July 10. Mabel asked me to lunch and we met at Marshall Field's and took a taxi from there to the Congress Hotel on Michigan Boulevard.

"On our way Mabel turned to me suddenly and said, 'Ned isn't going to marry me and I don't know what I'll do.' I couldn't believe it. Then she said, 'I was only kidding. Look at my ring. We'll be married in a little while. You're my dearest friend and I want you to be my matron of honor.'

"When we sat down to eat she told me the Colonel had settled six hundred and twenty-five thousand dollars on her. 'I had to sign my rights away for that but I think it was worth it,' she said. 'This'll give me fifteen hundred dollars a month for life.' "

Pfeiffer then asked Mrs. Stafford if she recalled the next time the agreement was mentioned.

"It was in June of 1918," Mary answered. "She and I were sitting in the Waldorf when she showed me a bank statement

273

and her new check for fifteen hundred dollars. She seemed very dissatisfied.

"'Mary,' she said, 'I don't think this is much money, do you?' Of course I didn't answer. Then she went to the safe and took out a paper and handed it to me. 'This is a copy of the antenuptial agreement I signed,' she said. 'Go on, read it.'

"I said I wouldn't. I already knew what was in it because Mabel had told me. So I handed it back to her. Lots of times later she told me about the agreement and how she'd signed off her rights but if she minded her P's and Q's with the Colonel, he might change his mind."

Under Pennypacker's cross-examination Mrs. Stafford admitted to several marriages, to an intimate life with the Colonel, and to a quarrel over money she had had with Mrs. Green shortly after Ned's death. She did not deny she had few assets before her friendship with the Greens began or that at the present time she was "comfortably fixed." Her satisfactory financial status was due, she reluctantly acknowledged, not only to a $100,000 trust fund set up by the Colonel but also to his wife's generosity.

"Mabel often used to hand me a thousand dollars and say, 'Go on, kid, buy yourself a couple of dresses.'"

While Pennypacker was able to impugn both Mary's character and motivation, he could not shake her testimony on the important point of the antenuptial agreement. The witness supplied so many supporting details to each conversation she claimed to have had with Mabel every time the agreement was discussed that it would have been beyond Mrs. Stafford's imagination to have invented them all.

With good reason, counsel for the Widow Wilks were fearful of putting their client on the stand despite the fact that her testimony could be valuable. Sylvia, a dour, unattractive woman in her mid-sixties, had developed a few of her mother's unpleasant characteristics. She had respect for neither the law nor its practitioners. She was forthright to the point of rudeness and cared little whom she might offend. She hated Mabel and might express this feeling for her brother's widow quite openly. She had utter contempt for the press, coupled with a horror about its right to invade her privacy.

Mrs. Wilks was also extremely shy, a near-recluse, was rarely seen in public and then only by the few who might catch a glimpse of this tall, erect woman, dressed in black and sitting behind the chauffeur of her aged Lincoln limousine. The thought of appearing in open court before so many strangers must have weighed heavily against Sylvia's desire to protect the Fortune from the onslaught of her detested sister-in-law.

As it turned out, Sylvia's counsel had no choice in the matter of whether or not Mrs. Wilks would testify. She was called to the stand by the opposition. By this time court had moved to a large meeting room in the New York Bar Association Building on West 44th Street, a most convenient spot for newspaper reporters who flocked to the hearings in large numbers.

"We had no idea what effect our client would have on Surrogate Owen," recalled Pfeiffer, "and with something akin to horror, Tweed, Jaques, Dillon and I sat back and watched Mrs. Wilks take the stand. Her answers to Brother Pennypacker's initial queries gave us cause for alarm."

After she was duly sworn, counsel asked Sylvia to state her full name.

"You heard it," she said. "You're not deaf. I won't give it again."

The patient Pennypacker, his Quaker heritage now serving in good stead, continued.

"If you please, Madam, would you mind saying what your full name is? It's merely for the record."

"I won't. It's not necessary. I want to get out."

"You will get out sooner, Mrs. Wilks, by answering the question."

"All right. It's Hetty Sylvia Ann Howland Green Wilks. Do you know it? You have seen it for the last six months in the papers. It seems to me you are very stupid. I don't want to be insulted."

At this, Pfeiffer rose.

"I don't think Mr. Pennypacker intended to insult you, Mrs. Wilks," he said apologetically.

The interrogation continued in the same vein. When it came to disclosing her residence, Sylvia became more truculent than ever.

"Where do you live?" asked Pennypacker.

"Several places," was her answer.

"Where is your residence, Mrs. Wilks?"

"New York."

"Where in New York?"

"I'm not going to tell you. It's not necessary to go into my private affairs."

Judge Owen intervened.

"Madam," cautioned the Surrogate, "that was a proper question. You will have to answer it."

"Your Honor," replied the witness, "I can always be found at the Seaboard Bank. That's all I'm going to tell you or anybody else."

Pennypacker tried again.

"I am asking your place of residence."

"I'm not going to give it to you. I don't want twenty-five reporters coming out to my house."

The Philadelphia Quaker shrugged his shoulders in despair and turned to the Court for guidance.

"Mrs. Wilks," said Judge Owen sternly, "you are instructed to answer that question."

The witness was undismayed.

"I'm sorry to disobey you, I won't answer. Everybody knows where I live."

"But if everybody knows, Mrs. Wilks," said the Surrogate, "what difference does it make if you tell Mr. Pennypacker?"

"That's my point exactly, Your Honor," replied Sylvia. "If everybody knows, why doesn't Pennypacker? He can't be that dumb."

Tweed came to the rescue.

"I think this question could be resolved, Judge," said the attorney, "if you will permit Mrs. Wilks to write her address on a piece of paper and hand it to counsel. She doesn't want it revealed to the public."

As Pfeiffer recalled, this was the time when Surrogate Owen's reaction to Mrs. Wilks was put to the test.

"If he allowed Mrs. Wilks to follow my colleague's suggestion then we could be reasonably sure the Judge would understand our client and be tolerant of her idiosyncrasies," said Pfeiffer. "On the other hand, if he insisted on a verbal answer we knew we'd be in for trouble. Fortunately for us, Owen was a knowing gentleman and, even more fortunate for us, he had a well-developed sense of humor. He was enjoying the entire proceedings; this was something new in his experience.

"I caught the ghost of a smile on his face as he granted Mrs. Wilks permission to write her address on a pad. There was absolute silence in the room as she tore off the sheet and handed it to me without a word. I passed the information on to the Court. Judge Owen glanced at the paper and turned it over to Brother Pennypacker. Not one of us said anything. The ridiculous part was that for months the nation's press printed Mrs. Wilks' address, 988 Fifth Avenue, quite regularly."

One further question annoyed Sylvia. She refused to tell her age and would admit only that she was "over fifty." Since she had previously testified she was two years younger than Ned, who died at the age of sixty-seven, counsel for Mrs. Green preferred to rely on simple arithmetic rather than press the point.

During the entire proceedings, at which Sylvia and Mabel were present much of the time, Sylvia never glanced at her sister-in-law while the latter continued to make audible comments about the former. Finally, stung to a retort by Mrs. Green's unflattering remark about Hetty, made from the witness stand, Mrs. Wilks rose from her chair.

"I have been persecuted by this old woman," she shouted. "She killed my mother and my brother. I am tired of it. I have state prison evidence against her. I won't stand much more!"

Following this purging outburst, Sylvia's testimony was obtained more easily. She supported Potter's discovery of the antenuptial agreement and vouched for its validity. She even answered Pennypacker's questions with little show of reluctance.

"Upon leaving the stand, finally," Pfeiffer said, "Sylvia turned to the Surrogate. 'I wasn't too bad, was I?' she asked. Then, to the Judge's complete astonishment, she gave him a broad wink. Shades of Hetty Green!"

Chapter Forty-four

Both sides continued to attack, counterattack, advance, or retreat, but after a little more than a year of battle it was apparent that the forces carrying the Fortune's banner were gaining ground. Mrs. Green's case suffered its most damaging blow with the appearance of George E. Warren, a Vice President of Chase National Bank.

Warren was a witness to the antenuptial agreement, and he clearly remembered the day, twenty years before, when Miss Harlow and Colonel Green entered the bank. He recalled that Mabel was fully instructed on what she was about to sign. Warren testified that the bride-to-be was cognizant not only of the fact that she was "signing off" her rights to the Green fortune but also that she had an excellent idea of its extent.

"The one question I clearly recollect Mr. Pierson [Ned's attorney] asking Miss Harlow," said Warren, "was, 'Are you aware that Colonel Green is the son of the late Hetty Green who was reputed to be the richest woman in the world?' Miss Harlow's answer was 'Yes.' "

Senator Pepper assaulted the banker's testimony but with less enthusiasm than he might have shown had not Warren been such an apparently disinterested, highly credible witness. At this point it was merely a question of believing either Mrs. Green's claim that the Colonel, Pierson, and Warren had obtained her signature to the antenuptial agreement through "fraud," or that the banker was lying.

A conference between opposing counsel was called at which Surrogate Owen reviewed the testimony up to date and declared he would like to wind up the case as quickly as possible.

"To discontinue useless, expensive litigation," the Judge said, "I would suggest an immediate settlement. I will recess until both sides have reached a satisfactory conclusion."

Sylvia was furious at this turn of events. Money meant so little to her that she informed counsel she would rather sacrifice her entire inheritance than allow her sister-in-law to receive a cent. It took hours of patient persuasion to convince Mrs. Wilks that in view of the tax saving and the cost of continued litigation it would be better to conclude the hearings with a minimal loss to the estate. Sylvia reluctantly consented and within a few days Mabel Green was richer by a half-million dollars, less, of course, the $200,000 fee claimed by her Philadelphia lawyers.

But this settlement by no means ended the "Green circus." The preceding February, Attorney General William McCraw of the State of Texas appeared at the offices of Milbank, Tweed, Hope and Hadley. He had been following Surrogate Owen's proceedings (then recessed for the Washington's Birthday holiday) with considerable interest, he said, because Texas had the greatest stake of all in the Colonel's estate.

"No doubt about it, gentlemen," he told Tweed and Pfeiffer, "the Colonel was a Texan. We're going to claim death taxes on his estate."

To which Pfeiffer replied, "That, sir, is your privilege. Go right ahead."

Not one for subtlety, McCraw admitted there might be an obstacle or two to surmount before Texas could get its hands on the late Colonel's assets.

"I don't have to tell you," McCraw went on, "that a couple of other sovereign states have the same idea as Texas. It's going to be a war, gentlemen, and we all can't win. There'd be nothing left for you fellows to divvy up between the two widows."

That this had occurred to the Widow Wilks' attorneys, Tweed admitted, adding that both the Commonwealth of Massachusetts and the sovereign state of New York felt equally strongly about claiming Colonel Green as a citizen.

"You ain't even heard from Florida," McCraw went on, "but I have and they want in. Cary Landis, their Attorney General, says the Colonel was a 'cracker.' No doubt about it in *his* mind.

"I got a proposition, gentlemen. I stopped off in Philadelphia yesterday and talked it over with Senator Pepper and a young fellow named Scott, and now I'd like you fellows to hear it."

"We're listening," said Pfeiffer. "Go on."

"All right," McCraw continued. "First of all, I've done some checking around with the Colonel's close banker friends in Dallas and Terrell. They tell me Ned Green got about fifty-five million dollars net from his Mamma's trust fund. You fellows probably know exactly but mine's only an educated guess. So then I did some more checking with Cary Landis and a couple other guys.

"We came to the conclusion that Ned was spending his dough at the rate of five million dollars a year for the last nine years. That was since he got his hands on the trust fund and three million dollars a year before. Walter Allen told me the Colonel's income was just under that three million so that he'd been dipping into principal at the rate of two million dollars a year. This means there ought to be somewhere around thirty-five million dollars left."

McCraw reached into his inside coat pocket and drew out a sheet of paper.

"I got just a few figures here," he said, "and I'd like you gentlemen to do a little simple arithmetic. First write down seventeen million dollars. That's the Federal bite."

Tweed and Pfeiffer obliged.

"Now I'm going to claim five million dollars for Texas. Write that under the seventeen million dollars. Cary Landis is going to do the same for Florida, so write down another five million dollars. I wouldn't be a bit surprised if New York and Massachusetts did the same thing, so put two more five million dollars to the column. Now add it up and what do you get?"

"Thirty-seven million," answered both of the Widow Wilks' lawyers.

"That's exactly right, fellows," McCraw said. "And it means there'll not be enough to go round for each state."

He paused.

"What do you propose to do?" Tweed asked.

"Since this makes it a controversy between the states," McCraw answered, "I propose to ask the United States Supreme Court to take original jurisdiction, under Article Three, Section Two, of the Constitution."

"You realize," warned Pfeiffer, "that if the Supreme Court accepts jurisdiction and decides that Texas was not the Colonel's true domicile, you'll get nothing."

"I do, indeed," said the Attorney General. "It'll be winner take all!"

What McCraw wanted from the Manhattan firm was help in drawing up a proper petition to offer to the highest court in the land. McCraw's experience was extremely limited in that area while that of Sylvia's counsel was wide. In addition, McCraw was not a particularly able lawyer. He was, however, a tireless politician. He was a big man, well over six feet, with broad shoulders, an enlarged paunch, and a florid complexion. He had a loud voice which he had difficulty adjusting to any space smaller than a circus arena, and of course he wore a ten-gallon Stetson wherever he went. At the age of thirty-eight he had

282

bellowed his way into the elective office of Attorney General. If he could win the now famous Green case for his native state, McCraw's supporters believed, their man would have an excellent chance to become Governor.

Would the Manhattan lawyers help? "Yes" was the answer but with a condition. The Attorney General for the State of Texas first had to present his own petition. If it failed, the Manhattan firm would render all assistance necessary to persuade the United States Supreme Court to accept jurisdiction but would take no steps beyond this point. At the outset, Pfeiffer informed McCraw that the Widow Wilks' counsel did not believe Texas was the Colonel's true domicile and would in no way assist that state to prove its point.

Despite McCraw's contention, built up by the Colonel's habit of referring to himself as a "Texan" (and frequently behaving like one), his Terrell voting "residence," thousands of his signatures followed by "Terrell, Texas," wherever an address was required, and other spoor Green left on his life's trail, Tweed and Pfeiffer were convinced Ned had not been a legal resident of Texas for a long time prior to his death.

"We appreciated McCraw's ingenuity," Pfeiffer explained, "and we hoped he would succeed in getting the court to take the case. For if he did, we were confident his state would not win. In this way the nightmare of liability to more than one state would be eliminated."

Shortly after his first meeting with Mrs. Wilks' counsel, McCraw appeared in the high-ceilinged, austere marble chambers of the United States Supreme Court to present his petition. His opening remark to the nine aging, black-robed Justices was long remembered after the brief moment of stunned silence with which it was greeted.

"Your Honors," drawled McCraw, who had modulated his voice from a bellow to a tempered blare, "this here's going to be a honey of a case!"

Chapter Forty-five

T HE United States Supreme Court threw out McCraw's petition only because of its technical deficiencies but did not deny original jurisdiction (Justices Frankfurter and Black dissented, saying the case should be referred to the States themselves). The majority opinion, written by Associate Justice Van Devanter, afforded McCraw the opportunity to file a new interpleader against Texas' sister states Massachusetts, Florida, and New York.

McCraw returned to New York, where he established head-quarters in the offices of Mrs. Wilks' counsel while a new petition was prepared. Since the three other contesting states had agreed to a policy of "winner take all" and therefore had nothing to lose by helping McCraw correct errors in his original interpleader, their Attorneys General were instructed to assist the Texan every way they could.

The chief reasons for the Court's rejection of McCraw's petition was the vagueness of his statement of tax liabilities. In the new interpleader, however, tax claims were as accurate as fiscal experts of the Internal Revenue Service and individual states could make them. At that, McCraw's "educated guess" came close to the truth. Actual claims against the estate of the late Colonel Green were:

United States	$17,520,987
Texas	4,685,057
Florida	4,663,857
New York	5,910,301
Massachusetts	4,947,008

The total was $37,727,213. Because the Colonel's net estate was only $36,137,335, there would be a deficit of $1,589,877.

McCraw's second try was successful. Justice Stone wrote the majority opinion, which held that since any one of the four contesting states might legitimately claim the Colonel as a citizen, "adequate remedy" could be provided only by the United States Supreme Court, which therefore would accept original jurisdiction. Experts on constitutional law say this rare combination of circumstances—a legacy sufficient to arouse the interest of the Attorneys General of four states yet not enough to pay what each demanded, plus an eccentric testator with the cash to indulge in peripatetic obfuscation—could happen only once in a lifetime. Thus the "Green Domicile Case" became famous in the annals of estate law.

As Trueman O'Quinn, an Austin, Texas, lawyer, put it in his excellent monograph which appeared in the *Texas Bar Journal,* September, 1961, "If Colonel Green had died worth 36 dollars, 36 thousand dollars, or even three million dollars . . . it is unlikely that there would have been more than passing interest in the question of his domicile.

"Certainly, it is improbable that four states would have gone to battle for such small stakes. But 36 million dollars was too tempting, and the publicity was too prodding, for the question to be passed over lightly by the tax conscious state officials.

"Colonel Green's residence was in much the same position as the title to an East Texas sandy farm before oil was discovered on it. It was not important until the estate and the farm became worth a lot of money.

"The moral is . . . don't amass a fortune of 36 million dollars. Be satisfied with less, if you don't want your love of Texas and your hatred of taxes to get mixed up and rescrambled in the courts."

McCraw's petition was heard March 15, 1937, and on the following June 1, John S. Flannery, a distinguished member of the Washington, D. C., bar, became the official representative of the highest court in the land. He was appointed Special Master and given authority to issue subpoenas, call witnesses, hear testimony, and take whatever other legal steps he felt were necessary to determine in which state Colonel E. H. R. Green's true domicile was.

It took Flannery some time to put his personal affairs in order, and it was not until October 10 that he pre-empted the seat of Surrogate Owen, who only the previous day had concluded what he called "thirteen months on the road as ringmaster for the Green circus."

A number of attorneys and supernumeraries who had been faithful attendants at the hearings and enjoyed Judge Owen's informality were fearful that their new "ringmaster" would be stuffy. None of the lawyers had any idea of how long the domicile hearings would last, but no matter how lengthy or brief, work under a formal Master would not only be difficult but distasteful to the array of assembled counsel on whom Surrogate Owen had "held a light rein."

"I didn't particularly give a damn," recalled Ernest Scott. "Our chores were about over and all of us from the Senator's [Pepper's] office would be leaving in the morning.

"We'd planned a mild celebration in the Adolphus where we wound up the Surrogate's show. It was to be a combination farewell dinner for Judge Owen and the rest of us who'd been together for thirteen wonderful months, and a welcome party to Mr. Flannery, the new Attorneys General, and their staffs.

"I suppose the hotel management was slightly timorous about what effect this temporary release from bondage would have on *our* inhibitions and *their* furniture. So they gave us a rather wretched suite of rooms for the celebration. They were dingy, the carpets torn and chairs and tables considerably the worse for wear.

" 'Farewell' was said with appropriate toasts, and since there were quite a few of us retiring, there were quite a few toasts. Then we began to honor new members of the 'cast.' There were a considerable number of these to be pledged.

"I imagine we were resentful, at least subconsciously, of the awful accommodations the Adolphus afforded and we weren't as neat as we might otherwise have been. There must have been about seventy-five of us there and I don't believe much effort was made to place used cigar and cigarette butts or ashes in trays, and I'm certain no one bent down to mop any spilled liquid or possibly a broken glass. At one point in the evening I recall looking around and thinking to myself, This joint really is a shambles.

"At that very moment Mr. Flannery, to whom no one had been paying much attention except to see that he got his proper share of refreshments, rose and slapped his hand down hard on a table at one end of the room. Absolute silence followed, the kind which precedes the entrance of a judge into his courtroom.

" 'Gentlemen,' said the Special Master, 'I want to remind all of you that officially this is the Supreme Court of the United States.'

"Then he grinned. Right then I almost wished our office had a continuing interest in the Green case. I knew my brothers-at-law were going to enjoy the proceedings."

Arrivals in Dallas, where the domicile hearings began under

Flannery's aegis the following morning, included the big guns of each of the four competing states, the legislatures of which had appropriated sums averaging $100,000 each for the ensuing contest. The Texas delegation continued to be led by McCraw. His chief of staff was Assistant Attorney General Llewelyn B. Duke, whose legal abilities were superior to those possessed by his chief. McCraw did most of the trial work himself and, in the opinion of his colleagues, injured his case by "running for office" every time he interrogated a witness.

Landis represented Florida for only a brief period before he was killed in an automobile accident. He was replaced by George C. Gibbs, a former Hoosier and a Floridian by adoption. Gibbs was far more vehement in his praise of Florida than most natives and would tolerate no criticism of that so-called Sunshine State. He frequently quoted his favorite poet, Edgar Guest, and assured all who would listen that when this rhymster mentioned "a heap of livin'," he was referring only to Florida. Pfeiffer earned Gibbs' undying dislike when he innocently suggested to a Florida witness that perhaps the view from Star Island might be improved by the removal of Al Capone.

New York was represented by Seth T. Cole, who had attended many of Surrogate Owen's hearings. He was a good but not outstanding attorney whose field was tax work. He was assisted by William M. O'Reilly, an excellent trial lawyer with years of experience in upstate New York courts.

Dever represented the Commonwealth of Massachusetts. His aides were Edward G. Proctor, an Assistant Attorney General, and Henry F. Long, Commissioner of Corporations and Taxes. Long had met the Colonel several times and until after Green's death was persuaded the master of Round Hills was not subject to Massachusetts taxes.

Counsel for Mrs. Wilks threw their lot in with Massachusetts.

The Internal Revenue Service, which had only an academic interest in the proceedings since Federal tax claims had already been established, nevertheless, with its usual vigilance coupled

288

with its normal distrust for everyone, was represented by counsel, Frank F. Korell.

As did counsel for Massachusetts, attorneys for Mrs. Wilks held to the theory that while a man can own more than one domicile, he may have only one "home." Colonel E. H. R. Green's home, they were certain, was South Dartmouth. This they set about to prove.

Once the Colonel's will had been found, the basic purpose of testimony before Surrogate Owen was to determine merely the validity of the antenuptial agreement. To achieve this it was necessary to show only the broadest aspects of Ned's biography. Details of his life were saved for the domicile hearings. In the opinion of Mrs. Wilks' counsel, it was important to furnish Flannery with a picture of Green's life, if not hour by hour then at least day by day, from his early years in Texas until his death at Lake Placid.

Since there was likely to be little dispute about the Colonel's home prior to the turn of the century, it was decided to concentrate on that period between January 1, 1900, and June 8, 1936, the date of his death. There are approximately 13,000 days in this span, and it was the job of Dillon Anderson, a youthful member of the Texas bar who represented Sylvia's counsel in Texas, to find out just where the Colonel had been on every one of them.

At the same time it was the Texan's task to sift the evidence he would be discovering in his biographical research to determine what would prove or disprove counsel's contention that their client's brother was a resident of Massachusetts.

Certain facts, as Anderson found out, were not likely to be controversial. He assumed, for example, that no one would question the Colonel's presence in Terrell those days he signed the voters' register there. The attorney also believed Green's recorded attendance at Boards of Directors' meetings in Dallas and New York would be acceptable proof. The Southern Pacific dug up old Texas Midland records of the *Lone Star*. Other railroads, from whom the Colonel had rented private Pullman cars through

289

the years, obliged with dates of these loans. Hotel registers, logs of the Colonel's fleet, correspondence between Uncle Ned and his protégées, friends, business associates, lawyers, beneficiaries, jewelers, numismatists, philatelists, builders and suppliers—wherever there was written evidence of the Colonel's presence somewhere, this was found, scanned, and used to fill in blank days in the Colonel's hegira.

As the weeks rolled by and the hearings went on, Anderson constructed a seven-color map, labeled Exhibit 1154, and presented it as evidence to Special Master Flannery. Each tint represented a state, city, or area. A quick glance at Anderson's map proved that, as the years progressed, the majority of Ned's days passed from yellow and purple (Terrell and Dallas) to orange (New York City) to navy and light blue (Miami and Star Island) and finally to the green of Round Hills. Miscellaneous communities—St. Louis, Bellows Falls, Lake Placid, etc.—were represented by ivory, but here the total was small.

If Flannery were to base his recommendations on the amount of time the Colonel spent in his various "domiciles," it would have been easy for the Special Master to state that Green's Texas residence ended in 1910, his New York citizenship in 1921, while Massachusetts and Florida divided the balance of his earthly days between them in nearly equal portions, the Bay State having an eight per cent edge.

For the representative of the United States Supreme Court the job was hardly so simple. His decision had to be based on where the Colonel maintained his *real* domicile. That Green kept signing hotel registers as a resident of Terrell, or calling himself a "cracker," did not make him legally either a Texan or a Floridian.

Nor was the Colonel's refusal to pay taxes in Massachusetts or New York sufficient to disallow claims that Ned actually lived in either state. What had to be shown was intent. For a simple definition of what domicile meant to two of the contesting counsel, you had your choice between Landis' "Home is where a man does his heap of livin' " and Tweed's "Home is where a man keeps his *lares* and *penates*."

The Commonwealth of Massachusetts, the Manhattan firm, and Dillon Anderson were dedicated to the belief that the Colonel's household gods for some years had been firmly ensconced at Round Hills.

Chapter Forty-six

I̲N̲ the nearly twenty-two months that elapsed between October 11, 1937, when the first witness took the stand before Special Master Flannery, and July 31, 1939, when the last was called, a total of 385 men and women testified in behalf of one or the other of the four competing states. Some 4,000,000 words of testimony were piled up; 2,855 exhibits were shown; and nobody knows how much coffee was consumed during the recesses, which grew more and more frequent as the evidence became repetitious.

Every single item of Ned's character—his eccentricities, his hopeless wanderings, his health, his humor, politics, sex, his relations with Hetty, Sylvia, Mabel, Mary, his work, his hobbies, and his loneliness—was dredged from the bottom of the Colonel's muddy life stream, carefully scrutinized, weighed, measured, and evaluated by Special Master Flannery, by four Attorneys General and their assistants, and by the Widow Wilks' counsel, then tossed back into the water.

Even the Colonel's old trousers were dragged into the picture once more, when the Attorney General for the State of Texas attempted to introduce them as an important bit of evidence. Mr. Pfeiffer objected.

"Why?" asked McCraw.

"Because, sir, of autoptic proference," answered counsel for the Widow Wilks, who hoped in this manner to enliven a deadly session.

"Because of *what?*" exclaimed the bewildered Texan, looking first at Pfeiffer, then at the Special Master, who was chuckling.

"You'd better give Brother McCraw an interpretation, Counselor, before I rule on your objection," said Flannery.

"In substance, sir," explained Pfeiffer, "the phrase means self-perception of a thing itself. If, for example, you were to introduce a person in the Court to determine his sex, color, or baldness, I could not possibly object.

"But you may *not* introduce the Colonel's pants by reason of the activity of Texas insects which would make autoptic proference of said trousers out of the question."

McCraw continued to wear a puzzled frown. After a nod from the Special Master, happy for a break in the tedium of repetitive witnesses, Pfeiffer continued.

"Do not look into your dictionary for the word 'proference,'" he said. "It is a word coined by Professor Wigmore, the great authority on the Law of Evidence. One judge I recall, in answer to an objection similar to yours, Brother McCraw, wrote his opinion in this manner:

"'If philological incorrectness is referred to, the objection is more tenable; for, while "autoptic" is a good word, with a pride of ancestry, though perhaps without hope of posterity, the word "proference" is a glossological illegitimate, a neological love-child, of which a great law writer (Wigmore) confesses himself to be the father.'"

"Objection sustained," said Flannery.

From Dallas, the domicile hearings moved on to Florida. Here, that state's Attorney General quoted Gray, "And hie him home at evening's close, To sweet repast and calm repose." Next he quoted Hood, "Peace and rest at length have come, All the day's long toil is past, And each heart is whispering 'Home, Home, at last.'" Finally he made his point by bringing out the fact that the Colonel took Hetty's desk, a Howland family heirloom, to 46 Star Island.

"This ancient treasure," said the Attorney General with a sob in his voice, "this symbol of Ned Green's rich American heritage, his beloved mother's desk, he brought with him to his home at Miami Beach.

"When the Colonel departed from God's country for colder climes, the two-hundred-and-fifty-year-old valued relic remained."

The Floridian turned triumphantly to Tweed.

"This desk, sir," he concluded, "is the real *'lares* and *penates'* to which my Brother Tweed so eloquently referred."

That evening, at a strategy conference Proctor called, James A. Dixon, Sylvia's representative at Miami and the Court-appointed "Curator" of 46 Star Island, said he vaguely recalled seeing Hetty's desk when he was at Round Hills.

"It seems to me," Dixon recollected, "that John Bullard showed me what *he* called Mamma Green's desk when I was up at South Dartmouth. I know Gibbs wouldn't lie. Do you suppose Hetty had two of these? Why don't you fellows check with John and I'll take a run over to Star Island this evening?"

The following morning Pfeiffer called Dixon to the stand.

"Did you examine the desk to which Brother Gibbs referred as a 'symbol of Colonel Green's rich heritage'?"

"I did," replied Dixon.

"Was it an antique?"

Gibbs sprang from his chair.

"I object. The witness has not qualified as an expert on antiques."

"Sustained," said Flannery.

"All right, Mr. Dixon," Pfeiffer continued. "Did you find out where the desk was produced?"

"I did, sir. There's a stamp on the back which says 'Made at Grand Rapids, Michigan.'"

Gibbs' jaw dropped and he raised no objection to counsel's next query.

"When was it made?"

"About 1925," said Dixon.

"I'm sorry, Brother Gibbs," Pfeiffer concluded. "But we verified the fact that the original Howland desk never left Round Hills."

At New Bedford, the Green circus performed on hallowed ground, the Superior Court of Bristol County.

"The Green case," William M. Emery pointed out in the New Bedford *Standard-Times* of February 6, 1938, "will go down in legal history as the third *cause célèbre* which had its setting in the old Colonial Court House. First was the litigation in which Daniel Webster, then at the height of his fame, was counsel about 100 years ago. This is also the courtroom where the famous Lizzie Borden murder trial took place."

Mr. Emery also noted the light tone he heard running through the trial.

"Mr. Flannery, Master in the Green case," continued this eminent genealogist and reporter, "has a keen sense of humor and is not disturbed by the loud laughter that often greets sallies of counsel. There is no sharp desk rapping in consequence, and the Master joins in the amusement of the lawyers and spectators."

The last man in the long parade of witnesses was Harvey Mansfield, executive secretary of the Miami Beach Club. His testimony in behalf of the State of Florida added little to the knowledge of the Special Master or the weary counselors-at-law, who by then had reached a state of ennui where nothing in the strange life of the late Colonel E. H. R. Green could titillate them. It was time for summations.

It took many hours for each Attorney General to plead his

case, but O'Quinn, in his précis of the Green case, boiled down their lengthy arguments into a few paragraphs.

"Florida," said O'Quinn, "stated simply that Green's domicile was in Florida at the time of his death and presented facts in support of this contention. . . . New York said that Green had abandoned his domicile in Texas in 1911 and became domiciled in New York. They said that the presumption existed that the domicile established by Green in New York continued and that the burden of proving it was changed rested upon the other states, and finally, that Colonel Green's domicile was in the State of New York at the time of his death.

"Texas . . . took this position; that intent is a dominant factor in establishing domicile; that long-continued absence is not alone sufficient to work a change of domicile; that physical presence and continuous living at an old domicile are not necessary.

"Massachusetts said that if a man has only one home, his domicile is there; but if he has a plurality of habitations, his domicile will attach to the one which is his principal establishment or headquarters. The final contention of the Massachusetts lawyers appears to have been the most effective. This contention was that domicile is where a person chooses to make his home and not where he chooses to make his residence."

The Special Master ruled for the Commonwealth of Massachusetts. His opinion was upheld by the august body that had appointed him. Mr. Justice Stone wrote the majority opinion. A dissent was filed by a newcomer to the bench, Mr. Justice Frankfurter, and concurred in by Mr. Justice Black.

Said Mr. Justice Stone, "While one's statements may supply evidence of the intention requisite to establish domicile at a given place of residence, they cannot supply the fact of residence there . . . and they are of slight weight when they conflict with the fact. . . .

"Whatever floating intention Green may have had after 1911 to return to Texas and make his home there, it is plain that it receded into the background after his mother's death and completely vanished when he began to build up his extensive estate at Round Hills. . . . When he had established himself there all the circumstances of his life indicated . . . that his real attitude and intention with respect to his residence there were to make it his principal home or abiding place to the exclusion of others.

"This is clearly indicated by the fact that it was the place most associated with his family history, by the scale on which he built, by his assembling there the furnishings and objects closely associated with his family life and by centering there all the activities related to his chief interests. . . . He spent more time there than at any other place . . . curtailing his stays only to avoid the possible danger of being subjected to Massachusetts' taxation. His conception of legal residence or domicile as a mental state whereby he could obtain certain political advantages and freedom from taxation does not weigh against this conclusion. . . ."

Defenders of the Fortune had won. For the Widow Wilks' counsel it meant a fee of $700,000, not incommensurate with the time and manpower involved. For McCraw it meant defeat by "Pass the Biscuits, Pappy" O'Daniel in the next Democratic gubernatorial primary, and the political oblivion that followed. For Dever, the victorious Attorney General, it meant a forceful boost in his career with enough power to carry him into the Governor's mansion. What the victory meant to Dever's constituents was neatly reckoned up by the Boston *Herald*, March 14, 1939.

"The Supreme Court decision in the Green Estate case will result in the largest single tax ever paid in Massachusetts, $5,250,000," said this newspaper. "This is: Approximately equal to all inheritance taxes paid in Massachusetts during 1938; equivalent to a yield of one cent on each gallon of gas used annually; and if used in the general fund it will reduce the state taxes in 1939 by some 30% benefiting the individual taxpayer to the extent of $1 for each $1,000 valuation."

For Sylvia Wilks, the victory meant least of all. The $30,000,000 she received as sole beneficiary of her late brother's will was

297

added to her $10,000,000 checking account at Chase National, where none of it drew interest.

"Actually," complained one of that bank's officers, "it was a nuisance. We couldn't invest it. We knew Mrs. Wilks only slightly but we knew her mother *very* well. We figured that possibly, just possibly, someday H. Sylvia Ann Howland Robinson Green Wilks might step up to a teller's window, present her passbook, and say, 'Give me all my cash now.'"

Chapter Forty-seven

Soon after the domicile hearings ended, Sylvia went to Bellows Falls to dispose of the Tucker House, which had been damaged badly by the 1938 hurricane.

"I invited her to dinner," recalled Mamie Bolles, "but Sylvia said she was very tired and would come over to my house later. That evening, one end of the piazza was occupied by some of my grandchildren and their high-school friends, and when I greeted Sylvia at the door I was conscious that in the shadow of the vines several pairs of eyes were scrutinizing my unusual guest.

"After a while I came out and asked them to sing for Sylvia. There were violent whispered protests but I said, 'Just sing as you do when I have no guest.' Few gatherings of young people at our house were without some free-for-all singing with my daughter

Gertrude at the piano; so they followed her into the living room and sang 'The Long, Long Trail' and other popular songs in good glee-club manner.

"Sylvia's pleasure was quite evident and she applauded heartily. I said, 'They are not used to applause,' and she replied, 'When people do well I think we should let them know that they are appreciated.' On leaving she said, 'I don't know when I have ever enjoyed an evening so much.' To her, a few hours with a friend away from critical eyes and a glimpse of young people in normal everyday fellowship was something to be remembered."

That Mrs. Wilks was not speaking idly about "letting people know when they are appreciated" was evidenced shortly before she left her childhood home for the last time.

"Sylvia was packing such of the furnishings as she wished to keep and giving away or otherwise disposing of the rest. One day she called me to the telephone and said, 'I am sending you a work-stand. It will be there soon.' It couldn't be the Chinese lacquer one! In a few minutes the truckman arrived and carried a tablelike object wrapped in a sheet into the house. 'Mrs. Bolles,' he said, 'will you let me unwrap this thing and look at it? I never saw anything like it and probably never will again.'

"It is now a hundred years since Edward Green's gift to his mother made the journey from the Orient to her home in Vermont. It was old when it started but its beauty is unmarred. The multitude of little golden people that swarm over the black lacquer, crossing golden bridges, feasting in golden gardens, and peeping from golden pagodas has indeed a mysterious story which was all mine to unravel."

After razing the Tucker House and deeding its grounds to the village for a public park, Sylvia returned to her Fifth Avenue apartment, which for the next few years she was to share with the Bancrofts. These natives of Bellows Falls were not only her loyal friends but had known and liked Hetty as well. Gradually Mrs. Wilks discharged most of her household servants at 988

Fifth Avenue, retaining only a day worker who came in twice a week to help with the heavy cleaning.

The furniture at 988 Fifth Avenue was heavy, ugly, and practical, but the linens, silverware, and china were magnificent. Most of these had been salvaged from the *United States* or bought by Mabel for Star Island. There were three closets in Sylvia's bedroom; two were filled with her clothing, made from fine material but hopelessly out-of-date and drab in color. Contents of the third closet were in striking contrast to the others. In this were the Colonel's four glittering swords and a dozen gaudy uniforms, pressed, cleaned, and carefully hung, one next to the others.

Once or twice a month Mrs. Wilks went to 111 Broadway to consult with Potter, whose chores were simple; Sylvia bought or sold little. When mortgages fell due and were paid off, Potter converted the proceeds either into government securities or other safe, long-term investments. It would be difficult to find a more depressing atmosphere than that in the three-room suite of the Windham Realization Company and the Westminster Company on the tenth floor of the Trinity Building at 111 Broadway.

There were four people in Potter's domain: Potter, in charge, sphinxlike, aloof, humorless; Anna Burke, his secretary, an aging widow, reserved, care-worn, spending her days at 111 and her nights in a dismal Jersey City flat taking care of her invalid mother; Lynagh, the bookkeeper, with the Greens since 1916, sitting on his high stool, back bent over the ledgers, with wisps of gray hair covering a narrow, balding head, white frayed cuffs jutting from a shiny black alpaca coat; Grace Van Riper, typist, single, young, and friendly when she came to 111 but now climbing into middle age, her early efforts at office camaraderie rebuffed, sitting behind an ancient Oliver, the clatter of which was almost the only sound to break the gloomy silence in this exchequer of the Fortune.

There were no office parties, no Christmas trees, no coffee breaks, no "sunshine fund" at 111. It was "Good morning" and

"Good night," and the Widow Wilks' appearances did little to change the somber air. The view from the four windows, overlooking Trinity Church, was equally dim. Below was the ancient graveyard.

Sylvia's visits to the Trinity Building usually were brief. They took place in her brother's office, dusted but otherwise undisturbed. A dulled shingle, "Private, Colonel E. H. R. Green," was still on Ned's door. Inside, a wooden hatrack clung to its burdens, a linen duster and a straw sailor tossed there carelessly so many years before. On the Colonel's desk was his jeweled pen and ink set, a clean blotter, a calendar pad, the day turned to August 21, 1921. The hour, marked on a nautical clock that had ceased to run decades before, was 11:52.

Sylvia owned fair-sized estates in Greenwich and Stamford, which she had inherited from Wilks, and a house she herself had bought at Shippan Point, with a fine view of Long Island Sound. Although she probably had more money than Hetty, the Widow Wilks was not "the richest woman in the world," and her movements to and from these Connecticut dwellings were ignored by the press.

Despite the fact that each house was completely furnished and staffed and had a fully equipped kitchen, Sylvia preferred to pack her own picnic lunches at 988 Fifth Avenue and eat them by herself or with an old friend on the lawns of her summer residences. Only rarely did she spend a night at any one of these houses. Usually she and her companion of the day left for Connecticut about 8 A.M. in Sylvia's chauffeur-driven Lincoln and returned to Manhattan before nightfall.

Sylvia's most frequent companion was her doctor, who by a coincidence bore the same surname as the practitioner who treated her grandaunt, Sylvia Ann Howland, a hundred years before. Except in name, profession, and ethics, the pair, Dr. Donald Gordon of New York City and Dr. William Gordon of New Bedford, Massachusetts, were not related.

It may be recalled that Dr. William Gordon received a legacy of $100,000 from his bedridden patient. Dr. Donald Gordon did even better. In less than six years he managed to extract an admitted $36,640 in cash "gifts" and $27,448 in fees from Mrs. Wilks in addition to persuading his charge to set up a $150,000 trust fund for him. Contemporary physicians, struggling with the economics of the day, might take note that Dr. Gordon used to charge his patient $100 every time he took a pleasure ride with her to Connecticut or elsewhere. In his defense, it should be pointed out that Sylvia was aware of the cost of his company.

Sylvia's likes were circumscribed—rare roast beef, Dwight D. Eisenhower, Dick Tracy, and Robert Moses. Her dislikes were a bit more catholic—cold cereals, counselors-at-law, all physicians except Dr. Gordon, Mabel Green, Bishop Manning, and Franklin D. Roosevelt. Since Sylvia was not one to gossip or engage in chit-chat, when her pet topic of the day, a like or a dislike, was exhausted, she was inclined to lapse into lengthy silences.

She was brusque but not unkind. She simply did not know how to display emotion; her tear ducts had long ago dried up. Touched by a note of sympathy sent by an old Bellows Falls music teacher after Ned's funeral, Sylvia Wilks' response was a check for $100. When Potter's wife died, Sylvia did not call on the bereaved husband; instead, she sent him a check for $10,000.

An impoverished aunt of an orphaned eleven-year-old daughter of one of Sylvia's New Bedford friends was able to penetrate Potter's barrier (he opened all of his employer's mail) to ask Mrs. Wilks for help. Sylvia responded by sending the girl (known only as "Little Anna") to St. Mary's, an Episcopal boarding school on the Hudson River, and paying all the child's expenses for eight years. She never saw "Little Anna," never answered the girl's letters, sent regularly, but when Anna was married Sylvia sent the bride a gift of $5,000. Money was the Widow Wilks' substitute for sentiment.

Years later, long after Anna had left St. Mary's, Sylvia, accompanied by her pragmatic physician, paid a call on that institution. The doctor waited outside.

303

"She asked for the Mother Superior," Dr. Gordon recalled.

" 'Why do you want to see her?' asked one of the Sisters who was in the reception room.

" 'I thought, perhaps, you might need a sewing machine here, the kind which does blind stitching for your veils, and I'd like to talk to your Mother Superior about it,' Mrs. Wilks said.

"The Sister, thinking Mrs. Wilks was a representative of the Singer Sewing Machine Company, tried to give her the brush-off. She said the Mother Superior was resting and besides they had enough sewing machines.

"Finally it dawned on the Sister that what Mrs. Wilks was attempting to do was not to sell a machine but *give* one away. She apologized profusely and summoned the Mother Superior, to whom Mrs. Wilks spoke.

"Mrs. Wilks came out of the school actually laughing, the first time she ever did that.

" 'You know, Doctor,' she said, 'I think I'll give St. Mary's a real shock. I'm going to order that sewing machine for them and besides I'll tell Potter to send them a check for twenty-five thousand dollars.'

"And as far as I know she did."

Potter died in 1949. Mabel, who retired from the public eye in 1937 to live alone in her spacious Long Island house, died in a Miami Beach hotel room in August, 1950. It was that resort's most unfashionable season and neither Miss Jefferson Bell, Mr. Lino L. Sertel, nor Mr. Alfred Barton was aware that the Widow Green was in Florida. It should be noted in passing that in keeping with Green traditions, three years of litigation followed the probate of Mabel Harlow Staunton Green's will, contested by several cousins.

Soon after, cancer struck Sylvia. Even the home remedies her mother had so strongly advocated—squill oil and Carter's Little Liver Pills—were ineffective.

Mrs. Wilks managed to be with Mamie again. "I hadn't seen Sylvia for years," Mrs. Bolles recalled, "and I had no idea she was ill. I was staying with my daughter Margaret in Darien, Connecticut. It occurred to me that Sylvia's home in Greenwich was not far away and I might be able to see her. I dialed her number and asked for Mrs. Wilks. A woman's voice answered, 'She is not here.' I asked when she would be at home and was answered, 'I don't know.'

"At first I thought it was the routine manner of a servant dealing with a stranger. 'Tell her,' I said, 'that Mamie Bolles is in Darien and would like to have her come to lunch.' That afternoon the telephone rang. 'This is Sylvia. I am at a drugstore in Darien. Please tell me how to get to East Lane.'

"It was a beautiful spring day and we were sitting on the lawn enjoying the lilac and dogwood blossoms, so we waited for her there. The shining Lincoln car with its chauffeur bore little resemblance to the old one-horse surrey of her girlhood days. Her physician, Dr. Gordon, was with her. He entertained my daughter while Sylvia and I enjoyed an hour as old friends do. Speaking of my invitation, she said, 'When you phoned me [it *was* Sylvia who answered, just as I suspected] I was in that house for the first time in five years.'

"In a flowered silk dress and black silk coat she had the appearance of any stout woman too busy to keep quite up to the latest fashion. I asked them to stay to dinner, saying I had an old-fashioned rice pudding in the oven.

"'Let's stay,' said the doctor boyishly; but Sylvia thought they had better get back to the city before traffic was heavy. We said good-by and so came to the end of a perfect day."

Chapter Forty-eight

H. Sylvia Ann Howland Robinson Green Wilks died of a malignant tumor on February 5, 1951. She was eighty years old.

"Mrs. Wilks' death," said the New York *Times*, "probably has brought to an end a fantastic concentration of family wealth. It was originally amassed by her mother, whose financial manipulations half a century ago earned for her the title of the world's richest woman and was zealously protected over the years.

". . . A conservative estimate put Mrs. Wilks' possessions at more than $100,000,000 in 1946. Now it is presumed that taxes, the dreaded enemy of Hetty Green and both of her children, will finally break the back of their fortune, since no immediate relatives survive. . . . If litigation should follow Mrs. Wilks' death, it would be no new experience for the Green family. . . ."

Not until later was it discovered that in addition to securities, Sylvia had $31,448,220 in a checking account at Chase National, $4,545,601 in a checking account at the Bank of New York-Fifth Avenue Bank, and $257,045 cash in a safe-deposit box which also held $2,000,000 worth of the Colonel's jewels.

"The wealth from which Hetty Green and her tall, austere, lonely daughter derived so little pleasure, aside from the satisfaction of possessing it and watching it grow," said Joe Epstein in the New Bedford *Standard-Times,* "was originally, in the words of Herman Melville, 'dredged up from the depths of the ocean.'

"Mrs. Wilks, final heir to the entire fortune which Hetty amassed and hoarded with complete disregard of the human values of life, lived most of her life in seclusion. . . . She had shared with Edward a childhood of poverty. . . . Disposition of the combined fortunes of which she was virtually a prisoner will provide a fascinating closing chapter to a family saga that rivals fiction."

Mamie Nims Bolles saw her friend for the last time on February 10, when Sylvia was laid to rest beside the bodies of her parents and brother in the graveyard adjacent to Immanuel Church at Bellows Falls. There were many mourners, recipients of Mrs. Wilks' quiet generosity. Services were brief.

Weary defenders of the Fortune were now ready to lay down their weapons. Sylvia's closest surviving relative was a cousin whom she had never met. Mrs. Wilks' will, three years in the making, would soon be probated and her vast estate broken into sizable chunks and scattered all over the country.

But assailants of the Fortune gathered their forces for a last-ditch battle and once more its tired legions were called to arms. The final assault began when Sylvia's will, which her attorneys claimed had been signed in 1948, could not be found. A testament, drawn twenty-five years before, was offered for probate May 17, 1951, in the New York Surrogate's Court by Mrs. Emilie Keene Elmendorf Colles, of 89 North Broadway, White Plains. Mrs. Colles was the granddaughter of the Reverend John Jay

Elmendorf who had married Edward Henry Green's only sister.

Mrs. Colles had in her possession Sylvia's 1923 will, in which Mrs. Wilks left everything to her brother except for $150,000 to Matthew Astor Wilks, who had signed away his other rights, and $5,000,000 to the Girl Scouts of America. Under provisions of New York State's intestacy laws, this meant that the Fortune, less taxes, would pass to Mrs. Colles. The Girl Scouts promptly joined forces with the White Plains matron.

Counsel for the late Widow Wilks, who had spent endless hours conferring with their client in the preparation of the latest will, were frantic. They knew it existed; they had stenographic records and copious penciled notes of meetings that Sylvia attended, together with her recommendations and suggested legatees. But all this meant nothing without the production of the later testament itself, and counsel had no signed copies of the document.

Ever since Sylvia's death, her safe-deposit boxes (and Mrs. Wilks had a dozen of these in Manhattan) had been searched. Then came the strongboxes and wall safes at 988 Fifth Avenue and in her Connecticut houses, but the will was not in any of these. After that, the contents of every drawer in every piece of Sylvia's furniture were scrutinized; every book she owned was opened with the thought that perhaps the will would be tucked away somewhere between the covers, and every closet shelf was emptied. Even the rugs were lifted.

"We were going nuts," recalled Alexander McKenna, a Vice President of Chase National assigned to the posse. "There were about ten of us looking at 988 Fifth Avenue, where we really felt the will would be. We broke into five groups of two. This was the afternoon of May 17. I was looking in an old tin kitchen cabinet, but all I saw there were three or four cakes of Ivory soap, and I didn't bother looking further.

"I guess we'd been covering each other's tracks. About an hour later I saw Ralph Pemple (a Chase V.P.) starting to go through that old cabinet. I said, 'Don't bother, Ralph, I looked there.' He

308

answered, 'I'll go over the same ground once more, maybe you fellows missed it.' The next thing I heard was Ralph calling out, 'Stop the music! I got it.' And there was the will under the soap I'd been too lazy to lift."

Mrs. Colles and the Girl Scouts of America then changed tactics. Their new strategy was to attempt to prove that Mrs. Wilks had been of unsound mind and was improperly influenced when she made her will. It took six months for defenders of the Fortune to rout the foe and to show the New York Surrogate that the late H. Sylvia Ann Howland Robinson Green Wilks was sane when she made her will and was not subjected to undue influence. To prevent further litigation in higher courts counsel for the estate prevailed upon Mrs. Colles to accept a settlement of $140,000. The Girl Scouts waived their claim and accepted $50,000. The hour when the fruits of the 325-year-old plum tree would fall was near at hand.

Chapter Forty-nine

THE final shake of the plum tree was a gentle one, but it sent the fruit flying in all directions.

"After you come back from lunch," said Harrison Tweed to his secretary, Miss Mary Walsh, about noon, January 29, 1952, would you call Mr. Pemple and tell him to close out the Wilks Estate."

By 3 P.M. the following day, a hundred million dollars in Wilks Estate checks had been signed by Mrs. Anna Burke, Executrix, cosigned by Ralph J. Pemple of Chase National, and verified by Messrs. Tweed, Pfeiffer, and Jaques. By 2 P.M., January 31, 1952, all checks, together with explanatory letters, were ready for distribution. Three hours later, the Green plum tree was bare.

To many the fruit was savory, to some it was bitter, and to a few it was indigestible. The sweetest of all plums was the smallest.

"I give and bequeath the sum of One Thousand Dollars ($1,000) to Mary Lahey of 1523 Unionport Road, Borough of Bronx, New York City, an occasional servant. . . ."

Mrs. Lahey was a widowed day worker who "gave" one day a week to assorted Manhattan ladies. For this she was paid thirty cents an hour. The Widow Wilks was one of the Widow Lahey's clients, but instead of using the cleaning woman every week, Sylvia shared her with another resident of 988 Fifth Avenue and so Mrs. Lahey went to Mrs. Wilks twice a month from 1944 to 1946, usually at a time when Dr. Gordon was taking his patient for a ride. It is not likely the two widows saw each other more than a half-dozen times. At the end of her nine-hour day, Mrs. Lahey was handed a sealed envelope containing $2.70, plus carfare, by James MacCotney, the building superintendent.

"I didn't even remember the woman," said MacCotney. It appears that Sylvia did.

MacCotney himself fared quite well at Sylvia's hands. Although he did no more for Mrs. Wilks than for other tenants, and admitted that the only cultural interest he and Mrs. Wilks shared was a mutual fascination with Dick Tracy, the superintendent nevertheless was a Wilks legatee to the extent of $14,000. This, prorated, meant a thousand dollars for each year Sylvia resided at 988 Fifth Avenue.

Before coming to the main portion of her last will and testament, Sylvia disposed of several million dollars in individual bequests, including the aforementioned $10,000 gift to Robert Moses "in appreciation of his work in creating public parkways."

All of this was exclusive of twenty-eight trust funds that Sylvia had set up on March 18, 1948, four months prior to signing the will itself; each of the trusts was worth $500,000. Among individual beneficiaries were such old friends of Sylvia as Mamie Nims Bolles of Bellows Falls, Vermont; Mrs. Ruth Lawrence

Briggs; the latter's aunt, Miss Ruth Lawrence; several elderly ladies who used to while an occasional hour with Mrs. Wilks; the ubiquitous Dr. Donald Gordon; and Mr. Charles Lawrence Cleveland of Lawrence Farms, Chappaqua, New York, and Mr. Edward L. Parker of South Orange, New Jersey, distant cousins of Matthew Astor Wilks, neither of whom had ever met Sylvia, Hetty, or the Colonel.

In addition to the individual legatees, these trust funds named charitable institutions, some of which benefited again in the will: the Seeing Eye, Inc., of Morristown, New Jersey; the Institute for the Crippled and Disabled of New York City; the Peabody Home for Aged and Indigent Women, the Bronx, New York; and the Sheltering Arms for Children of New York. And several institutions of a less dominant charitable nature were included: the Kent School of Kent, Connecticut, and St. Bartholomew's Church, Park Avenue, New York.

No one can know what thoughts captured the mind of the lonely Sylvia, aware that a malignant growth left her little time to dispose of the vast Green fortune. Yet something is revealed by the bequests in the will to people only remotely related to her and, in a very real sense, absolute strangers. A number of individuals were left bequests of $100,000 in cash. One was Mrs. Anne Barney Sharp, wife of a retired naval architect. Until recently the couple had divided their time between a beautiful New Rochelle home and their Park Avenue *pied à terre*. Mrs. Sharp's father and Hetty shared a common great-grandfather, Gideon Howland.

"Sylvia's gift was a complete shock," said Mrs. Sharp. "I didn't know her at all and neither did my husband, although he'd met the Colonel once or twice. The first we learned of the bequest was from reporters who somehow got to our New Rochelle house before the mailman."

Another legatee in the $100,000 class was Dr. Robert I. Walker, a highly successful New Bedford osteopath. (His wife, Dr. Mary Walker, also practices the same profession.)

"I'm amazed and delighted," Dr. Robert told Joe Epstein a few hours after opening his mail, February 1, 1952, "but I don't ever recall having met Mrs. Wilks."

Asked how he and Sylvia were related, the osteopath pondered for some time and then replied, "My grandmother, Sylvia Howland Almy, the wife of Benjamin Almy, was a cousin of Sylvia Ann Howland, the aunt from whom Hetty inherited a million dollars. That makes me a distant cousin of Mrs. Wilks."

After disposing of those odds and ends, which included ten gifts of $100,000, fifteen of $25,000, two of $10,000, and two of $5,000 each to various remote relatives, only one or two of whom she had ever met and most of whom were unaware of her existence, and another $350,000 to former employees and friends, Sylvia divided the remainder of her fortune into 140 equal shares. Each share was worth $642,155.93.

At one time Sylvia had seriously considered leaving her entire estate to Princeton University, but subsequently she developed a violent and inexplicable antipathy toward Woodrow Wilson and left nothing to the school he headed before becoming twenty-eighth President of the United States. In an uncomplicated will that she later voided, Sylvia divided her estate into three equal parts to be shared by Columbia and Yale Universities and the Massachusetts Institute of Technology, the funds to be used for medical research. In Sylvia's final will, Columbia and M.I.T. each were given four shares while Yale, for some reason, was cut down to two. However, Eli's loss was more than made up by Groton's gain; this elegant, well-endowed Massachusetts preparatory school received 4/140ths of the Wilks estate, or approximately $2,500,000.

Groton was not the only exclusive preparatory school to benefit: Kent, a $500,000 trust fund beneficiary, now received an outright gift of four shares; Blair Academy of Blairsville, New Jersey, one share; and St. Paul's, of Concord, New Hampshire, four shares. There is no clue to the reasoning processes that led Sylvia to conclude that these handsomely supported schools

313

needed more than $8,000,000 to carry on their operations. The only traceable connection Sylvia had with any of these institutions was through the accountant, Potter, whose nephew went to Blair and wrote "such interesting letters to his uncle."

The majority of Sylvia's gifts were sound beyond dispute: bequests to hospitals (two shares for Rockingham of Bellows Falls, four shares to Beekman-Downtown of New York), welfare institutions (two shares for the New York Association for the Blind, one share to the Legal Aid Society—a generous gesture, considering Sylvia's inherited dislike for members of the bar), public libraries (one share to New York and two for New Bedford), other universities (four shares to Harvard and two for Fordham), and other institutions developed for the common good.

Yet item number 63, the final bequest in H. Sylvia Ann Howland Robinson Green Wilks' last Will and Testament, one share to Trinity Church of Newport, Rhode Island, which has served America's very rich for generations, was perhaps the most whimsical gift of all. Why this? Nobody really knows, but Mamie Nims Bolles hazarded a guess. "Sylvia told me she and Matty once walked through Trinity's churchyard on a moonlight night." Perhaps for Sylvia that was sufficient.

One thing is certain—Sylvia had no wish to perpetuate the name or memory of her forebears. Considering the almost unlimited means at her command, the absence of any provision for a memorial cannot escape notice. Not one bequest to an institution of learning so much as hinted at a testimonial to the generous donor. No gift to a public welfare or philanthropic society suggested recognition of any kind. Sylvia, who could not expunge the events of this strange history from her own memory, obviously wanted the world to forget. In its own time, not hers, it would.